PREFACE

This account is written with a view to placing on record memories of my life, for the possible future interest of children, grandchildren and perhaps the wider family. I wish I had cross-questioned my parents and grandparents more about their early years. My father left a written account of what he called 'the more interesting period of my life' which ended, we find, four years before I was born. My mother did not talk readily about the past, saying what was the point, we have to live in the present. So here is an attempt at a story. In July 1953 Doreen's lifeline meets mine.

The title of the book is a joke family motto, 'Always Young' in Latin, possibly originating as the title of a collection of ancestral photographs compiled by Great Uncle Christopher Young.

Doreen will tell you that some of the dates and places in this account are inaccurate, and she will be right. For accuracy, go to her journals, written at the time. However, apart from some obvious flights of fancy, all the events recorded actually happened.

Anthony Young
Norwich 2016

SEMPER JUVENIS

Always Young

ANTHONY YOUNG

ISBN-10: 1519328923

ISBN-13: 978-1519328922

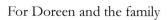

For Doreen and the family

Other books by the author

Slopes
Tropical soils and soil survey
A framework for land evaluation (with Robert Brinkman & FAO)
Soil survey and land evaluation (with David Dent)
Agroforestry for soil conservation
Guidelines for land use planning (with FAO)
Agroforestry for soil management
Land resources: now and for the future
Thin on the ground: land resource survey in British overseas
territories

Books for schools

A geography of Malawi (with Doreen Young)
World vegetation (with Dennis Riley)
Slope development (with Doreen Young)

CONTENTS

ACKNOWLEDGEMENTS

I should like to acknowledge the considerable help received from Howard Smith in bringing this book from draft to publication.

1

BEFORE THE WAR: HAMPSTEAD 1932-39

It is usual to begin autobiographies with notes on grandparents, uncles, aunts, and the like, but if I were to do so we might never get started. So let us begin with a short introduction to my parents' lives, leaving other relatives for later.

My father, Sidney Michael Young, was born on 13th June 1900, so his years matched those of the century. This meant that he was called into the army in the last year of the First World War but never reached the front line. Intellectually precocious, with a copious memory, he was called to the bar at Gray's Inn at the unusually early age of 21, practised in Shanghai 1924-27, but became seriously ill with dysentery and was forced to return to England. Lacking the capital to set up in legal practice he acquired a junior post (for which he was over-qualified) as legal assistant in the Inland Revenue at a salary of £350 (2016: £12 500).[1] He was to travel up to Somerset House until 1951, by which year he had become Assistant Solicitor General, or joint Number Two, in the legal branch of the taxation service, at £1200 (2016: £30 000). At the same time he met Mum, I know not how for there was no previous connection between the families. In any event, the courtship must have been rapid, for he married her at All Souls, Langham Place, on 27th October 1928. Dad was quiet, kindly, and somewhat intellectual in a literary direction. He always treated me, within the limits set by age and maturity, as an intelligent equal.

My mother, Joan Berrett Lack, was born on August 26th 1899, and thus was slightly older than Dad. The Lack family had for several generations prized education highly, and Mum's talent at school proved to be in piano playing;

---

[1]   Money values before the inflation of 1970 onwards appear absurdly low, so I give the approximate equivalent purchasing power in 2016.

the school sight-reading prize was a beautifully bound volume of the works of Chopin which she won year after year. She afterwards studied privately with Anthony Bernard, one of the pioneers of early music in Britain (before Christopher Hogwood and Neville Mariner), and became a profes- sional accompanist. Those for whom she played included the English soprano Dorothy Bennett and the Russian bass Kiriloff, and she broadcast on the BBC some time during the period when it was at Savoy Hill (1923-1932). Mum gave up professional work either on marriage or when I came along.

Wedding of Sidney Michael Young and Joan Berrett Lack
All Souls, Langham Place, October 1928

I was born on 25th September 1932, a Sunday. On the same day, in the same year, were born the brilliant but eccentric Canadian pianist, Glenn Gould; and the one-time Director of the Women's Royal Naval Service (WRNS), Commandant Daphne Swallow.

This was during the Great Depression, when world economies had been in a low state of activity following the stock market crash three years earlier. On a platform of bringing his country out of this, Franklin D. Roosevelt won a landslide victory as US President in November 1932. The Lindbergh child kidnapping took place. Hitler was gaining support in Germany and was to become Chancellor on 30th January of the following year. One author has called the 1930s 'The Dark Valley'.

In sport, the Olympic Games were held in Los Angeles, the only city to bid for it. Because of the economic depression only 37 countries sent athletes; USA won 474 medals, more than the next four countries put together. Due to an error by an official an extra lap was run in the 3000 metres steeple-chase. Bobby Jones played the first round on the Augusta National golf course which he had designed as the venue for the Masters.

It was the year of the opening of the Sydney Harbour Bridge, and the first appearance of the Olympic swimmer Johnny Weissmuller as Tarzan. France won the Davis Cup for the sixth year running. At Cambridge, James Chadwick discovered the neutron, for which he won the Nobel Prize. Ravel's piano concerto for the left hand received its première in 1932. The Times New Roman typeface was first used.

In Britain, life was hard for the unemployed, of which there were many. The middle classes on the other hand, provided they had a job, lived rather comfortably during this period, since labour could be commanded, and goods produced, cheaply. There was no inflation between the wars, indeed, £1 in 1919-25 would buy some 20% more from 1931 right up to 1939.

At the time of my birth we were living at 64 Goldhurst Terrace, NW4 (now NW6), a Hampstead residential suburb between Kilburn High Road and Finchley Road, not far from Swiss Cottage tube station. The birth certificate, however, gives the place of birth some miles away at 11 Alexandra Park Road, Muswell Hill, close to Alexandra Palace. I assume this to have been a maternity home.

The manner of my birth was told to me by Mum many years later, when I had enquired why I had no brothers nor sisters. "I couldn't have any more children, I haven't got a womb" was the reply. At the time of birth, Mum was told that to save her own life she would have to lose the baby. Her response was, "Send for my brother" who was Victor Lack FRCS, a noted obstetric and gynaecological surgeon. Uncle Vic presumably removed the

3

offending uterus together with the living baby, a fortunate circumstance from my point of view.

The Christening took place on November 12th at another All Souls church, Loudoun Road, NW8. With Great Grandfather Sidney Young, Grandfather Sidney Michael Young and Father Sidney Michael Young 'junior', family tradition might have determined my name, had not Mum disliked Sidney[1]. So Anthony was chosen, after Anthony Bernard, Mum's music tutor. It was to have been Anthony Michael, but Dad noticed the initials would be Amy, and knowing that schoolchildren are unkind, abandoned this. All three Godparents were from the Lack family: Uncle Vic, Terence Newth and Auntie Diddie.

The assistant nurse at the birth was Nurse Smith, and at some early date she was taken on as my nanny. This was Sybil Irene Smith, but always known to us as 'Nan', and this name stayed for the rest of her life, others presumably thinking it was short for Nancy. Initially a paid nanny, for a time she came to live with us virtually as one of the family.

Nan is the origin of the earliest story about my life, and my closest contact with royalty. Outside an entrance to Harrods Queen Mary emerged, turned to this uniformed nanny with the old-style carriage pram, and said, "What a pretty baby!" I have to admit that Nan was sometimes given to exaggeration, but that is her story.

Memories of life at Goldhurst Terrace are fragmentary. I think a Mrs Abbott lived on the top floor, so perhaps our maid, Maud, was not live-in. Presumably Dad was commuting to Somerset House from Swiss Cottage tube station. Being an only child is now believed to be good for intelligence, but the absence of repartee with a brother or sister was the first factor in my woeful lack of social skills. Not being sent to a playgroup, nor to school until well after the age which is now customary, made this worse.

Just what did I do all day? There are photographs of first steps at 11½ months, of walks in Golders Hill Park and Hampstead Heath (where I do remember Whitestone Pond), of our first holiday at Old Thorpe House,

---

[1] Dad was known as Sidney until 1928, but because Mum did not like the name he became Michael for the rest of his life – except on visits to his parents!

Thorpeness, Suffolk, in May 1935,[1] and at Felpham, near Bognor Regis, in August of that year. These show a happy, seemingly bright child with a high forehead, usually smiling, in contrast to the dour mien which became my rest position in later life, and dressed in a recognizably middle class way. I am playing water games in the garden, looking down rabbit holes, operating a wind-up gramophone, and there is one labelled 'first golf stroke'. At Felpham we must have met a family with whose daughter, Ann Hearn, I played with on the beach, but nearly all of the other photos show me playing on my own or with my parents.

At some early age, out of the back garden there was some kind of pathway, allowing one to play with neighbours. I made friends with a boy whom I was told was Timothy 'Weekly', and by coincidence was to encounter many years later. I had published my second book with Cambridge University Press in 1976. Mum mentioned this to a friend, also a Mrs Young, in Letch-worth, who said how interesting, as her son worked for them. It was thus I learnt that my contact in CUP, Timothy *Wheatley*, was this early playmate.

Two small incidents had a lasting effect. Walking home along Goldhurst Terrace it came on to rain heavily. This must have been early, for we still had a push chair into which I was placed. I protested vigorously at this, to no avail. Since then I have always, like Marcel Proust's grandmother, enjoyed walking in the rain. On another occasion my parents called the telephone operator, asked for Granny Young's number, and handed me the phone to speak to her. For some reason I didn't listen or didn't hear anything, but started saying, "How are you Grannie? Thank you for my present" and so on, then handed the phone back in a panic. It proved to be the operator saying that there was no reply. I was terribly embarrassed by this mistake, but from this apparently trivial incident developed a dread of telephones which lasted well into my working life.

It was found that I was left handed, like Dad and Uncle Geoffrey, but whereas they had been 'corrected', i.e. made to write with the right hand (with psychological effects, so they thought), that practice had gone out, and I am considerably abler with the left than the right hand. What doesn't occur to parents, however, is to teach you two-handed things the left handed

---

[1] The first house on the right as you enter Thorpeness from the west, adjacent to what is now the golf course practice ground but was then the 17th hole.

way, so perhaps when first playing beach cricket I was shown to put the left hand on top, and do every two-handed action, such as using a spade, axe, playing cricket or golf, the right-handed way. This may even be an advantage for such games, and is not uncommon among professional sportsmen. Dennis Compton would bat right-handed, bowl with the left, and a disproportionate number of top tennis players are left handed. A curiosity is that I use a knife and fork at table with the knife in the right hand, but transfer it to the left to spread butter. As for spoon and fork for pudding I always preferred spoon and right thumb. So that gives us a left-handed only child, with a name coming at the end of the alphabet, but there are more eccentricity factors to come.

Some time about 1938 we moved to 59 Southway, NW11, in Hampstead Garden Suburb (where, it was said, Harold Wilson was living before he became Prime Minister). The house is architecturally undistinguished but the garden suburb was planned along the lines pioneered by Ebenezer Howard in Letchworth. Perhaps the move was to be near my chosen first school, Henrietta Barnet, just at the end of the road. It is quite well known today, having opted to join the state school system, in which it regularly appears near the top of the examination 'league tables'. But, you may think, isn't it a girls' school? Correct, but at that time they took boys in the reception class. Attempts to get the school to tell me the dates of my attendance have not been successful, but I don't think I went to school until the age of six – socially disastrous again!

Our form mistress was not double but triple-barrelled, so when the register was taken we were expected to say, "Yes Miss Bruce-Kings-Mills". I started piano lessons there, including the playing of scales with a penny on the back of the hand. Very early on, it could have been the first day, there was naturally a reading lesson. At first I could not understand what was going on, for I could read fluently, having been taught by Dad in bed in the mornings using an old-fashioned book based on the "A is for Apple" method. When this ability was discovered I was put in a sort of open caravan in one corner of the classroom and given a child's version of *Robinson Crusoe* to read, which rather frightened me.

Meanwhile Dad would have been advancing into the professional grades of the legal service of the Inland Revenue. Mum certainly kept her piano up, for as soon as I went to bed she would begin scales and arpeggios; she had a box from which she would withdraw coloured pieces of cardboard, indicating for all keys whether they should be practised as 3rds, 6ths, octaves or 10ths. Nan went temporarily out of the picture at Southway.

The Lack family had entered motoring quite early. A photo "Cornish Tour April 1921" shows a Humber open tourer, and Grandfather Young's engagement present to Mum was an Austin 7. Neither Dad nor Mum ever took a driving test, as you could get a license if you had driven at all before they were introduced. I don't remember the Austin, but in 1936 we bought a Morris 12, grey and black, DGY 901. This remained in the family, 'laid up' on bricks through the war, was passed on me in 1959, and sold a year later. There is an early and uncharacteristic photo of me cleaning it. A road on which we had occasion to drive was the Watford Bypass, the meaning of which I did not appreciate, thinking it to refer to any three-lane two-way road, common at the time, on which overtaking in both directions was by use of the same central lane. The fastest I had travelled before the War was once when, doubtless with my encouragement, Dad took it up to 70 m.p.h. My position when motoring was standing in the middle of the back with one hand on each front seat, an instance of the different safety standards of the day.

Later I asked Dad how one managed about parking in towns before the war. He said you drove to the shop you wanted to visit and parked outside it. Buying petrol at that time was not from a branded service station but from a dealer who had a row of pumps, each with petrol from a different company. We always bought Cleveland Discol. The attendant would pump one gallon by hand up into a glass tube, release a valve to let it flow into the tank, then repeat for further gallons.

Starting a car in winter could be quite an adventure. First remove the radiator cover (a sort of lined coat) and either the trickle charger (for the battery) or Peter the Heater, a low wattage heater placed in the engine. Then pull out the choke and the throttle, and try the starter motor several times. If this does not work, open one side of the bonnet, and place your finger on a button on top of the carburettor and let it go tick-tick until a spurt of petrol covers your hand. Try starting again. On failing this, get out the starting handle and put it in a hole in the centre of the front bumper; then holding the handle *not* with your thumb in opposition, to avoid harm if it kicks, turn it vigorously several times. If still no luck, put someone in the driving seat with hasty instruction what to do, recruit bystanders, put the car in second gear, push until 5-10 m.p.h. is reached then shout, "Now", meaning "Raise the clutch". This should produce a spark, whereupon the driver must simultaneously take it out of gear, rev madly, and brake to avoid whatever is in front. If the person at the wheel is a non-driver this can be an exciting moment.

My personal safety was further compromised by receiving as a Christmas present, when about six, a bow saw, a fully adult version with coarse sharp teeth, presumably to saw up logs for firewood. Later, in the early war years, this was supplemented by an axe to split the logs, with which I spent many hours.

Early on I started to suffer from the hayfever which was to be such a burden for the first 50 years of my life. From May to July my nose would be streaming, eyes watering, and some asthma. Any sort of outdoor activity, such as camping, barbecue, barn dance, was anathema; all I wanted to do was to stay indoors with windows shut – socially disastrous again.

Before the War

Meanwhile in the world at large the economy was slowly recovering, led by Roosevelt's New Deal. Hitler had gained power in Germany, and was redu-cing unemployment by building up armaments. A young child knows nothing of such world events but of course Dad was more than aware, and around 1939 he decided to move out of London to avoid anticipated bombing – surprisingly prescient, considering how little of this there had been in the First World War.

2

IN THE COTTAGE: RUSHDEN 1939-41

At the outbreak of war we moved into a small and isolated village in north Hertfordshire, Rushden.[1] An isolated building facing the village green, Players Cottage had been named as such by the two ladies from whom we bought it who were retired players (actresses), but it was known to us simply as 'The Cottage'. Thatched, with an oak-beamed ceiling and walk-in larder, it could have been several hundred years old. The windows were small, "to keep out the light and fresh air of which," as Osbert Lancaster remarked, "its occupants had had more than enough during the day".

When we first moved in there was electricity but no running water nor, therefore, inside sanitation. Water could have been obtained from a well served by a pump in the garden, but mindful of the biological activity in this, we carried it in buckets from a standpipe in the middle of the village green – just as one was to see Africans doing many years later. My bath was a galvanized iron oval tub, with the water warmed in kettles. A pipeline to our house followed fairly soon. At the bottom of the garden was another African institution, the drop-down loo, a pit with seat in a wooden hut. We called it the Elsan after the odorous disinfectant that was poured into it. I must have had some geographic awareness by this time, for adjacent was a spring, in winter intermittently feeding a stream which could be traced down on maps, and I took delight in the thought that our Elsan was a source of the Thames.

With a shortage of agricultural labour during the war, the land girl system was started. Those from towns lived in hostels or were billeted on families. Our contribution to this patriotic effort was to take in Nan again thus

---

[1] No connection with the Northants town of the same name. There is a privately printed book, *Recollections of Rushden*, by Linda and Edward Hill, 1999.

making a virtue out of necessity. She became essentially one of the family, helped to look after me, and I am sorry to admit that for a time I preferred Nan to Mum. She met and was later to marry Norman Stewart, head cowman on Mr Rowley's farm. After the war we would visit them, with their children Ian and Anne. Nan died in 1993 aged 92, Norman in 2002. Nan and Norman were a fine couple, seeing to the education of their children. Ian went into agrobusiness, Anne became a university lecturer, specializing in women's rights.

Players Cottage, Rushden, Herts
Back garden put down to vegetables as 'dig for victory'

Indeed our social circle, if such it can be called, featured Nan's and Norman's relatives more than our own. Nan's older brother Reg taught me how to play the 3-chord accompaniments (the bass in split 10ths) which were sufficient for most popular songs of the 1940s and 50s, such as 'The White cliffs of Dover,' 'Maresey dotes and dosey dotes,' and that challenge to Beethoven's 5th Symphony, 'Open the door Richard'. Her younger brother Roy came to stay at the cottage and we played cricket on The Green, although being four years older he was not the ideal playmate; Roy later rose to a managerial position in the banknote firm, De La Rue. Norman's niece Sheena was the first girl for whom I can remember entertaining feelings of attraction, although never expressed. Alf, identified in my mind as where the sacred river ran, in fact ran a garage, a possible source of black market petrol.

We all bought bicycles. Dad announced that he had not ridden one since 1919 and was unsure what would happen, but of course that skill never goes. The rest of us learnt by the energetic system of someone running behind you holding the saddle, not saying when they had let go.

Mum smoked 20 du Maurier a day, so it was not unreasonable that I should try it. When Dad discovered this he increased my pocket money from 3d to 6d a week on condition I gave it up. Since then I have scarcely ever taken even an experimental puff. Beer, traditional bitter, didn't initially taste very nice, but I appreciated this was a taste worth cultivating.

At the end of the road past the cottage lived Percy Portsmouth, a monumental sculptor of some note, who had been Professor of Sculpture at Edinburgh University. He was looked after by an Austrian housekeeper, Eileen. There were dark stories of her being seen at night with a hurricane lamp, signalling the whereabouts of Rushden to enemy planes. She was required to report to the police weekly, and was known in the village as Eileen the Alien.

Of the outbreak of the Second World War, the fall of France, the retreat from Dunkirk, and the threat of invasion, I was largely unaware. This should be qualified by the fact that one learnt to distinguish our planes from German planes by their silhouettes: Spitfire, Hurricane and Lancaster from Fokker and Messerschmidt. Living only 35 miles from London, bombing was rarely audible, with the single exception of one which fell in a field beside Clothall Church, a few miles away; the crater remained for many years, but cannot be seen now. For the period when we were losing the war, I did not give much attention to it.

This situation changed on October 23rd 1942 when, at the Battle of El Alamein, we started winning. From then on I took a keen interest in the war, especially by cutting out and displaying in my room the wonderful hand-engraved maps which *The Times* used to illustrate its accounts. Thick curved black arrows showed the advance of our troops, and also those of the Russians; spotting in advance a town on which the latter were descending, I listened eagerly to see what the BBC newsreader would make of Dnieperpetrovsk. For a time tabloid newspapers were only four pages, a single folded sheet, with business news and sports news each occupying only part of a page. Evidence of the conflict was to be seen in the Italian prisoners of war, 'the Eyeties', who worked on Mr Rowley's farm, wearing blue overalls with large red circles on the back.

With the well-organized system of rationing, food was never a problem for anyone during the war, but we were able to supplement this. Most of the substantial cottage garden was turned over to vegetables. One could also make direct farm purchases, technically black market I suppose, but living in the country this was regarded as sensibly helping each other out. We bought large numbers of eggs, which were stored for the winter in an earthenware pot filled with isinglass.

My education at this time was erratic but academically effective. In Rushden it began with engaging the vicar's daughter as a governess. Lessons in summer might be in the garden, otherwise in 'the shed', a wooden outhouse heated by one of those tall, round unstable paraffin heaters which limited the life expectancy of the elderly. We started on French, which was to become my worst subject at school, and arithmetic which I found easy. Facility at quick calculation was supplemented through evening games of vingt-et-un (pontoon) and nap. One to one tuition of a bright child undoubtedly led to educational progress, but once again was socially useless when it came to interacting with others of my age.

Things weren't much better when I started at Grove House School, Baldock, a private school with just three classes. It was OK in the middle class where I started, but then I was promoted to the top form which consisted of girls only, along with one other insufferable boy called Julian, who would scrawl on one's exercise books. We were put at the back of these serried ranks, with the mistress seemingly far away in the distance.

For a time I went to Rushden Church, usually Morning Service, occasionally Evening (Holy Communion was for a dedicated minority). I remember first, being irritated that to follow the service you had to jump about from one part of the Prayer Book to another; and secondly, surprised when I realised that the order of service was the same week after week. This exercise did not induce any religious belief, although I was to have another try at it some years later.

My contribution to the war effort started in 1940. Harvest before the days of combines was labour-intensive; the binder threw out sheaves, which had to be lifted into stooks to dry. Then a tractor and trailer went round the fields collecting them. Offering to help with this work, I was too small to throw the sheaves up onto the cart, so instead was put in charge of an ancient Ford tractor with a viciously severe clutch, having only a tiny distance between off and fully engaged. Getting the knack of this I worked all day, and without asking was given a few shillings payment. The great benefit was learning the basics of driving at the age of nine. This was later supplemented by being allowed to change the gears of our Morris from the passenger seat, so that when the law finally allowed, I am told that I simply got into the car and drove.

I suppose that Dad's job in London gave us a small petrol allowance. One gave a lot of lifts to servicemen in those days, going to or from leave. If there wasn't room in the car they stood on the running boards and held on, like Indian railway passengers.

There were a few children of agricultural labourers with whom I sometimes played, picking up a fearsome rural Hertfordshire accent. At the other end of the social scale the Pleydell-Bouveries lived on the largest farm there. My second contact with royalty, or thereabouts, was to join the former in throwing lumps of earth at them as they were out trotting in an open carriage.

There was an old man who lived at the end of a side lane who lent me bound copies of the *Boys Own Paper* for several years of the 1890s. The stories in these show a somewhat distorted idea of school life, which had a lasting psychological effect on me.

It must have been at Rushden that we found a bundle of 1938 newspapers in a barn, and were amazed at how many pages they had. These included a report of Stan McCabe scoring 232 not out for Australia (to save them from defeat in the last innings?) which I cut out and stuck in a scrapbook. This started an interest in sport, and I had soon resolved to cut out accounts of all major sporting events, sticking them into books labelled 'Sports Cuttings', about eight of them. These were kept for quite some years but eventually discarded.

One day we found some lead flashing that had come off an old roof. Someone knew that the melting point of lead was low, so we melted it down on the gas cooker, getting lead ingots by using tobacco tins as moulds. No-one seemed to worry about the hazard aspects of this.

It was at the cottage that I gained my love of dogs. The first was a golden labrador, Simon (named, I know not why, after Sir John Simon, lawyer and Chancellor of the Exchequer), a beautiful dog, my favourite breed. Labradors are very good at retrieving (especially from water) but have an inborn antipathy to walking to heel, as may be seen if somebody has one on a lead. Photos suggest that Simon first came to us when at the London house in Southway. He must have died, though I do not remember this, since at the cottage we acquired two springer spaniels, first Sally and then, possibly from the Stewart family, Jock. Sally lived on well into Letchworth days. But dogs should live in the country where they can run around, not always be taken for walks. I have retained a great liking for dogs (except small ones, cocker spaniel and downwards), and an affinity with them. Friends are sometimes surprised at how their pets will respond to commands which they did not think they knew about, like raising a front paw to shake hands. If a dog comes up fiercely growling I tell him he is bluffing, and he backs away in consternation at this unexpected reaction. One day, I suppose, I shall get bitten by a dog that thinks it's me that's bluffing.

Playing in the country was a privilege. We would go down to the stream, find where it was undercutting the bank, and hope to see a change after heavy rain (budding physical geographer again). The winter of 1941 brought heavy snow and Rushden was cut off, all available labour going out to dig clear the road by hand, but great for sledging. I had (and long retained) a particular liking for climbing trees, sizing them up from below like a mountaineer: where is there a route past the trunk onto the first branch, is there a section without branches where one must shin up the trunk, and how high can you get? I would get right near the top of the big conker tree outside the vicarage. No-one cried "Be careful!"

3

SCHOOL: LETCHWORTH 1941-50

Two moves now led to a longer period of stability: I started at St Christopher School, and my parents moved to Letchworth. These moves were not simultaneous. I started at St Chris in the Autumn Term of 1941, but for at least one term, possibly more, lodged during term-time with the Headmaster of the Junior School, 'Pop' Ogilvie, in Whitethorn Lane. His younger son, Colin, about a year older than me and in the same form, became a friend for a time, although later his education and career was to go in a different direction; Colin became an engineer, worked for oil companies in Arab states, married a German wife and retired to Cyprus. My parents' move to Letchworth was some time in 1941-42.

Letchworth

Letchworth Garden City, Hertfordshire, was the First Garden City, to be followed by Welwyn, Hampstead Garden Suburb, and later countless suburban developments. The garden city was the brainchild of Ebenezer Howard (1850-1928), a practical idealist who saw that one need have neither the crowding of close-packed towns nor the isolation and lack of services of country villages. "Town and country must be married, and out of this joyous union will spring a new hope, a new life" he wrote in *Garden cities of tomorrow* (1898). Enthusiasts recruited at his lectures formed the Garden City Pioneer Company in 1902, and set about looking for somewhere to build it. A greenfield site with a small hamlet and manor, midway between Hitchin and Baldock, was identified, and 3818 acres purchased for £155 587. Not Howard himself but Barry Parker and Raymond Unwin were taken on as architects, and their design of 1904 is largely the same as the street layout of the central area today. A 'Plan of Present Development' of 1906 shows our road, Field Lane, the shape that it is today but without housing.

Letchworth attracted idealists, including Arcadians, Theosophists, Quakers and vegetarians, and became something of a byword for eccentricity. Women were to be seen in smocks, men in shorts and, most shocking of all, sandals. An early decision by the Company was that the city should be dry – was this unique in England? At any rate, it brought prosperity to pubs at Willian, Norton and other villages outside the boundary, and per capita consumption of bottled beers, delivered from Hitchin, was among the highest in the country; capitulation to the demon alcohol was finally achieved in the 1950s. Letchworth attracted industry as well, including Kryn and Lahy, makers of cranes, and Spirella corsets. There was also 'Tabs', the British Tabulating Machine Company, which turned its expertise in cash registers to the manufacture of computers for the 'bombe', Bletchley Park's early computer for decoding intercepted German wartime communications.[1]

St Christopher School

St Christopher School was in the true pattern of Letchworth, pioneering or eccentric depending which way you looked at it. It had been founded in 1915, initially with 6 boys and 7 girls (one of whom was still living in 2002). The founder was Dr Armstrong Smith, but in 1925 it was taken over by one of the greats of teaching, H. Lyn Harris, jointly with his wife Eleanor. They remained as Headmaster and Headmistress throughout my time there. Lyn had deep-set piercing eyes, total sincerity, and the commanding presence which is the first qualification for a teacher. By the time I joined it was a well-established private school, coeducational, part boarding part day, with Montessori, Junior and Senior sections. The ideals of its founders, shared by all the staff, were a reaction to the strictness of much schooling, state and public, at the time, and especially against conformity, the following of the accepted ways. St Chris stressed the development of the individual, a relationship of friendliness between pupils, and doing things your own way. From its beginning there was absolutely no corporal punishment. It possibly handicapped its recruitment by serving only vegetarian food, although boarders were not prevented from buying meat products in town. Today the

---

[1] An account is given in Mervyn Miller (1989) *Letchworth: the First Garden City.*

way things were done doesn't sound all that revolutionary but in the early days, and still in the 1940s, it was in advance of its time.[1]

The forms in the Junior School, from top downwards, were Groups D, E, F, G and Transition, this last referring to the transfer from the Montessori section.[2] For the Summer Term of 1941 I was placed in the F Group, the youngest in the class – there we go, socially disastrous again. Maths classes were held at the same time for all the higher groups, allowing transfer according to ability. I spent one day in maths Group F, two days in E, and the remainder of my seven terms in Group D. The weekly mental arithmetic class was a special favourite. The master called out problems and the first hand to go up gave the answer and got a point. Those with three points became outsiders, and a proportion of questions were for 'no outsiders'. Thanks to card-playing or early tuition I was great at this and would generally become a double-outsider.

In September 1943, while the world was deeply engaged in world war both in Europe and Asia, I moved into the Senior School, and there came to meet the teachers who would for the most part remain for the rest of my time there. This was for two reasons. First, any man who was teaching in the early 1940s was unfit for, or exempt from, military service (one had lost an arm in the Spanish civil war). Secondly, any teacher who remained at Chris for more than a short time had to be totally committed to its ideals and methods, and thus they stayed. Hence unlike most schools nowadays, there was very little turnover of teaching staff.

Many of them were talented teachers. Hetty Maxwell (English), of Irish extraction, possessed that gift of walking into the classroom and without saying a word, freezing the misbehaving back row to stone. Humpy (G. W. Humphrey, Maths), on finding out what I knew already, would say, "You don't need to come to class today".[3] In School Cert 'Ad Maths' and Higher Cert he didn't believe in offering excessive coaching, giving perhaps only

---

[1] For a history see Reginald Snell (our English, Latin and German master), *St Christopher School 1915-1975*, published by the author.

[2] Madame Montessori came to talk at the school once. She spoke in Italian, translated by her son. All I can remember is that she said that children aged 13-14 were not very interested in study, and it might be better if they took a year or two off and went to work on a farm, which received a big cheer.

[3] A frail but lively 90-odd year old Humpy attended the school reunion in 1999.

one class a week, believing that if mathematics didn't descend upon a pupil like manna from heaven, then they shouldn't be taking the subject at all. This attitude produced many mathematicians of distinction, notably my lifelong friend Philip Drazin, Professor of Applied Maths at Bristol.[1] It meant, however, that my own mathematical career came to a halt, for although I had a flair for the subject up to School Cert (O Level), at that stage I abruptly struck my ceiling. Maurice Williams (History), a debonair man with a moustache and wavy brilliantined black hair, fairly soon married another English mistress, Betty.

One should point out that teachers who did not wish to be addressed by their Christian names need not be; Mrs Manson (Belgian, teaching French) was one such, actually Simone but we hardly knew this. "Mr" Fernyhough hid his Christophian ideals beneath an appearance of being an old-fashioned schoolmaster, and woe betide anyone who referred to him within earshot as Bugsy.

Another totally dedicated master was Reg Snell (Latin, German), who spent his whole teaching career at Chris. One day he was taking a Current Affairs class in the LASR (Lower Arundale Sitting Room), standing with the group around him, those who couldn't find a chair seated on the floor. I arrived late, ran across the room, and went into a skid across the polished floor. I stuck Reg on the ankles, knocking him to the floor. Without a word he got up and strode out of the room, leaving me to the censure of others. Coming back in a few minutes later, he brushed aside my attempted apology.

For Gym (PT) the boys had Eric Schuckhardt who had been coach to the Czech Olympic team. A Jew, he was put into a concentration camp by the Nazis, escaped – including by swimming the Rhine – and reached England. Eric wasn't all that great at team sports, but put a discus in his hand and it sailed away into the distance without apparent effort. The girls had a tiny young woman, Rene Hughes/Coram – she married another master. Inter-Christophian marriages were quite common, both between staff and

---

[1] Philip was equally dedicated to research and to teaching. He continued in post until 65, then on compulsory retirement immediately took up part-time teaching at the University of Bath; but very sadly, died of cancer of the throat soon after.

between pupils after leaving – indeed, one of the supposed morally impeccable staff members mentioned above left his wife to marry a pupil.

The most popular teacher in the school, and one who was to exercise an influence over my later life, was Oscar Backhouse, the Geography master. He taught in Room 16, a wooden shed outside the main school building, and we would race to get the best places at the two wooden tables. Oscar came from Yorkshire (and was to retire there) but for some reason the only qualification he held was a New South Wales Teacher's Certificate. His methods might not meet the approval of today's inspectors. First, he talked us through the topic of the day; a sketch map in coloured chalks was already on the board. Then he would say, "Now let's take a few notes, shall we?" and dictate them. This meant that not only had we heard the material twice, but had it down in orderly form for future reference. Contrary to today's educational theory, this in no way discouraged individual thought and effort.

In the Sixth Form, Oscar sent Michael Chisholm and me across to Cambridge once a week for coaching. We both sat the entrance exam for St Catherine's and Selwyn, Michael Chisholm got in, I did not. I was to gain a chair at the University of East Anglia, David Harris from the class above us one at London, while Chisholm persuaded an appointing board, how I cannot imagine, to give him a chair at Cambridge. Oscar may well be the only master to number three professors of geography (more or less) among his pupils.

One of the keys to teaching at St Chris was the system of optionals. From C group (2nd form) onwards one had about 12 periods a week in which there were no taught classes. You worked on your own, either in the large Library or in classrooms where staff members would sit (marking books). You did the work they had set, and you could go up at any time and ask them questions. In the Library you just worked in silence, supervised by the (full-time) Librarian, a frail elderly lady whom I now recognize had Parkinson's disease. Your optionals sheet was initialled by the staff member, and inspected at Company Time. We were not above occasionally forging the Librarian's signature. The proportion of the week devoted to optionals increased progressively until in the Sixth Form one might have fewer than 12 taught classes in the week. This meant that on going to university, Christophians were already accustomed to working on their own. I cannot imagine why all schools do not adopt this system.[1] It also meant that, being a bright child, I never did any homework at home until the age of 15.

Lyn Harris and his wife Eleanor were Quakers, but did not push religion at us. To this day I have never entered the School Chapel. Morning Talk (assembly) was conducted in what I now realize (but did not at the time) was the manner of a Quaker meeting. The Head Master and/or Mistress entered and greeted the school. A piece of music was then played or sung, followed by a silence of length proportional to its solemnity. This was followed by a reading of some kind and a shorter silence, or less often an address from the Head. Notices for the day followed, first from the Head, then staff, after which any member of the school could stand up and announce something, such as the AGM of a society.

I said that this 'act of worship' (as required by law) contained little of religious content, but there were two exceptions. At the beginning of term the Head would read in stentorian tones, "Though I speak with the tongues of men and of angels..." (Corinthians I.13), either in the dramatic language of the Authorized Version or in the Revised Version which rightly replaces 'charity' with 'love'.[2] And at the end of term he read the 23rd Psalm ("The Lord is my shepherd") and we sang "Jerusalem", a moving experience although a somewhat surprising choice since the school certainly did not advocate old-style patriotism. Indeed, during the war they supported ex-pupils who wished to become conscientious objectors as the Headmaster had been, spending time in prison in the First World War.

From time to time Lyn Harris would speak on morals or behaviour, and such was his commanding presence and respect that anything he said went deep into the hearts of pupils. Service to the community was central, and the James Leigh Hunt's poem *Abu Ben Adhem* was sometimes read. An angel appears to Ben Adhem saying he is compiling a list of those that love the Lord. Adhem replies, "Write me as one who loves his fellow men". Subsequently the angel returns with a list of those whom the Lord had blessed, "And Lo, Ben Adhem's name led all the rest".

---

[1] They have abandoned it now.
[2] When asked to read from this at Doreen's mother's funeral I took the Authorized Version but substituted 'love'.

Another recurrent theme was standing out against others around you when you thought that what they were doing was wrong (e.g. bullying). Individuality, making up your own mind rather than following others, was part of the ethic, and very useful for future researchers. These last two aspects were combined in a little-known poem, *In this our world: prejudice* by Charlotte Perkins Stetson. It gives a mental picture of a hiker climbing up a mountain path to find it blocked by a prejudice, some great floppy creature, like a huge sea-lion, draped across the road. He reasons with it rationally, flies into a passion and and shouts at it, begs it to move, but all to no avail. Then:

> I took my hat, I took my stick
> My load I settled fair,
> I approached that awful incubus
> With an absent-minded air
> And I walked directly through him,
> **As if he wasn't there!**

The One-Act Play Festival was a feature of the Summer Term. The idea was to take our minds off the worry of studying for exams. I think it was ten plays on each of two successive nights, which got a fair proportion of the Senior School either onto the stage or participating as stage hands.

There was a play in French in which I took the part of a doctor whose solution to every ailment was a cataplasm (hot poultice). After he leaves, the patient and attendants throw this out of the window. However, medical complications require that the doctor is recalled. He enters, and the new problem is explained. "Ah, j'ai exactement la chose. Un bon cataplasme. Il a tombé du ciel!"

Music was not good, and there was no school choir nor orchestra. Sidney Twemlow (Twink), the music master for most of my time, wasn't really in the St Christopher mould, and wisely left (later to become Director of Music for Norfolk County Council). The lady who replaced him caused interest one summer by wearing an open-mesh string blouse without anything underneath. I sung as a jury member in *Trial by Jury*, and have retained the whole work in my head to this day.[1] Despite the limited music we had two children of British composers there, Jonathan, son of William

---

[1]   Recently I joined the chorus of jurymen when Chrysogon's choir sang it. The judge's robe was my scarlet PhD gown.

Alwyn, and Rachel, the dark-complexioned vivacious daughter of Alan Bush, a composer with communist leanings.

To mark the 1945 General Election the school held a mock election. The conservatives, represented by a not very popular boy, Anthony Woolf, came last. John Williams (son of Francis Williams, editor of the *Daily Herald*), a popular boy who was later to become a solicitor, came in second place for the Labour party, and might have won (as nationally) but for the powerful personality of the Liberal candidate, Jonathan Alwyn.

I went on only one overseas school trip, to Montreux on Lake Geneva at Easter 1947. The journey there was by overnight French railway, very basic at that time. There was no food on board, and when we changed trains (Geneva?) we discovered how minimal continental breakfast was. The Chateau Chillon, which Lord Byron visited and later wrote the poem *The prisoner of Chillon*, was visible from our hotel. The magnificent snow-covered mountain scenery, the Rochers de Naye, was my introduction to photography. We were very limited in funds, and I was naïve enough to be talked into lending some of mine to John de Soyres, which ran me short. The trip was led by Maurice and Betty, who were courting at the time; one evening they went off in a rowing boat but headed back to the wrong set of lights on the shore, returning very late.

School dances were very different from now. A gramophone record was put on 'the amplifier'. The school repertoire of dances was limited to quickstep, waltz and slow foxtrot, rumba, samba and tango, and jive. You went up to a girl and asked for this dance, then after 3 minutes either conducted her back to her place or stayed on the floor for one more. The volume was such that talking was easy. I find this system immensely more enjoyable than the modern style, in which you are not holding you partner, or smooching, most of the time, and the deafening noise prevents conversation.

But we are at school to learn things, aren't we? My academic progress was somewhat erratic. I never had any difficulty with schoolwork, French excepted, and in particular liked exams, generally coming top, and being annoyed that results were communicated individually and not read out. Only children like exams, you can shine in them without social skills. Early in the senior school we took an intelligence test, the results of which were meant to be confidential but somehow reached us. I scored 144, and when being told off by the Head for misbehaviour he would begin with, "Now you are an intelligent boy, Young…". This score was bettered only by Kenneth Johnson – who was to go to art school, where he showed some talent, then spent his entire life as Letchworth Librarian, living with his mother. Kenneth wrote a poem about me, full of rhymes with Young ("His praises I have sung", etc.). My response was a shorter verse, ending, "Twould need a poet very bright/To find a rhyme for Kenneth Johnson".

He did, however, have one influence upon me. My handwriting in early schooldays had been the cursive style, with nearly every letter joined up, loops on all strokes above and below the line (h, l, g, even t), and a hook for 's'. One day Kenneth put up on a notice board in the corridor an informative piece on lettering which I found convincing, and forthwith changed to a print style, with most letters separate, no loops and a proper 's', and have stayed with this.

Being left-handed, handwriting is somewhat clumsy and slow. It seemed so unnecessary to write out in full 'the, and, to, -tion, -ing' and the like, so for class notes I invented a private shorthand; not on the phonetic system, as Pitman, but with line or hook symbols for the 50 or so commonest words and suffixes. I used this at university and for private notes all my life, so anyone who wants to dig into these will need it.

By the School Certificate year I had fallen into bad ways, not paying much attention in class, skiving in a place called the Bunk Room (an illness rest room), and still doing all my assignments (homework) in optionals. In June 1947 I took School Cert at the somewhat early age of 14 years and 9 months. I could easily have passed it, but at that time you had to pass six subjects at one sitting (counting Eng Lang and Eng Lit as two). I got five credits (Bs) but failed both History and French, and thus was not awarded any passes at all, putting me into the 'failed School Cert' or blue collared section of the country's youth, who would thereafter hew wood and draw water. In 1950, O Level put an end to this sheep and goats situation. This failure had a radical effect upon my attitude and work habits, and at the retake in November, still only aged 15, I got the necessary six credits plus a Very Good (A) in Geography. Examination aids were that as it had been the life of Gladstone in July we assumed correctly it would be Disraeli in November; and an evening inspection of the physics lab before the practical revealed a set of Wheatstone Bridges. Two years later I added, most improbably, a VG in Latin, having learnt the English cribs of the two set books (Caesar Gallic Wars II and Virgil on beekeeping) by heart in bed at night. *Hic rebus cognoscit*, as Caesar himself remarked, I passed.

I was then supposed to study Maths, Physics and Geography for Higher Certificate (the last of these before the introduction of A level), but didn't progress well with Maths. All mathematicians reach a ceiling, and mine was found to be here. I might have made better progress if there had been more manipulative maths (statistics, computing) around at the time. Meanwhile I had found my métier in Geography, and Oscar knew that he, too, had reached his ceiling. Together with the egregious goody-goody Michael Chisholm I travelled once a week to Cambridge for coaching by a young don, and we had soon covered a good deal of the university first year syllabus. The leading college for geography was St Catherine's, for which we took the entrance exam and went for interview; I didn't get a place (learning afterwards that my Physical Geography paper was very good, the Economic one less so), Mike did; he was later to become Professor of Geography at Cambridge.

Rather surprisingly I never took Higher Certificate, but went off to do National Service in April 1950, my only notion of the future being that Dad had introduced me to a chartered accountant who offered to take me on afterwards. But a few weeks into basic training I received a phone call to say I had a place at St John's College, Cambridge, to which I had not applied, to read Geography. There are three possible explanations of this. First, that Dad had access, through a colleague in Somerset House, to Cup Final tickets, which the Master of St John's was eager to acquire; confronted with this late in life, Dad denied any knowledge of it. Secondly, the headmaster had a long-standing connection with St John's, his influence being strengthened by the fact that his eldest son, Simon, was in the Lady Margaret first boat. On reflection, the duller third reason might be that my entrance papers to St Catherine's had been passed on. In any event, the outcome is that I am possibly the only person in the country with MA, PhD who lacks the minimum requirements for entry to university, two E-grade passes at A-Level.

St Christopher did not go in for intensive coaching, although it was sound in its teaching. To this day it appears about midway in the FT 500 best independent schools, never attaining the multiple A's that gets the top places.

However, it would produce individuals quite outstanding in their field, winning Oxbridge scholarships, in one case to both of these. It was not strong on encouragement of team spirit, nor did it encourage going along with policy when you disagree with it which is sometimes necessary, e.g. in the civil service. On the other hand it was very good at making you think for yourself, hence the success in producing academics. We had hardly heard of most of the redbrick universities; those who were not up to Oxbridge might go to Bristol, Exeter or, in not of an academic bent, Loughborough.

As far as sport was concerned I had a frustrating time, being mad keen but with no great natural ability. My football was indifferent, and hampered by occasional knee trouble. Cricket, for a boy without any social cachet, was a bore: sent in to bat No. 10 or 11, not often asked to bowl (slow left-arm leg breaks), and put to field at a position found only in school cricket, long stop (in case the wicket keeper missed the ball). In athletics I was a natural sprinter but was low on stamina; for some years after I hankered a wish that I had devoted effort to training for the 100 yards, though in retrospect there are better ways of spending one's time. Up to the age of 50 or so I've loved a really fast sprint.

I got a somewhat distorted view of the balance of British society, since naturally at a part-boarding fee-paying school most pupils were middle class (though not one of my best friends, a plumber's son) and of course there were no Catholics, who would choose their own private schools. On the other hand Jews were over-represented, e.g. among my contemporaries Schneider, Sachs, Mendel and Woolf. It was also unusual at that time to have Africans. Ian Orchardson (Chunky), son of a Kenyan mother and a Scots father,[1] ran the school's first 5-minute mile and became an Assistant Registrar at London University. The Coussey girls, Christine and Marie, daughters of the Gold Coast's first African judge, broke most athletics records in every age group, and when the Captain perceived that there was no rule against doing so, he selected them for his House cricket team.

Christine Coussey had a classmate called Ingrid White, maybe of Scandinavian extraction but anyway who was a blonde and extremely white. One day they read that Bernard Shaw, who lived at Ayot St Lawrence, Hertford-

---

[1] President Obama is also half and half, but with a Kenyan Luo father and an English mother.

shire, had said something unorthodox (I cannot recall what) about school-children. They rang his Secretary, said they would like to thank him, and got invited to tea.

Contemporaries of mine included Philip Drazin, Professor of Applied Mathematics at Bristol; sons of a North London electrical contractor, one of his older brothers became Professor of Maths at MIT, the other, called in their family 'the dull one', Reader in Philosophy at Oxford. A boy I did not particularly like, Paul Mendel, became Director of the Council for Christians and Jews. Another fat self-opinionated boy, whom I did not like at all, showed remarkable persistence in putting on a notice board, every week, reviews of the films showing locally; he went up to Cambridge, rescued the fortunes of the Rex Cinema by telling the Manager what films undergraduates wanted to see, and later talked himself into becoming the film director and minor media celebrity Michael Winner – in which capacity, despite the encouragement he had received, he took frequent opportunities to denigrate the school. One boy who spent his break periods balancing stationary on a bicycle now runs a radio station in California. Then there was a boy who was no good at academic work, useless at school sports, and had no personality, in other words he was just a squit; he became the main-stay of Britain's Ryder Cup golf team for 20 years, Neil Coles. The chain of children's holiday adventure centres, PJL holidays, was founded by Peter Lawrence; because he had some health problem he was advised to take an outdoor job. There have been no politicians that I know of, and only a few military personnel other than for WWII service, in which we lost at least one boy. Overall, looking through the Old Scholars' Notes, one finds a greater range of careers than in most schools, with an emphasis on the creative and on service to the community, but industry, engineering and the professions are also well represented.

At home and friends

Our house in Letchworth was in Field Lane, a typical curving road with grass verges and rowan trees, good for cycling. No. 27 was a bungalow with a small front garden and a good-sized back garden. Inside it was distinctly limited for space: living room, small dining room, main bedroom, my room at the back, kitchen and larder, hall. To get from the lavatory (which had no wash-hand basin) to the bathroom meant going through the kitchen. It served well enough for living during a period of general austerity, although there was nowhere to put guests. A great feature was its closeness to the school, only 200 yards, allowing me to walk there and even home to lunch, thus never partaking of the vegetarian meals which the St Christopher served.

In Field Lane, Letchworth
Last photo without glasses!

Home life was not eventful. Dad commuted up to Somerset House from Hitchin Station, steadily getting promotion in the legal branch of the Inland Revenue. On weekdays on return from school I was given high tea (scrambled eggs, Heinz spaghetti, etc.), whilst Dad dined when he returned around seven o'clock. In the War years we didn't travel much, then later came visits to grandparents, uncles, aunts and cousins.

My out-of-school activities were centred on a group of day boys (known to the boarders as day bugs) who formed a minority in the school, and were not meant to be there out of hours except for club activities. My two best friends were Leon Fish and John Manson. Others in the group were Francis (Wuffy) Davidson, of socialist persuasion – he liked to play Monopoly "to work out my capitalist instincts"; Colin and Romilly Bowden, John Robinson and Jack White.

We used to make fireworks using materials which the chemist's shop must have known full well were for this purpose. I forget some of the ingredients, but the ones made with potassium nitrate were comparatively safe, requiring ignition to explode, whilst those made with potassium sulphate could be set off by compression, as when stuffing them into an old shell or cartridge case. It seems to be a theme of my youth that safety was not an over-riding feature, and in this respect with good reason. I was in the adjacent garden when John Robinson screamed, "Help, I've blown my fingers off!" and indeed he had blown off the thumb and first finger of his left hand – which did not stop him playing a good game of cricket. At Wuffy's house there was table croquet, an effective miniaturization, and at Leon's table tennis, an eighth-size snooker table, and a back yard suited to two-man cricket. Why this choice of friends? Well, Wuffy was on the plump side, and Leon, John Manson and Colin were all lacking in self assurance, like me.

Leon, John and I shared a passion for sport, most readily done by following Luton Town Football Club (the Hatters), or nearer to hand the amateur sides of Letchworth and Hitchin. Luton was 13 miles away and to begin with we went by bus, queuing for what seemed ages. During the War the teams included 'guest' players, servicemen who were stationed nearby. The first game I saw was in 1942, Luton 2, Brentford 2, the Luton side including the England full back Eddie Hapgood. Most of the spectators were standing, and we would queue up to get in early and run into the stadium to get a good position behind a barrier. Footballers then were paid £4.10s a week (2016: £140) in the First Division, less in the Second and Third (in wartime Third Division North and Third Division South, to reduce travelling).

Later we cycled to Luton. One went everywhere by bicycle in those days, when it was very much safer. If a car came along the road, both you and the driver took care. True, once there was one of three occasions in my life when there was a small chance of getting killed. Entering Luton you freewheeled down a steep hill, reaching about 25 m.p.h.; lying in the road was a coiled bed-spring and I only just swerved in time to miss it. Cycling was extremely convenient and relatively safe, without helmets or other devices.

I was a boy scout for several years, not a very good one although appointed a patrol leader. Meeting in the hut beside St Paul's Church, initially we were Air Scouts, with the interest of recognizing planes, British and German, from their silhouettes. Then they decided that without a nearby airfield we could not justify remaining so, and became regular scouts. Our 'Skipper' was a wonderful man, willing to devote so much time to us and with a natural command. An activity which ended most meetings was British Bulldogs: all run from one end of the room to another whilst the boy in the middle catches the smallest and lifts him off the ground; whereupon there are two boys in the middle, the game continuing until all except one have been so lifted. That wasn't all that dangerous although a variant in which you had to be flattened onto the ground was less pleasant in the later stages. As for vaulting over a line of boys, heads beneath the legs of the one in front, trying to support as many as possible, that cannot have been good for the back. In Junior School we played rough riders, piggy-back, try to charge or pull the others onto the ground, no damage done when you are not too tall.

The County Scout Marathon required teams of three to cycle, navigating by map, a route of 25 miles, camp overnight, and arrive the next day for inspection, with marks awarded for cheerfulness, the condition of your bicycles, and the log book you had kept. I found myself allotted the rear position on a tandem (cheerfulness joke prepared in advance: a puncture kills two birds with one stone). Supper included sandwiches made with huge radishes, and the next morning I had a serious stomach ache. There was nothing for it but to cycle home where the doctor called, gave me a pain killer, and when the next morning the pain had not gone I was taken to hospital, diagnosed as having appendicitis, and my appendix removed.

In 1947 I was selected, with two others, to represent Letchworth in the Hertfordshire troop for the World Scout Jamboree. Skipper thought I ought to have more badges than I had, and I instantly became Cook and Cyclist – not the last time my progress in life was to be achieved not strictly according to the book. There was a preparatory camp for the Hertfordshire contingent, attended by the Chief Scout, Lord Rowallan, at which we learnt our County song with its immortal refrain. Being the first after the war, and held at Moisson, on the Seine downstream from Paris (it is near Monet's garden), this was called the Jamboree de la Paix. To begin with it was good fun, with a few national demonstrations, like American scouts showing lassoing and accuracy with long whips. However, there was a fierce heat-wave in Europe that summer, and soon all one wanted to do was to go swimming the Seine. Regrettably, after a few days someone got drowned and that was the end of swimming – but not of large numbers of boys going down with sunstroke.

The Hertfordshire troops were 33, 34 and 35, hence the camp song:

A song for Hertfordshire scouts at the Jamboree de la Paix 1947
To the tune of There is a tavern in the town

Oh, Thir—ty Three and Four and Five
Four and Five!
Will try—to keep the flag alive
Flag al-i-ive! So-o
Let your voices swell into a choir
And sing—this song of Hertfordshire.

I guess I gave up scouting after the failed School Certificate episode.

Shortly after the War my parents had arranged a holiday at a guest house somewhere on the East Coast. They went off by car, but I wanted to attend the end of term School Dance. The next morning I locked up the house and cycled something like 100 miles there. When I went to wash, the sweat wouldn't come off properly, I thought because it was so deeply impregnated into me. It turned out that the owner had, during rationing, invented a soap substitute, which as I afterwards observed looked like cheese, felt like cheese, tasted like cheese, but wouldn't lather.

My girl friends, on the other hand, were all boarders. They were few, and with hindsight it cannot be said that their marriage prospects were ideal. Elizabeth Mallinson was my idea of glamour, so much so that I realized I stood no chance against socially adept boys, and only worshipped her from afar. Then there was Susie Younger, a freckle-faced redhead, daughter of the Minister of State Kenneth Younger, but beyond once playing doubles tennis as Young and Younger I did not pursue her; which was just as well, as she became a missionary, setting up a home for reformed prostitutes in Korea. Somewhat more progress was made with a girl called Claire. After going to bed, I waited until my parents thought I was asleep, then climbed out of the window of the bungalow, through the next door back garden and to the school, meeting her by pre-arrangement in the gardener's potting shed where we engaged in some enjoyable mutual activities – but stopping short of the whole way, as nearly everyone did at that time. She became a piano teacher. Another became one of the early policewomen.

I spent a lot of time practising the piano, particularly in holidays. Mum, a professional accompanist before marriage, and teaching piano after Dad left home, did not teach me, nor did I learn at St Christopher but from private tutors, latterly in Hitchin. The high points of ability, reached at around 14 years old, were Mendelssohn's *Introduction and Rondo Cappricioso* and Debussy's *Jardins sous la pluie*.

Whilst glad to have been able to sit down and play all my life, I have several regrets about my musical education. First, not to have acquired perfect pitch as a young child, which I understand is the only time you can do it. Secondly, not to have been taught music theory nor playing by ear, both of which I would have enjoyed, neither in Musical Appreciation (MusApp) at school nor in conjunction with piano lessons (hence the gratitude to Nan's brother Reg). I wish someone had tried to give me the knack of playing accurately, perhaps it is laying the fingers on the keys before striking. Then I wish even more that I could sight read better; I don't look even one bar ahead of what I am playing.[1] Finally, I would love to have also learnt the violin. Unless you are very good indeed, playing the piano is a private activity. But a competent violinist is always in demand as the bread and butter of amateur orchestras.[2]

In the album there is a picture of me on a drop-handlebars bicycle dated 1947 and labelled, 'Last photo before glasses'. We had been to the London theatre, Dad had made some remark, and I responded, "Do you mean that you can see the expressions on their faces?" This led to a visit to the opticians and glasses, one more handicap to sporting success. By the time I was fully grown the correction had reached -5 to -7 dioptres, when I could more or less exchange glasses with Dad. Maybe the eye is large (in short sight, light rays come to a focus in front of the retina) because I have such a large head, even XL hats don't fit properly.

---

[1] Liszt was once asked to demonstrate his sight reading, watched by musicians. It was found, by when he nodded for the page to be turned, that he memorized seven bars ahead.

[2] But inheritance is necessary to become a top violinist. It has been pointed out that nearly all the world's great violinists are Jewish, many of them Russian Jews, a surprising number born in Odessa.

Early reading included the *Just William* books[1] and several Arthur Ransomes. *Swallows and Amazons* I enjoyed and read more than once, followed by *Swallowdale*; but then I started on *Missee Lee* and it was obvious to me that these children could not have sailed up the River Yangtze, so it did not really happen. This was a great let-down, the beginning of my disillusionment with fiction. On the whole I prefer to read about what happened (including to real people, as in biographies), not what an author decides should happen. Pelican books, the non-fiction arm of Penguins, were a great staple; in those early years they had the knack of choosing authors who made virtually any subject interesting, science, history, or whatever.

For newspapers, we took Beaverbrook's *Daily Express* and *Sunday Express*, and Dad brought home the *Evening Standard* from the train (I guess he must have read *The Times* on the up journey). In the *Standard* I read the reports from magistrate's courts (real life) and the short stories (OK, fiction, but with the pleasure of seeing the 'point' at the end). Then there was the column by Beachcomber (J. B. Morton) in the *Daily Express*, the subtlety of whose humour I could not always appreciate, and a similar one by Nathaniel Gubbins in the *Sunday Express*. The latter featured a funny Nazi, "Ziss iss Funf speaking"; Colonel Chinstrap, "Water my dear Sir? Never touch the stuff"; and messages sent up by the writer's stomach, in response to wartime and post-war diet (e.g. powdered egg, whale-meat steak). He observed that drama was often spoilt by the entry at a critical point of a Sporting Englishman, thus:

> Sir Jasper: Aha! Now I have you in my power.
> Millicent: Alas, I am lost! What shall I do?
> *Enter a Sporting Englishman*
> S.E.: What about a game of golf?

> Stephan Stinkowski: Peter Pushkin has shot himself, Ivan Ivanoff has drowned himself, Dmitri Dmoitrikoff has gassed himself, Anna Avan-other has poisoned herself. Nobody understands the Five-Year Plan. *(Pointing a revolver at his head)* There is only one way out.
> *Enter a Sporting Englishman*
> S.E.: What about a game of golf?

---

[1]   By Richmal Crompton whose niece I later came to know in Norwich. She was also Richmal, married to Paul Ashbee, archaeologist.

Fifi: Zo you tink I am ver nice, hein?
Claude: You are adorable, intoxicating … Let this night be ours, just you
and I.
As before

It was also at about that time, or perhaps into the 1950s, that my ideal of
the perfect female was set by fashion photographs, particularly those of
John French. The essential of this was extreme elegance. I have never
caught up with the modern age in this respect, deploring the casual appearance which came in with Mary Quant and others in the 1960s.

I had a try with J. W. Dunne's *Experiment with Time*. Dunne believed that
dreams allowed you to see into the future; some people thought they could
get the Grand National winner in this way. What you do is to place a pad of
paper and a pencil on a bedside table and train yourself, immediately on
waking, before opening your eyes, to write down your dreams. It is amazing
the span of events that can be recalled in this way, but I never found any
plausible correspondence with the future. John Manson and I also tried tele-
pathy, transmitting the suits of playing cards, but without statistically significant results. Indeed, not a single instance of the supernatural, paranormal
or the like has ever entered my life, which is disappointing.

Entertainment

With no television, we went to the cinema once every week or so – like
most of the population. There were five: two in Letchworth, two in Hitchin,
one in Baldock. The first film I ever saw was in Rushden days, Helzapoppin
(1941). The opening was worrying in that I did not understand that the
roasting of bodies on spits in Hell was not for real; but I did appreciate the
situation when a character fired a shot at the painting of a ship on the wall,
which fired back a few times and then sank. By reading Dilys Powell's
concise criticisms in a text box on the back of the Sunday Express you
could readily tell which films you would like and which not (the worst film
I've seen was about Mickey Rooney in an American borstal, but that's
because John Manson and I had gone into the wrong cinema). We sat in the
2/6d (2016: £3.50) seats, not the cheap ones at the front. I am quite
prepared to sustain the view that this was a golden age of cinema, with a far
higher proportion of good films than nowadays – artistically good, making
use of film techniques, and not least, entertaining. The leading box-office

actor for three of the War years was George Formby, and my taste in humour as a boy coincided with that of the adult public at large. Films started to go wrong with *Laurence of Arabia* (1962) and *Dr Zhivago* (1965), becoming too polished, too much, "Let's make a great film".

Most feature films lasted about 1½ hours, not the 2-3 hour blockbusters which are common nowadays. But you also got at least two and sometimes three further films. First, a newsreel, usually Pathé, similar to the present TV News, very popular during the War. This was sometimes followed by a Documentary, almost any subject, e.g. a pottery, or the London-Scotland mail train (with music by Benjamin Britten). Then came the 'B film', a genre which has entirely disappeared, possibly a crime story or a film equivalent of the short story. It is surprising that with so much TV time to be filled, these are never revived. So finally, 30-40 minutes later, you reached the feature film. This was just as well, since the queues could be so long that you did not get in for that time. Indeed, you might not get in until the main film was under way, and have to sit round until the next performance to see the beginning – when the queue started moving very slowly you knew you were in the situation now found in multi-storey car parks, waiting for couples to leave so that you could be shown (by the usherettes) to the only two vacant seats in the large cinemas of those days. Danny Kaye's record, *Manic Depressive Presents*, finishes with, "This is a film that ends in the middle, for the benefit of those who came in the middle ... THIS IS THE ta-daaa END!"

Theatre in North Hertfordshire was represented by the St Francis Theatre just round the corner from us. I came in at the end of variety theatre, the bill including singers, dancers, comedy, ventriloquists, acrobats, jugglers and conjurers, with a large number, 1 to 10, displayed on a board at the side to the stage to show which act of the programme had been reached. Among the classic acts, I distinctly remember seeing the sand dancers, Wilson, Keppel and Betty, dressed as Egyptian hieroglyphs in profile doing a synchronized dance on a sand tray; and Harry Hemsley, sitting behind a newspaper while his family of children conversed. We also went up to London theatre, seeing the Crazy Gang: Bud Flanagan (minus Ches Allen, retired), Nervo and Knox, and Monsewer Eddie Gray with his handlebar moustache, juggling clubs.

I saw Sid Field, with his straight man Jerry Lewis, twice, his car sketch in Letchworth, the snooker sketch in London. Unlike in the TV era, these sketches were taken round the country for years, and thus the timing became finely honed. Regrettably I never saw Max Miller, the greatest standup comic of all time, only now preserved on a few recordings and one film.

From *Worm's Eye View*, about soldiers billeted with a landlord, I acquired a lifetime love of farce (and also how correctly to warm a teapot – swirl it round). Years later, I can recall seeing *A Flea in Her Ear* (Georges Feydeau) where there is a character who, in the production I saw (script, or producer?) had a speech impediment. When the usual farce climax of accelerating lunacy was reached, people rushing in and out of doors, inappropriately meeting or not meeting and so forth, in a moment of quietude this young man advanced to front stage and announced, "There's humfing hunny hoing on around here, I can heel it in my bones!" *The Government Inspector* (Gogol) is great, as too is a modern farce, *Noises Off*.

The pre-television era was the golden period for listening to the radio, and I must have started listening to the weekly comedy programmes at the Cottage: *ITMA* with Tommy Handley, and *Mediterranean Merry-go-Round* which over three weeks rotated between Charlie Chester[1] (based on the army), Eric Barker (navy) and the most sophisticated, Richard Murdoch and Kenneth Horne (air force). I am quite prepared to agree that much of it doesn't sound as funny now, but again my sense of humour as a 10-15 year-old coincided with that of the adult public at large. It was the era of the catch-phrase, the mere saying of which raised a laugh and sometimes, as with Mrs Mopp's "Can I do yer now, Sir" on ITMA, applause. For a time it became impossible to remark, "I have an idea" without eliciting the responses, "You havn't, Murdoch", "I have, Sir". Murdoch observed that whereas military personnel were frequently glorified, the less glamorous occupations lacked their own songs, so came up with the following ditty:

---

[1] In the 1980s Charlie Chester appeared in cabaret at the Norwood Rooms, Norwich, telling jokes intended for North of England working men's clubs. For political incorrectness it is hard to beat this one, being racialist, environmental and East Anglian: "I was standing on the beach at Lowestoft the other day when 47 Pakistanis swam ashore, disguised as an oil slick".

36

From *Much Binding in the Marsh* c.1944

I'd like to be—an oxy-acetylene welder
Welding the whole day through.
There's no—life like an oxy-acetylene welder's
And well does he know that's true.

I weld all day and I weld all night,
Just give me a bit of oxy-acetylene—I'll be alright.
And one day all my dreams will come true
When she says "Oxy-acetylene welder, I love you".

By and large, Robb Wilton does not now sound funny. He had a catch phrase, "The day war broke out…" It may have been him who had a verse monologue in which the ship's Captain calls upon him to make a selfless sacrifice for the good of the rest of the crew (Lancashire accent), "And we're all of uz saived – except except won – and that's you".

I have always liked the circus, having a weak spot for acts of human dexterity, the acrobats and jugglers, and for mime-based humour, the clowns. We went occasionally to touring big tops, and at least once to a major circus, probably Chipperfields, where I was lucky enough to see the Cairoli Brothers. One came on playing a clarinet, the lower part of which was rubbery and waved around; on being hit this came off, so he continued to play the upper part, and the same again for the mouthpiece (you can do this with a clarinet). But then with an almighty swipe his entire head came off and what was left ran out of the ring, still playing.

Sadly I never saw the greatest of clowns, the Swiss-born Grock (Karl Adrien Wettach, 1880-1959), who specialized in musical gags as he could play 24 instruments. One of the funniest things I have ever seen – only I havn't, just read about it – is when he approaches an enormous grand piano, sits on the music stool, and finds he cannot reach the keyboard; with massive effort he heaves away at the piano, but cannot move it. Eventually he becomes aware of the mounting crescendo of advice coming from children in the audience, pauses, listens, and as he comprehends a seraphic smile breaks over his face – and he pushes to stool towards the piano.

Leon Fish

A thoroughly genuine, unassuming person at school, Leon Fish was to go on to lead the most admirable life of anyone I have known, an outstanding example of courage in overcoming both personal tragedy and physical handicap. He lost his mother whilst still at school, his father some years later, his first child in infancy, and suffered from a crippling illness for more than half his life. Despite all this, he remained cheerful and uncomplaining, brought up a family, and led a full career.

After National Service in the Suez Canal Zone, he joined his father as plumber. At the age of 28, multiple sclerosis was diagnosed. He met a most wonderful girl, Jean, a year later, who married him knowing the likely progress of his condition, and they had two sons. Leon took pleasure from the fact that they both obtained single-figure golf handicaps.

When illness forced him to give up his business he became a Sales Administrator to a firm of builders merchants. A Director (also from St Chris) said that thanks to his previously having been on the receiving end, he developed a particularly good rapport with customers. Moving to a new Letchworth house for the disabled, working from a wheel chair he personally refitted the central heating system.

For the last nine years of his life his deteriorating condition necessitated a move to the Hertfordshire Cheshire home in Hitchin. He was soon coerced into becoming Chairman of the Residents Committee, and thus *ex officio* on Management Committee. The Manager reported that Leon was a quiet man, but when he spoke, everyone listened and respected his opinions.

4

THE FAMILY

Having declined to start this account with the relations, we cannot any longer avoid the hold-up that this will cause. Not that we visited them all that frequently because of travel limitations during and after the War, for on moving to Letchworth none of them lived close. Nor were they all that many: at the time of which I am writing, 3 grandparents (Mum's father had died before I was born), 4 uncles, 4 aunts and 5 cousins, not much of a showing compared with Dad's 22 aunts and uncles, and 32 cousins. I never met these Great Uncles and Aunts, for a sympathetic and amusing account of which you must go to Dad's autobiography.[1]

The Youngs

Grandfather and Grannie Young lived at Westhumble Place, Dorking, Surrey, a fine house in its own grounds just below Box Hill (Darryl was to have his wedding reception close by). Grandfather (**Sidney Michael Young senior, 1871-1955**) had had a profitable business as a quantity surveyor at a time of much building activity, the firm of Young and Brown being well-known. My recollection is of an amiable, jolly man – his portrait shows some resemblance to Groucho Marx. As a small boy we once went for a walk together. I must have asked on which side I should walk, his reply being (in a true Cockney accent), "Well, if you walk this side o' me I can't

---

[1]   A genealogy of the Young family is given in *A history of the families of Young and Goodall (Isle of Wight)*, written by my great grandfather Sidney Young FSA, privately printed in 1913. Dad's own account of his early life is in *Sidney Michael Young: recollections of a lawyer in London and Shanghai 1900-1928*, written by him about 1983 and edited and reproduced by me.

see yer, and if you walk that side I can't 'ear yer". Dad confirms what a nice person he was, adding that as a younger man he played the banjo.

Grannie on the other hand, (**Hilda Hardcastle Buchanan, 1877-1963**) was rather formal and correct. She had supernatural powers over animals: a casual aside, without emphasis, was sufficient to make a dog slink out of the room onto its mat. Dad's opinion of his mother was not favourable, for good reason, and he considered that if she had lived in an earlier century she would have been burnt as a witch. She held Victorian ideas of the amount one should eat, and once made me ill (possibly a precursor of an inflamed appendix) by over-feeding me until I was sick. I went to bed and was brought arrowroot, which after one mouthful was surreptitiously sent down the lavatory. After Grandfather's death she went to live in a succession of South Coast hotels, leaving when she had established that the head waiter was a thief or possessed other undesirable habits. A hotel once changed hands complete with Mrs Young in residence. Visiting her with Doreen, I was taken to task for the unkempt state of my hair, and for referring to her in the wrong way when speaking to a servant – it should have been "Mrs Young", and only "My Grandmother" to family.

Their four children were all sons. Dad was the first to be born, thus taking his father's name and spending the rest of his long life as 'junior'. Second was Jack (**John Lancelot Young, 1902-c.1963**) who was mentally handicapped, probably as a result of an injury during birth. I only saw him once, helping in the garden. Dad says that he was a mild, gentle man but in need of care, and that Grandfather spent much of his savings finding suitable private homes for him.

The younger boys had positive, assertive characters, perhaps in response to the need to stand up to their mother. Uncle Geoffrey (**Geoffrey Ernest Young, 1909-1994**) was a larger than life character. Like all his brothers he was six feet tall, but in Geoffrey's case this was accompanied by a weight of some 16 stone, a powerful physique with a prize fighter's neck, and a booming voice. After Westminster School he went to St Catherine's College, Cambridge to read Forestry. His graduation, however, must have been about 1930 when the Great Depression was at its height, jobs in the Civil Service had been cut by the Geddes Axe, and work with the Forestry Commission was out of the question. Despite lack of appropriate qualifications – these were not considered necessary for managers in those days – he took over his father's firm. His management competence not being high, the directors found opportunity to buy him out well before retirement age, thus providing Geoffrey with a comfortable income and the opportunity to indulge in his interest in arboreta and botanical gardens.

After having been bought out of the firm at a time when investment was highly profitable, Geoffrey increased his wealth in many ways. He lived with his parents into middle age. He never learnt to drive a car, considering it less expensive to take a taxi when necessary. After weekends he would walk onto Box Hill and pick up empty soft drink bottles, not out of environmental concern but to collect 3d or 6d for their return.

The Box Hill walks also provided him with a lifetime supply of biro pens, for which free writing paper would be collected from Fortnum and Mason or other London stores, on which his letters would be written. (I follow his practice with respect to combs, at the time of writing having a reserve supply of eight.) Receipt of his letters presented a problem, as his handwriting was close to indecipherable ("Because I am a corrected sinistral"). It was no good trying to work it out letter by letter, nearly every oscillation was much the same; you needed to get a little drunk and optimistic, then look at sentences as a whole and see if a meaning could be constructed from the few distinguishable letters.

His train story comes from a time when railway carriages did not have corridors but separate compartments. One day Geoffrey was on his own when three young men got into the carriage and started smoking. He pointed out that it was a non-smoking carriage and asked them to desist. One of the boys said, "We're going to do you". "Oh no you are not" he replied in his booming voice, "And I will give you three reasons. First, I happen to be a Special Constable (which was not true, but he had once been). Secondly, I shall pull the communications cord and officers of the railway company will arrive and detain you. And thirdly, I happen to be bigger and stronger than any of you; and I shall seize upon one of you, throw him around the carriage, and if possible maim him for life; *and you don't know which one of you it will be*". They remained very quiet before getting out at the next station.

At one time the family lived on the north side of Regent's Park, and Geoffrey would cross the park on his way to Westminster School. They had a very intelligent mongrel dog, Taxi, whom Geoffrey would take with him for a walk. On reaching his bus stop he would boom, "Go home, Taxi!", pointing in the appropriate direction. At one stage it was found that Taxi was arriving home earlier than before, so Geoffrey's brother Edward followed and secretly watched. Taxi went to the bus stop, sat down, waited for the appropriate bus and hopped onto the platform, leaving when he reached home. When questioned on the veracity of this story, Edward swore it was true.

In middle life Geoffrey married the gardener's daughter, **Olive Nethercott (1913-2000)**, too late to have children, and went to live at Budleigh Salterton. Aunt Olive tolerated his mannerisms and cared for him to the end of his days. He was wont to say, "Olive and I agree upon everything", and as she was a small and mild woman this was indisputable. When Dad left home, Geoffrey's disapproval was such that he never afterwards spoke to him nor, I think, to his other brother who was more sympathetic.

Geoffrey liked to say, "Cast your bread upon the waters, and you'll get a ham sandwich in return", which encouraged Doreen and I to pay him intermittent visits. Of course he left his money in trust to care for Olive, but on Olive's death the whole lot went to two deserving and penurious organizations, Westminster School and St Catherine's College, Cambridge, none of it passing to the family, which does not seem in accordance with his declared philosophy.

I saw very little of Uncle Edward (**Edward Buchanan Young, 1910-2000**) during my childhood – when taking a photo at my wedding he had to say, "I'm your Uncle". I only came to know him well in his later years. He worked for Shell as Officer in charge of Training, and said that he had introduced modern participatory methods at a time when this was not common. During the War he served as a Captain in the Royal Armoured Corps, landing in France on D-Day at D+36 minutes, i.e. 7.36 a.m., driving a half-tracked vehicle carrying 250 gallons of petrol, one of the first vehicles onshore. On D+1 he went to a farm, bought two camembert cheeses and posted them to his wife, Auntie Francis (**Francis Sprague, 1909-1992**); one arrived promptly and was consumed, the other spent too much time in the June weather. Some notion of the distinctive Young sense of humour may be gained from the fact that at his home in Chiswick the lavatory was lit by a 150-watt bulb, in order that he could display on the door Tennyson's line, "In that fierce light which beats upon a throne".

At some stage Edward became an Anglo-Catholic, a fact which plays a part in the story of the Young family portraits. There are seven of these covering five generations, the first from about 1730. The three earliest came into the possession of one of Dad's cousins, John Harrison Young (b.1928), who still holds them; Dad considers that this was a loan, but attempts to retrieve them failed. The others were held by Dad, but when he and Peggy (his second wife) went to live in South Africa were lent to Edward, on the clear understanding that they were to pass to me. So one day I rang Edward who agreed that that was the case, and would I come and spend Saturday night with him, taking the portraits the next day. After an excellent dinner, the next morning Edward announced that Francis and he were off to Mass ('Marss'), and would we please let ourselves out. Doreen held that we could not rip the portraits off the walls whilst Edward was on his knees praying, so we left without doing so. Some years later, after the death of Francis and Edward's intending move to be near his son in Dorset, we did succeed in collecting them.

Edward had three children, all boys. (Thus Grandfather had four boys, who between them had four boys including me.) Arising from his high church beliefs he felt obliged to name them after the Saint's Day on which they were born, thus my three cousins on the Young side were necessarily Bernard, Andrew and Valentine. They were all educated at Bloxham which, early in the life of 'league tables' for examination performance, distinguished itself by coming actually bottom in the list of public schools. Bernard (**Bernard Young, 1938-1993**) and Andrew **(Andrew Young 1941-)** both went into professions which serve the community, Bernard as a prison governor, and Andrew in the police force. Valentine (**Valentine Young, b.1945**) emigrated to Sydney, ran a business manufacturing and selling food-mixing machinery, and married an Australian, Helen. They are most amiable and hospitable people. At times there has been some animosity between these brothers, which I cannot understand and has never affected my relations with them.

Three generations
Sidney Michael Young with his son and grandson

The Lacks

Mum's family, Lack, is of a very different nature. I have given an account of them, with earlier generations, in a family history. My grandfather on this side, **Frederick William Lack (1862-1918)**, was Manager of the Brixton Branch of Bon Marché. He died shortly after the end of the First World War – Mum once said he drunk too much. He appears to have shared a characteristic of the Lack family through several generations, a concern for education of his children. During my early years Grannie Lack (**Mary Keer Berrett, 1863-c.1950**) lived at 57 Baldry Gardens, Streatham, cared for by her two daughters. Although in her early sixties when I first saw her, as was common in those days she looked and dressed like an old lady.

Auntie Hilda and Auntie Diddie were delightful ladies. Hilda (**Hilda Mary Lack, 1891-c.1972**) was trained and perhaps practised as a primary school teacher, but most of her life was spent looking after her widowed mother.

Diddie (**Mercie Keer Lack, 1894-1985**) was so called because when she was born, her elder sister could not pronounce 'Mercie' and said 'Did-di'; and so within the family she remained Diddie to the end of her days. Being somewhat dark she was also sometimes called Gypsy. Like her sisters she was educated at Clapham High School. This had linked to it an Art Training College, from which she obtained a Diploma/Pedagogic Certificate in 1915. She then held three posts as art mistress: County School for Girls Tunbridge Wells 1918-1924, Putney High School GPDST[1] 1925-July 1939, and Queen Anne's Caversham September 1939-July 1958.

The last move came about because in 1939 Putney HS was evacuated to Caversham, with a greatly reduced number of pupils. The Putney School Magazine takes up the story:

> Miss Lack is one of those generous people who spend themselves in unobtrusive services, and we were delighted that as we had so few pupils for her, the Queen Anne's School happened to be in need of an Art Mistress, so we have had the pleasure of seeing her at Harlech lunch on most days of the week. She is now entirely with Queen Anne's School until our numbers return to normal.

A colleague at Queen Anne's Caversham was Dorothy Bartholomew, later to become Headmistress of Norwich High School.

She produced sensitive watercolours, including two we possess showing a blacksmith and his forge, and colour woodcuts. She also recognized early the value of photography as an art form, taking many distinguished black--and-white compositions, printed in her own darkroom.

On the death of their mother, Hilda and Diddie moved to a house on Cockshott Lane, Froxfield, on the top of the Chalk scarp near Petersfield, to enjoy their own lives at last, looking after the large garden. They would welcome us, and later our children, most warmly. All the Lacks spoke with

---

[1] Her commencing salary was £146 plus £22.10s for needlework; 1934 salary £236.16s (2016 respectively £8400 and £11 800). In recent years GPDST dropped the P(ublic) to become GDST, the Girls Day School Trust.

pure but unaffected voices and possessed a natural charm. After Hilda died, Diddie moved next door to Mum in Field Lane, Letchworth but this was not a success, the two sisters seemingly having little to say to each other.

The Sutton Hoo burial ship

In the Summer of 1939, between two teaching posts, Diddie and her colleague Barbara Wagstaff, the Gym Mistress, were on holiday in Suffolk, with the objective of photographing Saxon remains in churches. They heard about the excavation of the Sutton Hoo Saxon burial ship, and asked if they might stay and record this. As the British Museum had not by then sent a photographer, permission was readily granted. They stayed, making a day to day record of the excavation. From 9th to 24th August Diddie took 297 photographs and Barbara 150. They had also acquired two rolls of Agfa colour slide film, which was briefly on sale in England before the outbreak of war. Each took 36 slides, "Miss Lack with slightly more success than Miss Wagstaff" (says the record) and a short film. This is the only photo-graphic record of the excavation which first revealed this outstanding archaeological site. It is remarkable that she should have stayed there for two weeks, when the Autumn term at her new school would start in the month following.

In retirement, she was happy at the continuing requests (and small royalties) for Sutton Hoo photographs. On her death, she bequeathed them to the British Museum, and they continue to be displayed, there and in the Sutton Hoo museum, to this day.

Uncle Vic (**Victor John Frederick Lack, 1893-1988**) pursued a distin-guished career in medicine, a profession he shared with three other members of the Lack family, Thomas Lambert, Harry Lambert (ENT) and Christofer (Psychiatry). His father died when Vic was 25, when he must have been starting on his post-graduate studies, qualifying as a surgeon three years later. Vic became a noted obstetric and gynaecological surgeon, and teacher and examiner of midwifery. He worked mainly at London Hospital in the East End, and had a commitment to improving the lot of women in childbirth, which at that time was generally not good.

Vic married **Beatrice Snell, 1905-1982** (Auntie Babs) who was a concert pianist, playing particularly Chopin. She gave up her career on marriage or the birth of children, but of course could be persuaded to play brilliantly at home. Babs dressed in an elegant style, and had an even more delightful voice, which I must stress was classy but not affected.

When Vic was working they lived in St John's Wood, in a house which backed onto that of Dame Myra Hess, whom they could sometimes hear practising – I asked what was the pattern of this practice and was told it might be long passages played straight through until she came to a bit that was not yet right, which would be played over and over again. When he retired he chose a country house in its own substantial grounds, only to find it later surrounded by Harlow New Town. So he moved again, to a similar large mansion – in the rural solitude of the village of Milton Keynes!

I was once remiss enough to enquire of Diddie why she and Hilda had not married; she replied, "We couldn't all get married then, so many of the young men had been killed in the War". So Vic's two children, Richard and Jeremy, were my only cousins on the Lack side, one a year older, one a year younger than me. Both went to Charterhouse. Richard (**Richard Lack, b.1931**) began his career in Jamaica, as a Safety Officer for Kaiser Bauxite mines. Bauxite mining means extracting the aluminium from thick weathered surface formations, then depositing the waste in red 'lakes'. He married Phillippa (**Phillippa Goffe, b.1939**), an artist in silks, with a part-Jamaican ancestry. When political conditions rendered Jamaica hazardous he moved to a similar job with oil shale extraction in North America, then became Chief Safety Officer for San Francisco Airport. He acquired distinction in the field of industrial safety in North America, and edited a book about it.[1]

Jeremy (**Jeremy Lack, 1933-99**) read economics at Cambridge, found it to be a boring subject, and went into film editing. Working his way up in this field he became Director of Documentaries for Tyne-Tees Television, marrying Pam (**Pamela Leithead, b.1940**) who also worked there. Whatever Jeremy did, from model trains and butterfly collecting as a boy, to early antique china and his garden, he did extremely well.

---

[1] *Essentials of safety and health management* (2001). Second edition as *Safety, health and asset protection* (2002).

The Lack family at our wedding 1957
Front row: Joan, Diddie, Hilda, Babs; back row Vic, Jeremy

The wider families

All five of my cousins have children, most of whom have married, so our children have about 12 second cousins on the Young side and 7 on the Lack side. But we all move around the country so much these days that they have rarely met any of them. There is a large Young family tree dating back to 1558, the first nine generations living in or near the village of Carisbrook in the Isle of Wight – what a different life that must have been! My great great grandfather **Joseph Young (1794-1872)** moved from the Isle of Wight to Chatham and married **Catherine Pratt**, the sister of **Anne Pratt** (1806-1893). Anne was foremost among the Victorian botanical illustrators with a copious output of publications, the magnum opus being *The Flowering Plants, Grasses, Sedges and Ferns of Great Britain* (1854 and subsequent editions).[1]

There is a Lack family tree with some 110 names, every one a descendant of William Lack (1795-1859), Saddler and Harness Maker of Swaffham, Norfolk. These include the artist, **John Gildon Lack (1823-1892)** who studied with Howard Carter, thus giving a vicarious association with the Tutankhamen tomb excavation; and the distinguished ornithologist, **David**

---

[1] I have placed an account of Anne Pratt on the Internet: a blog entitled *The Anne Pratt Circle* and also via my web site www..land-resources.com.

Lambert Lack (1910-1973), who has been called 'The father of evolu-tionary ecology'.[1] One of my mother's cousins, **Reginald Lambert Lack (1891-1916**) was killed fighting in France in 1916, the only member of the Young and Lack families to lose his life in the two world wars.

Two features of these families are of note. First, all my cousins, on both the Young and Lack sides, are boys. Secondly, all branches of both families are unusually long-lived.

Family trees of the Young and Lack families are given following Chapter 20.

---

[1]   Ted R. Anderson, *The life of David Lack* (2013). David's best-known book is *The life of the Robin* (1943).

5

YOU'RE IN THE ARMY NOW 1950-51

So to return to my own life. For some years after the end of the War, every 18-year old male had to do a spell of National Service, for most of the time 18 months. It cannot be said that this was a successful or rewarding period. I have the greatest admiration for servicemen, who make life secure for the rest of us, and whom I have always found to be exceptionally well-mannered and considerate, not only the officers but privates and even, off the parade ground, NCOs. But the military mentality, with its unquestioning following of orders, is far from my own, and I did not do more than get by.

If you had university in view you could apply for early call-up, so service to my country began on 13th April 1950. There was a medical exam and preselection before joining up, and I put in for the RAF. I reached as far as an interview with a RAF officer, but before saying anything he looked at my papers, walked out of the room muttering, "Why can't these people do their job properly?", and came back in saying, "Go back and have your eyes tested again without glasses, and for Goodness sake read that top letter". This I could not do, so that was the end of my air force career.

A parallel event had taken place when Dad joined the army in the First World War. He was told that he would be admitted into the Inns of Court Regiment provided he passed the medical A1. His eyesight being as bad as mine there seemed little chance of doing this, but his excellent memory came to the rescue. Whilst he was being examined for heart, lungs, etc. he saw that the eye test was coming up and, with glasses on, memorized the entire test board.

Perhaps on the grounds of holding School Certificate I was assigned to REME, the Royal Electrical and Mechanical Engineers, a regiment in which brains played some part. Preparation was in two parts, basic training and trade training. Of basic training, or square bashing, the less said the better. Mine was at Honiton in Devon, lasted 6 weeks, and introduced me to the apparent stupidity of traditional military training, with its drill, polishing of boots, inspections, and constant fear of getting into trouble – aspects which seemed especially pointless to us who were not going to be doing this for life. My superiors must have treated me with some leniency, for I only got into trouble once (for picking up two portions of butter instead of one). On the parade ground I knew how to "go through the motions", a favourite army phrase, well enough not to be disciplined, but unfortunately made it look as if I was sending up drill. Being tall, the commands "Tallest on the left shortest on the right-SIZE!", "From the right NUMBER!", "Odd numbers one pace forward even numbers one pace backward MARCH!", and ending with a "Ri-hi-hight DRESS!" put me into a prominent end position. As Company showing in the passing out parade was competitive and my presence would have put paid to any chance for C Company, I was assigned to kitchen duties.

REME telecommunications training course, Bailleau Camp
My hat is too small

Besides square bashing, there were more intellectually challenging parts of training. The Instructor Sergeant announces, "Today's lecture is on intervisibility". Marks two crosses at top and bottom of a whiteboard. "You are at A, the enemy is at B. Question: Can you see the enemy?" Draws three concentric circles in between. "Of course you can't, there's a bloody great 'ill in the way. That's intervisibility." As a model of informativeness and conciseness this is hard to beat.

This was almost the first time I came into contact with members of the working class – the middle/working class distinction was much clearer in those days. As the only member of the 18-man squad barrack room with School Certificate I was addressed as 'Prof', but not made fun of, indeed, sometimes consulted on spelling when letters were being written home.

I am sometimes asked why I did not go to WOSBE (War Office Selection Board) to seek officer training. I was six months younger than most of the conscripts, but more importantly, knew that I had no leadership qualities whatever. Put in a group of five, faced with a pile of oil drums and planks, and asked to order the party to construct a bridge across an (imaginary) river when all the others were trying to do the same thing, I would have got nowhere. More realistically it might have seemed good to ask for a transfer to Intelligence, making use of my geographical knowledge, but to get that you needed to sign up for the regular army.

There was aptitude selection for different REME trades, and it occurred to me that training as a vehicle mechanic would be of some use in civilian life. However, selection was based on two components, an intelligence test (I am good at these), and a practical test in which you were presented with six objects which had been taken to pieces and asked to assemble them. I only managed one, it might have been a bicycle pump, but while I was still fiddling about with a mortise lock, those with a different upbringing had put together the lot, so that was the end of my vehicular ambitions. Being good at intelligence tests, I was assigned to the highest graded REME trade, tele-communications mechanic.

A longer period of trade training followed at a telecommunications training camp in Hampshire. The preselected members of this group were very different from those at basic training, all necessarily educated; one was the son of Herbert Bargett, Choirmaster of the Huddersfield Choral Society. The military elements, drill and so on, still took place, but most of our day was spent at lectures and practicals. In the early stages I made good progress, for they did not assume the prior God-given knowledge of elec-tronics that gifted schoolfellows seemed to possess, but started from basics. "Electrons move only from the anode to the cathode" our teacher announced, to which someone called Mellors called out, "Disciplinary action will be taken against any electron found proceeding from the cathode to the anode", and another added, "It will be charged – with 40 000 volts". At each stage of the course there was a theory exam, in which I would get 90%, but also a practical exam in which they gave you a b------d up tele-printer (or similar) and asked you to repair it. As I had spent much of the time in practical classes speeding up my touch typing, this I was unable to do. Nevertheless, perhaps after heart-searching in the examination board, I was passed as a qualified Telecommunications Mechanic, "22351554 Craftsman Young, Sir!" It is fortunate for military communications that the wars in which our country engaged did not take place when I was on the list of reservists.

We took a vow together that in the future we would never say, "Well, after all, the army wasn't so bad", since overall it was. However, droll events did sometimes happen. Once there was a practical class based on 6-foot high items of automatic telecommunications equipment, set on benches behind us. The instructor was droning away at the end of the hut, whilst for rest I leant on the bench behind me. Suddenly there was a loud explosion at the far end of the hut, followed by a smell of burning. Turning to look behind me I saw two very thick wires, one red and one black, intended to convey mains power into my piece of equipment, but which I had loosened and bought into contact with each other. I hurriedly and surreptitiously repaired the situation.

There was one bath in the camp, not much used, and usually offering only lukewarm water. Once, however, the soldier in charge of water heating must have received a rocket, for when I turned on the tap, an explosion of super-heated steam burst forth, continuing for some time before it gave place to water at 95° C. Seeking to moderate this, the adjacency of the pipes was such that the cold water alone was too hot to get into.

There were three REME camps in close to each other in this part of Hamp-shire, named after First World War battles, and commemorated in an immortal song.

A song for REME Ballieu telecommunications training camp
To the tune of the Eton Boating Song

Hazebrouck turns out bullshit, Borden turns out tanks,
But we are men of Ballieu, Dozey bloody cranks.

Push-pull together, We operate in Class B
Output united, From second harmonic free.

Other camps may scorn us, They talk a lot of rot
At scientific progress, We know we are SHIT HOT!

Push-pull together, etc.

A communications boffin will explain the second verse to you. I certainly can't.

A phone call received during basic training informed me that I had a place at St John's College, Cambridge to read Geography, surprising in that I had never applied to go there. Another phone call was received by the CO who summoned me, gave me a week's leave, and told me I was to go home and not do anything stupid. On arrival I found Mum in great distress, Dad having left home. He had gone to live with Peggy Francis, a talented bilin-gual stenographer 13 years his junior. Peggy had been living in a flat close to us, at the junction of Field Lane with Sollershott East, and I suppose they had met whilst commuting up to London. She was often invited into our house, and I would play piano duets with her. Such was (and still is) my insensitivity to personal matters that the nature of this situation did not strike me, for I had not been aware of anything wrong with my parents' marriage. So to put it bluntly, after 22 years of marriage Dad left Mum and went off with a younger woman.

So from the age of 50 onwards, Mum was going to live a lonely life. Dad sought a divorce, which was not easy in those days. He went through the distasteful but common procedure of taking Peggy for a weekend to a South Coast Hotel and tipping the chambermaid to recognize them and be prepared afterwards to testify. However, proceedings could only be started by the injured party, and this Mum refused to do – as she reasonably said, she had no wish for a divorce so why should she ask for one? So Dad and Peggy went to live, at the first of many places, as Mr and Mrs Young. It was quite some years before Mum was persuaded to take the unpleasant step of suing for divorce.

Naturally I was sympathetic towards her, took the view that Dad had done wrong, and in the early years did not visit him often and tried not to see Peggy at all, slowly moderating this attitude. After 26 years together (longer than Dad's first marriage) Peggy contracted cancer, Dad caring for her at home until the final days. She died in 1976, leaving two elderly people leading separate lonely lives. After coming to my wedding they never saw one another again.

To return to the army, Craftsman Young was posted to Ashford, Middlesex, but discovered this was simply a transit camp en route for Malaya, where the communist insurgency called for the presence of British troops. I promptly asked for and was given a compassionate posting and spent the rest of my 18 months at Ashford. Unfortunately there was no establishment there for telecommunications mechanics hence no benefit derived from my lengthy training and valuable acquired skills. By a feat of powerful logic, however, the powers that be decided that if telecoms was the highest graded REME trade and Instrument Mechanic the second highest, I could be usefully assigned to the instrument shop. I think some of my colleagues repaired clocks from time to time, but being unqualified to do this I spent much of the day devising games with nuts and bolts on the workbench.

Later it was found that a civilian engineer was repairing radio trucks and on completing each one, required someone to speak into the microphone from the back to the driver's cabin, so my communication skills were put to some use. This was a skive to beat all others, for you spent the whole day hidden in the back of the truck, where I would deal and practise bridge hands. This was because I had joined Hounslow Bridge Club, who played duplicate every Monday evening. Incredibly, John Manson travelled by train and tube from Letchworth to Hounslow to partner me, and back on the midnight train. I had learnt from a Penguin book by Terence Reese, which taught a version of the Acol system which has long been modified but which I still play, to the occasional dismay of opponents.

So what did I get out of the army? Well, many years later in a bar in Kathmandu a notice said 'Reduction in price for serving or former members of the armed forces'. When the barman asked, "Your service number, Sir?" I rattled off, "22352554" hoping this was not my credit card. More substantially, to learn the drill movement, "Change Step", useful when you are walking with your girl friend and find you are not in sync.

The government had increased the period of National Service from 18 months to 2 years, bringing gloom to all. We counted the days to demob like convicts, "279 days to go", until eventually the welcome day arrived. But with the university term about to start I was given early release on 28th September 1951, serving only 17½ months. One was not technically demobbed but transferred to the Reserve, in which I subsequently attended a summer camp in Stirling. My Discharge Certificate says that I was, "Extremely well educated, far above the average type[!], is being released from the service to enable him to complete his studies, to which he devotes most of his time and energy".

INTERLUDE: WORDS

These Interludes are not part of the life story, but an opportunity to display likes, dislikes and prejudices. There is some repetition from the main text.

FAVOURITE BOOKS

Fiction

When it comes to fiction I have a problem. Deborah Mitford relates that once when her father was ill in bed she thought she would try to cheer him up by reading to him, and chose Hardy's *Tess of the d'Urbervilles*. At one stage this has a sad section, and her father clearly became distressed. When she said, "Don't worry, Farve, it's only a story" the reply was, "You mean the blighter made it up?" and from that point he never read a book for the rest of his life. I feel much the same: if I know that something in a novel is not what really happened but "the blighter made it up" my interest wanes.

I first had this reaction as a boy, maybe aged 10. I had enjoyed reading Arthur Ransome's *Swallows and Amazons* and *Swallowdale*, assuming these were true accounts of childrens' adventures on Lake Windermere. Then I got *Missee Lee*, in which they go up the River Yangtze, and to my dismay realised that it could not possibly be a true story.[1]

So if I am to get to the end of a novel, it has to be good. Here are some of the more memorable.

Detective stories Although Agatha Christie is so formulaic, you must read *The murder of Roger Ackroyd* for a reason that cannot be revealed. Dorothy Sayers is more varied; let us have *Gaudy night* which, if I recall correctly, also has a feature unusual in detective stories. Another distinctive feature is found in

---

[1] On reading this, my grandson Oliver expressed a very different, almost diametrically opposite, view: "For me, fiction is one of the great tools for ethical thought, as it allows you to explore ideas freely".

E. C. Bentley's 1913 story *Trent's last case* (I hope it isn't too much of a spoiler to mention it has something in common with Hitchcock's film *Vertigo*).

Novels I have read most of Jane Austen but with a struggle, admiring some of the gently disparaging asides, but many were too subtle for me. The Bronte's *Jane Eyre* and *Wuthering Heights* both of which make an appearance, for different reasons, later in this text. After a few attempts, only one Dickens, *A tale of two cities*. An effort to complete James Joyce's *Ulysses* succeeded only with substantial skipping, and did not impress me. And in Proust's *A la recherche* … I scarcely got past him going to sleep without his mother's kiss (though I do have one thing in common with his Grand-mother, who liked walking about in the rain). No Trollope except for *The way we live now*, about a corrupt financier, still relevant today.

Several Thomas Hardy, Joseph Conrad, Graham Greene and Evelyn Waugh. Greene's *The power and the glory*, about a catholic priest in a Spanish American country who is hunted down by its dictator, is gripping. Conrad's *The secret agent* was great, notably the way a character gives much thought to some-thing, then comes out with a terse remark; on first reading I was confused by whether Verloc was a spy for Irish anarchists or the British, but have since learnt he followed that dangerous profession, the double agent. Another case where I didn't cotton on to a key fact was Salinger's *The catcher in the rye*, where I missed the key words, "Before they sent me to this goddam place" (a mental hospital).

Not a very modern selection, is it? But for best novel I'll choose the four volumes of Paul Scott's *Raj quartet*. We have them signed by Scott, thanks to an acquaintance with my father. It becomes a double whammy because the BBC television adaptation became the best TV series before or since.

A SOCIAL CALL AT THRUSHCROSS GRANGE

From *Wuthering Heights*, Chapter 11

Edgar Linton comes downstairs to the parlour to find that Heathcliff has called and is chatting up his wife Cathy. Edgar tells Heathcliff he is pois-oning Cathy's mind and demands that he leave, adding that if he has not gone in three minutes he will be thrown out by force. Heathcliff, in a voice of derision, replies, "Cathy, this lamb of yours is in danger of splitting its skull against my knuckles. By God, Mr Linton, I'm mortally sorry that you are not worth knocking down!"

Edgar asks Nellie, the housekeeper, to fetch armed servants. Before she can do so Cathy (with her flair for pouring oil on troubled waters) runs to the outer door, locks it, and throws the key into the hottest part of the fire. Cathy tells Edgar that he deserves to be beaten up for thinking evil of her. Heathcliff wishes Cathy the joy of the slavering milk-blooded coward that she had preferred to him.

Edgar strikes Heathcliff across the throat, goes through the inner door and fetches servants armed with bludgeons. As they approach Heathcliff seizes the poker, smashes the lock on the outer door, and leaves.

It is to be hoped that Mr and Mrs Linton will soon return this call.

Short stories

Short stories are a type of fiction I like because they don't take long to read and make just one unexpected revelation at the end. Here are some tops:

Guy de Maupassant: Several stories set during the Franco-Prussian war of 1970-71. Two concern attempts by women to get revenge on the invaders. In one a young woman gets herself infected with syphilis and passes it on to as many German officers as she can. In another an old woman knows who has killed her son; lacking strength, she makes a model of a man and trains her dog that the only way it can get food is from the neck of the model; then starves the dog before finding the killer.

Henry James: The gift of the Magi Widely recognized as one of the best, and very moving.

Allan Sillitoe: The loneliness of the long distance runner.

Rudyard Kiplng: A wayside comedy A masterpiece of compression, set in a small Indian hill station where only five people live (that excludes the Indians of course). A lesser author would have written this as a novel.

Woody Allen: The Kugelmass episode An ageing Jew seeks just one more affair and goes to a magician, who lets him meet Emma Bovary; he takes her shopping in New York; students of English literature say, "Who is this bald Jew kissing Emma on page 154?"

Non-fiction

Biographies The lives of famous people are often interesting when they were young and finding their way, becoming rather dull in their mid-twenties as one success builds upon another. For lasting interest, how about *Shostakovich* by Elizabeth Wilson (all written as extracts from people who met or knew him); and the little-known *Chaliapin*, described as, "An autobiography as told to Maxim Gorky"? Then there is the amazing Portuguese spy *Garbo* (Juan Pujol), who ran a network of 27 spies in England, all imaginary, to collect information for the Germans, and received both an OBE from Britain and an Iron Cross from Germany.

The strangest man is a biography of Paul Dirac, with whom I have a fellow feeling, first because he was socially non-adept and secondly, his room in St John's College was on the staircase on which I had tutorials. Hence when it comes to quantum theory, for me it is, "Down with the Schrödinger equation, up with the Dirac!"

History Not a great interest apart from one area, World War II. Many years ago I hit on Chester Wilmot's *The struggle for Europe*, an account of D-day and beyond. Recently my interest was renewed by a biography of Hitler left in a holiday cottage, and have since read more on him and also on Stalin, two of the most evil beings the world has even known. TV documentaries, based on newsreels and memories of survivors, reinforce this. How could the German people believe in this caricature of an orator? And how is it there were so *many* who were prepared to follow the ways of the SS? Another candidate for the lowest level of Hell is Stalin. How he came to power is not so surprising, given the terrible conditions of Tsarist Russia. More of a mystery is how Russia, while going through the successive periods of serfdom, Stalin's terror, the German atrocities, and even now not much to envy by European standards, managed to produce so much outstanding literature, music and ballet. Other candidates for most evil are Mao Tse Tung and Pol Pot.

Science As a boy I would get hold of almost any Pelican Book, the non-fiction branch of Penguin, and read it no matter what the subject. Then early on I hit on George Gamow's 'Mr Tompkins' series, accounts of science for the non-specialist. The best is *Mr Tompkins in wonderland* in which he goes to lectures by 'The Professor', does not understand them, then dreams of what happens when the speed of light is ten miles an hour, or Planck's constant is raised from 10^{-34} times whatever to some everyday value (approaching cyclists shrink in length, billiard balls when struck dissemble into clouds, your car leaks out of the garage).

Nowadays, accounts of science readable by laymen have come to dominate my reading. James Gleick's account of chaos theory, James Watson's retrospective account of where DNA has led us, and my favourite TV presenter Jim Al-Khalili on quantum theory. The very large, astrophysics, and the very small, sub-atomic theory, are equally fascinating. Not one member of the general public in ten thousand (and even fewer religious leaders) has any conception of the size of the universe, nor the scaling down needed to reach the sub-atomic level. Asking Howard for something that would be challenging he produced *The road to reality* by Roger Penrose. I don't pretend to understand 95% of the maths, but 'read through' trying to make out what emerges. On Desert Island Discs this would be my 'one book'.

What is so fascinating about science today is what is not known. I maintain a scepticism about 90% of the substance of the universe being the never-detected dark matter, just so that some equations will work. Jim Al-Khalili, no less, ended a TV series on quantum theory by saying there is something fundamental that we don't yet understand.

POETRY

Poetry of the Wordsworth-Shelley-Keats-Tennyson type has never been my line. But I am happy to go along with some of John Betjeman's:

> *The varsity students' rag*
> *Slough* – "Come, friendly bombs, and fall on Slough," Betjeman's view of modern architecture
> *Indoor games near Newbury* – motoring between the wars; I set the first two verses as a song
> *Seaside golf* (the finest golfing poem)
> *I. M. Walter Ramsden* – 'Dr Ramsden cannot read *The Times* obituary today/He's dead."
> *In a Bath teashop* – Six lines only, the most moving poem I know.

In a correspondence in *The Times* about the best limerick, someone wrote, "The best limerick is the one about the Bishop of Birmingham, but is it not suitable for publication in this newspaper". I agree.

Clerihews are less well-known. I like:

> Sir Christopher Wren
> Was dining with some men
> He said, "If anyone calls,
> Tell them I'm designing St Paul's".

A number of classic poems appear in the text, some written by me, others recorded in print for the first time.

THEY SAID IT!

From undergraduate times I collected printed sayings which I found cogent, striking, curious or funny. You may not share this view.

A teacher affects eternity; he can never tell where his influence stops. *Henry Adams*

Science is the organised scepticism in the reliability of expert opinion. *Richard Feynman*

The great advances in science are made by those who question the consensus or see beyond it. Martin Rees, *The Times*, 2016.

APPROPRIATE AUTHORSHIP:

Methods for collection and analysis of water samples. *Rainwater, F. H. and Thatcher, L. L., US Geological Survey Water-Supply Paper 1454 (1960)*

The analysis of transformations. *Box, G.E.P. and Cox, D. R. 1964 J. Roy. Statistical Soc. B26: 211-52*

Vegetation of the Peak District. *C. E. Moss, 1912*

MISCELLANY:

The glorious succession of 'ifs' which runs through all our lives. *Peter Haggett, speaking at a 2001 reunion of 1951 Cambridge geographers.*

Hope isn't an economic policy. It comes below wishful thinking, and only a little above doing a rain dance. *Rick Hall*

No great discovery was ever made without a bold guess. *Isaac Newton*

Even worse, perhaps, is the illusion that if management takes decisions, imposes rules and sets standards, then the decisions will be implemented, the rules enforced and the standards closely monitored and maintained. *The Times 18.9.1995*

If a guy is out of step, perhaps he is listening to a different drummer. *Charles Ives*

Blessed is the man who, having nothing to say, abstains from giving us wordy evidence of the fact. *George Eliot*

I do not know with whom Aidan will sleep. But I do know that fair Aidan will not sleep alone. *Marginal note found in a a Mediaeval manuscript, set as a song by Samuel Barber.*

C'est ce que nous croyons savoir qui nous empêche d'apprendre. (It is what we think we know that prevents us from learning.) *Claude Bernard*

I failed to get into Oxford. At my interview the Dean of Christ Church asked me, "In Pinter's plays, would you say the pauses between the lines were important?" As soon as I left the room I realised the answer was, "You couldn't have the pauses without the lines for them to be between." *Peter Bazalgette, recipient of a Royal Television Society award.*

SOME PROFESSIONAL ONES:

I know these slopes, who knows them if not I? *Matthew Arnold*

Take not too much of the land, weare not out all the fatnesse, but leave it in some heart. *Pliny, Historia Naturae*

Most subject is the fattest soil to weeds. *Shakespeare, King Henry IV Part II*

No amount of soil analysis takes the place of sugar cane. *Discussion remark by a staff member of Booker McConnell, at an FAO conference*

Jivak, the ancient physician, when asked by his teacher to bring a plant which was of no use to man, returned empty-handed, remarking that there was no such plant. *Notice displayed in the National Botanical Research Institute, Lucknow*

One important principle is that for every serious land-use plan prepared by one part of a government, there will be another part of the same government that objects. *East African Agriculture and Forestry Journal*

A number of soil survey organizations are being expected to discover areas, usually of more or less 'undamaged' forests, in which peasant production of such crops as cocoa, bananas, etc. will … be an unqualified success from the start. This is nothing less than turning soil scientists into pedological procurers who are given the task of finding attractive virgin lands for agricultural rape. *C. F. Charter, a renowned passage in Soils and Fertilizers 1957, 127.*

ENVIRONMENT

Tamino: Nun sag' du mir, in welcher Gegend wir sind?
Papageno: In welcher Gegend? (Sieht um sich) Zwischen Talern und Bergen. (Now tell me, where are we? Where are we? (Looks around) Between the valleys and the mountains) *Emmanuel Schickenader, libretto for Mozart's The Magic Flute*

RESEARCH GRANTS:

I have never received a farthing of the public money – my hands are clean. *Coke of Norfolk, originator the the Norfolk four-course rotation.*

The *new* Norfolk four-course rotation, based on fertilizers and farm price subsidies: barley-barley-barley-trip round the world. *Anthony Young. Stolen by Dennis Greenland for his address to the International Congress of Soil Science 1972.*

PUT-DOWNS:

The discussion initiated by Peet and Horvath of Sinclair's paper concerning the relevance of von Thunen's writings is as likely to obscure the real issues as it is to illuminate them. *Michael Chisholm, Annals of the Association of American Geographers 59:401.*

I doubt if there is much significance in Mr Spender's remarks on Beanley Island, on which I do not think he has ever set foot. *Professor James Alfred Steers, in discussion of a paper in Geographical Journal 89: 212.*

AND A NON-ACADEMIC ONE:

Lucian Freud spent six months painting a portrait of a friend. When it was finished the subject commented, "You've made my legs too short". Freud replied, "Your legs *are* too short".

LET'S MAKE IT CLEAR:

The cabinet's left and gone to it's dinner
But the Secretary stays growing thinner and thinner
As he cudgels his mind to record and report
What he thinks, that they think, they ought to have thought.
The Times

Reading the bald words on the page gives the wrong impression of what I thought I was saying in response to what I thought I was being asked. *Alastair Campbell, submission the Chilcot Inquiry on the Iraq war.*

AND LET'S GET IT RIGHT:

It is the solar system that is thought to have been formed 4.6 billion years ago, and not the universe as we stated. *Corrections and Clarifications, The Times 8.8.2014.*

ACCIDENTAL VERSE:

And in base six palets wavy
Argent over all a fesse
Dovetailed counter-dovetailed on the
Last thereon a lion passant
Gules

The Armorial Bearings of the Federation of Rhodesia and Nyasaland, 1960.

A MUSICAL ONE:

When Schubert first heard Beethoven's quartet in C minor he remarked, "After this, what is there left for us to write?" *Programme note.*

AND THE LAST WORD ON SCIENCE:

Although I can confidently tell you that the future will be amazing I can also say, with scientific certainty, that I have absolutely no idea what it holds. *Jim Al-Khalili, at the end of a TV talk on chaos theory.*

TIM MINCHIN'S GUIDE TO LIFE FOR STUDENTS

Summary of an address when receiving an honorary degree of D. Litt.

You don't have to have a dream: pursue short-term goals
Don't positively seek happiness: make someone else happy
You can't take all the credit for your successes: some of it is luck
Exercise! Inverse correlation between depression and exercise
Be hard on your opinions: question your own strongly-held views
Be a teacher! Not as a profession, but spray your knowledge
Define yourself by what you love, not by what you hate
Respect people less powerful than yourself
Don't rush; and don't panic.

T-SHIRTS

Not usually recognized as a form of literature. Here are some favourites:

On a young lady

PLEASE SPEAK SLOWLY
I'M A NATURAL BLONDE

On a young man

JOIN THE BRITISH ARMY
VISIT EXOTIC PLACES
MEET EXOTIC PEOPLE
AND SHOOT THEM

On a small girl

IF YOU THINK I'M PRETTY
JUST WAIT TILL
YOU SEE MY MUM

6

UNIVERSITY: CAMBRIDGE 1951-54

St. John's College

What a wonderful contrast! Within a week or so of demob, here I was at St John's College, Cambridge, doing what I like best, learning things. St John's is the finest of Cambridge colleges, with five courts in my day: First, Second, Third, Chapel and New, this last dating from 1631.[1] It lies next to Trinity, separated by a gap of three feet, but if a tourist asked a Johnian where to find Trinity he might receive the answer, "In Oxford, I believe". College is where you live, dine, have tutorials, and where your Tutor and Director of Studies have rooms. I was put in digs for the first year, in Park Street, close to college. Also living there were two undergraduates from Durham School (old Dunelmians) including their tacitly acknowledged leader, Derek Batey. I joined them in dining hall (and for coffee in our rooms or digs afterwards) and they formed a nucleus of my college friends. Derek read History, became a successful solicitor, but later abandoned the law to become history master at his old school.

In the second year I had rooms in Chapel Court, on the first floor and facing Bridge Street. This was a unique position, and once we were woken after 10.30 p.m., when the gates were locked, for someone to suspend his girl friend from the window and lower her into the street. In the third year my rooms were in New Court, on the top floor of 'I' staircase. There was a lavatory on the staircase but only three bathrooms in the College. You donned a dressing gown and strode across the open space.

---

[1] Due to a donation from a manufacturer of motor parts a sixth, Cripps Court, has since been added behind New.

Many years later I discovered from the university alumni magazine that I had shared the New Court bathroom with Manmohan Singh, Prime Minister of India in 2004-2014. I did not personally encounter him because he did not wish to be seen without his turban so would cross the court to bathe at 5.00 a.m.

Opposite me was Professor Jopson, a short, bald-headed bachelor. He was a comparative philologist of the old school, and having himself a flair for languages held it to be appalling that young dons taught this subject without being able to speak the languages. A tale related was that one day he came upon a friend fishing. "What are those?", he asked, and was informed they were maggots. "Ah, maggots" he replied, "I've never seen them before", and proceeded to reel off the word for maggots in about 20 European languages.

My first tutor was Sir James Wordie, who had been Chief Scientific Officer on Shackleton's 1914-16 expedition which attempted to cross the Antarctic. Early on he became Master of the College, and my Tutor from then on was a philosopher, Renford Bambrough. The Tutor was primarily for your overall academic guidance and 'moral welfare', and many students only saw theirs to report arrival at the beginning of each term. He would also issue weekend exeats, required to be absent from College, and which I would obtain in order to see Mum. I had a more substantial discussion with him when I felt a moral urge to follow Uncle Vic into medicine, and enquired whether, if I were to stand firm on this, it would be possible. He said in principle it would be, but pointed out the prior need for science A levels, and suggested that my conscience would equally be set at rest by staying with what I was doing, reading Geography and doing it well.

Formal dinner was taken in Hall every night, in three sittings because St John's was such a large college, the Dons attending the third sitting. It was the scholars who read Grace, but we can all rattle it off, "Oculi omnium in te sperant, Domine…". Memory of this led to temporary fame in 2009 when at the St John's College Golfing Society dinner it was found that the golfer in holy orders who normally said grace was absent and a volunteer was called for; I tentatively put up my hand, managed to cope, and since then have been the resident grace-sayer.

It was at dinner in hall when your attendance at the university was checked. The porters came round, initially with a list and photographs; for a few weeks they might ask your names, but after that they recognized everyone. I once met a man who went back to his college after about 40 years, to find one of the porters whom he knew still present. "Do you know my name?" he asked. "No, Sir" was the reply, "But come with me and I'll show you where you sat in Hall."

The only academic activity which took place in College was one's weekly tutorial. During the first term my intended Director of Studies was on sabbatical in Ceylon, so his place was taken by Glyn Daniel. He was an archaeologist, TV personality ('Animal, Vegetable, Mineral', not the parlour game but identifying objects) and College Bursar, which meant buying the wines. How did he cope with knowledge of first-year Geography? By listening to what the undergraduates read out in their essays. For the rest of the three years tutorials were with Benny Farmer – always 'Mr Farmer', at College and for some years later – a small man of Welsh origin from a family of modest means, who had acquired an interest in Ceylon from War service, and continued his research there. He was later to become the founding Director of the Centre for South Asian Studies at Cambridge.

Loping around college, a year below me, was medical student Jonathan Miller, whom I saw in the Footlights review which led him towards such a distinguished career in the arts as an opera director. The astrophysicist Fred Hoyle was a young don at St John's whom I heard give a lecture on continuous creation, now highly neglected as compared with the Big Bang. However, several times in life views I have held which have been regarded as absurd at the time but some years later adopted as the norm, so let me put on record that continuous creation seems intellectually more satisfying than the Big Bang.

When asking for money, the College sent me a list of 'Ten Johnians who changed the world'. I have added two more 'world-changers' (Hoyle, Miller) plus two not in the same class but with whom I had personal contact (Wordie, Jeffries).

    1781   William Wilberforce campaigns against the slave trade
    1798   William Wordsworth's poetry starts the romantic movement

1914-16	James Wordie, Chief Scientific Officer on Shackleton's Trans-Antarctic Expedition
1924	Edward Appleton proves the existence of the ionosphere
1924	Harold Jeffries, doyen of geophysicists, publishes *The Earth*
1932	(a good year!) John Cockroft splits the atom
1949	Maurice Wilkes creates EDSAC programmable computer
1949	Fred Hoyle names the Big Bang (as a term of disparagement)
1951	Maurice Wilkins produces X-ray images of DNA
1958	Vivian Fuchs leads first overland crossing of Antarctica
1960	Jonathan Miller appears in *Beyond the fringe*, later becoming opera director
1960	Louis Leaky finds *Homo habilis*
1977	Fred Sanger develops method of sequencing DNA
2004	Manmohan Singh becomes Prime Minister of India

Did anyone of note go to that place next door, where was it, Trinity?

Religious interlude

The first term at college was also the time of my religious phase. It had sunk into me that Christian teaching supplied an outstandingly good moral guide to the conduct of life. It also seemed that Christians were fortunate in having a ready-made, free counsellor (as they would now be called) in time of need, besides the more dubious assurance of some kind of afterlife. The music inspired by the Christian faith was great, too. There was just one snag: despite attending church in Rushden, and going to a Quaker school, I had not got the slightest degree of belief.

Nothing daunted, I set out to acquire this, attending Chapel and nightly saying my prayers (with a worrying feeling of being Christopher Robin). Not surprisingly this didn't work. Going to hear Billy Graham at St Mary's church the following year failed to lead me to commit my soul.

After that time I continued to go to Sunday church sometimes, sing the hymns and also say the prayers with one exception: being in a profession dedicated to the truth, it would be hypocritical to say, "I believe in…" when for a substantial part of the creed I don't, so I remain silent. It would be still more two-faced to take communion.

The above was written ten or more years ago. Since then I have firmed up my ideas on religion. I am now absolutely clear that there is no objective God. A subjective God, that is, one that has been envisaged in the minds of human beings, clearly does exist. Peoples all over the world have 'created' such a being. On the whole, barring extremism, religion is a force for good. In particular, it is hard to find a better guide to morals and behaviour than the Christian religion. I'm not sure how we would teach children to do to others what they would like done to themselves without the carrot and stick of religion. Could one just say, "That's wicked", a sort of Mrs Do-as-you-would-be-done-by morality?

Two other problems. First, the fact that the Christian story has inspired a fair proportion of the best architecture, painting and music. Secondly, I don't like what I see of atheism. There are highly intelligent people in the Church, but if they claim that there is an objective God, external to ourselves, I regret to say they simply do not know enough science.

I reached this conclusion independently. Many years later came the publication of Richard Dawkins' *The God Delusion*, and the debate in the media which followed it. So what was at the time a minority viewpoint has since become common currency. This was to become a not infrequent experience in life.

If asked what is my religion, my reply is not that I am an atheist nor an agnostic. My religion, defined as my set of beliefs, is science.

Whilst on the subject of more-than-science, there is the supernatural. I was afraid of ghosts not only when young but at least into my late teens, even when logic told me they could not exist. Matters were not helped by an episode in the film *Dead of Night* in which the reflection in a mirror shows the room not as it is now but as it was many years ago; when looking at this the man starts to strangle the girl, and is only stopped by her grabbing a table lamp and smashing the mirror. Mirrors at night were something to be avoided for years after. Occasionally as a boy I experienced that "I've been here-and-now before" feeling, accompanied by a sort of buzzing sensation. As already mentioned, when at school John Manson and I thought it would be terrific if we found we were telepathic, but trials at guessing the suits of cards never gave a statistically valid result. For the whole of my life, however, I have never had any experience, or evidence, of what appears to be supernatural, which is disappointing.

Likewise the fact that with all modern scientific search techniques, absolutely no evidence of living beings on other planetary systems has been detected. There are such a vast number of stars, many of which must have planetary systems with some form of life.[1] This is not only disappointing but surprising. It is most likely to be single-celled organisms, by analogy with the bacteria-like organisms (prokaryotes) which were the only form of life on earth for three-quarters of its existence. To have intelligent life, something that has the idea of transmitting into space the squares of natural numbers, is another matter. The discovery I would most like to live to see would be to find whether any such life is based on the extraordinarily complex, and apparently wasteful, system of having DNA in every cell.

At Cambridge

---

[1]   As I write, stars with planets in the right temperature zone for water and life are being identified.

Geography

With a career in research, the academic side will interpose itself in this account from time to time. I will try to warn those with no interest where this is about to happen, so beware of subheadings such as Geography, Geomorphology, Soils, Land Resources, and Agroforestry.

There may have been a day when learning was centred upon Colleges, with the Tutor advising which lectures you really should go to but that attitude, to whatever extent it existed, was before the War. I also just missed a golden age, 1946-50, when large numbers of demobbed soldiers became under-graduates, filling the place with the enthusiastic desire to learn that is still found in mature students.

By this time the Department, in my case the Geography Department in Downing Place, was of more importance to us than the College. In all three years our teaching consisted of some 10-12 lectures a week, nearly all of which we attended, and one or two practical classes. The first year syllabus was, as often the case, not inspiring, since 'Introductions' to Physical and Human Geography were inevitable, and universities still taught Regional Geography, in our case of North America. There was also, *mirabile dictu*, a course on the History of Geographical Discovery and Exploration; it wasn't easy to write anything interesting or original about this, and it was dropped soon afterwards. As mere consumers, we were happily unaware of the way the teaching staff agonize over syllabus changes. The second year was also fairly straightforward, introductory courses in the more specialized branches of the subject.

As at school, I rather preferred the lecturing style, "There were three reasons for this, a, b and c", which far from shutting out original thought gave you a solid platform from which to continue. John Patterson, talking about North America, was particularly good in this respect. The basic book on this, J. Russell Smith and M. Ogden Phillips, *North America* (1925, revised 1940-2) will have been utterly forgotten by now, but I cannot bring myself to get rid of it. Nor have I discarded Wilfred Smith's *Economic Geography of Great Britain* (1949), describing a time when the position of the coalfields dominated manufacturing activity, delightfully old-fashioned geography.

Our Professor (at that time there was only one, permanently Head of Department) was James Alfred Steers, an excessively studious and shy man, but said to be kind and solicitous by those few who got to know him. Commissioned by the government to survey the coastline of the British Isles he had walked along the whole of it – on a field trip I once asked if this reputed achievement was truly the case, and he self-deprecatingly said that a few reaches had been covered by boat. In the second year he gave a course of lectures on it, jumping from one aspect to another. He would walk into the room, place his notes upon the lectern, and without looking at the class nor waiting for newspapers to be folded away, the latest cricket score ascertained and otherwise for the noise to die down, announce, "I want to say a few words to you today about hibbleobbledibobble". Before you knew where you were, it became apparent from the blackboard that whatever this was, a knowledge of the stratigraphic succession in the Middle Triassic was an essential prerequisite for its appreciation.

His wife, professionally Harriet Wanklyn, was also a lecturer, but during my first year she was away. To give her lectures they recruited an eccentric man of independent means who had spent nine years successively getting firsts in History, Geography and Anthropology. He soon made it clear, with remarks about the statistically-established validity of the greater size of a certain organ among negro races, that he disliked the presence of women in his audience. One day it was agreed that all the men should stay away, leaving him with an audience entirely of women (which, to be fair, was very few in those days, maybe 10 out of a class of eighty). He walked in, quickly looked at the room, and remarked, "As there is nobody here, today's lecture will not take place". Complaints by some of the women to their tutors resulted in discontinuance of his lecture course.

The lectures told you what chunks of knowledge you were meant to be acquiring. What mattered for one's learning, however was the weekly tutorial: two students with the tutor, for an hour, each having written an essay, beginning with one reading his out, then discussing it (the other essay being read by the tutor and returned the following week). I would read broadly around the subject covered, not just the essay topic, and in this way progressively get to know a small sample of the ridiculous number of books which lecturers always 'recommend'. There were four geographers in St John's my year, hence two tutorial groups, all with Benny Farmer who reckoned to be able to handle both the physical and human branches of the subject. Nowadays students maybe gain by being sent around subject specialists, but then they lose greatly by being in larger groups – seminars are not a substitute for the tutorial.

We didn't have any course grading (continuous assessment), thank goodness. Your weekly essays were written in their own right, the tutor's assessment never included an exam mark. This meant you could do as you wished: write them brilliantly or in a pedestrian way, slapdash if you hadn't begun to prepare until the evening before (a common circumstance), or occasionally not at all. Neither brilliance, stupidity nor absence would have the slightest effect on your degree class, which was determined solely on the marks in exams at the end of the year (plus, in the case of Geography, a dissertation). Quite soon after I went into university teaching, continuous assessment became the norm, and students more interested in the 'mark' you gave them than in discussing or improving the content of their essay.

Of my three college colleagues, John Wyatt pursued a career in hospital administration and Gus Weedon became a computer salesman. The third was someone who had got in from a public school and was extremely stupid, getting a Third Class degree in his Second Year, which takes some doing. For Part II (the Third Year) he switched to read English. I lost track of him, until at a College reunion many years later when I recognized his name, counted along the Hall table to where it was listed, went up and introduced myself, enquired if he was whom I thought, and asked what he was now doing. "Oh, Principal of Cheltenham Teachers Training College."

For the first two years, Prelims and Part I, I had been a reasonably assiduous student but without natural brilliance, drive, nor excessive hours of study. Without difficulty – of all my worries in life, passing examinations has never been one of them – I got II.1s. In the Third Year, Part II, my attitude changed as a result of three factors. One was a particularly inspiring Lecturer in Geomorphology, Vaughan Lewis (he was later tragically killed in a car accident when on sabbatical in Australia). As he admitted, his lectures were sometimes muddled (for 'left' you might have to read 'right') but they were inspiring, one reason being that he sent you directly to primary sources, that is, journal articles, and not to books; one could do that more readily at that time, there was nothing like the vast mass of publications that now exists. We even went back to Nineteenth Century American geologists, like Gilbert and Powell, who had first seen the Grand Canyon, written about it, and made very detailed drawings. This was inspiring stuff. A second and apparently trivial reason was seeing a Dirk Bogarde film called *Accident* in which he portrayed an Oxford Don, who seemed to lead a pleasant life and to be reasonably well paid, which was true at that time and at Oxbridge. The third reason lay in meeting a certain person, as I shall relate below.

Taking these together, I resolved to have a go at getting a First in my final year, with a view to life in university research. I still didn't have the natural brilliance but began to work more solidly through the day and into the evenings. As far as I can tell, when it came to the Finals exam results there was a problem. There were about 80 students in our year, and Geography had the reputation of awarding very few Firsts; and I now know that examining boards look for gaps in the percentages to separate the degree classes. The problem lay in two students, Peter Haggett and Ken Warren, the former both brilliant and hard-working, the latter just prepared to work longer than the rest of us. When the exam results came out, my guess is they went Peter Haggett – large gap – Ken Warren – smaller gap – us ordinary mortals. In any event, the Firsts went in Prelims to Haggett and Warren, and in Part I to these two plus my ingenuous but studious school classmate Chisholm, while in Part II the examiners came to their senses and gave them only to Haggett and Warren. Benny Farmer told me I got, "A good II.1", at a guess approaching First standard in Physical Geography but well below Haggett and Warren in my second selection, Economic Geography.

The 1951-54 cohort was a good one for geographers. From a class of about eighty, seven became academics: Peter Haggett (Bristol), Kenneth Warren (Oxford), Michael Chisholm (Professor at Cambridge), Gerald Manners (London – I think he built up a good consultancy sideline in environmental legislation), Gerald McGrath (Kingston, Ontario), Deryck Belshaw (University of East Anglia), and me. Aided by the fact that we graduated at the start of a period of university expansion, this may be an all-time high (though the intake of 1941, graduating at varying post-war dates, has also been suggested).

What I was basically doing at university was, "Read about it. Now write an essay on it". This has remained my basic skill for the rest of my life, whether writing reviews of research for academic journals, in consultancies for international organizations, or when taking part in setting up the fledgling scientific discipline of agroforestry.

University life

I wasn't in the dilettante generation, doing little work for most of the year, then scraping a degree by intensive work for four weeks before the exams, with the connivance of their tutors who could guess(?) the exam questions.[1] The degree class didn't matter if you were going on to 'manage' the family firm. The *Salad Days* song, 'Find yourself something to do, boy' epitomised this attitude: the Classics or History that you had been reading were irrelevant when a place in the upper middle classes was yours for the taking. Of course it was never entirely like that. Evelyn Waugh writes that you must not imagine that all undergrads were heavy drinkers – "There was a drinking set, and I was of it".

However, most undergraduates are expected to follow some other line, be it the Union (debating club), sport, music, drama or other activities. In this respect, I have to say that I did not make best use of the unrivalled opportunities presented by time at university. Why I did not join the Music Society, and at least sing in the Choir, I cannot imagine. Many weekends I got an exeat and cycled the 25 miles to Letchworth to keep my mother company. Despite the experience of National Service I was still, if not a social misfit, then certainly not a very good fit.

Having played table tennis at school, this seemed the best sport to continue – what a waste of a golden opportunity to acquire a good standard at either tennis or golf. I took my lunches at the YMCA and, on afternoons when there were no practicals, played table tennis there, achieving a sufficient standard to play for the College. Unfortunately on leaving university I discovered that this sport is played largely by members of a social class to which I did not belong. There was a small payoff. One of the other regular players was a quiet maths scholar who spent a lot of time constructing rubik cubes and the like. He was later to become Sir Roger Penrose OM FRS, Rouse Ball Professor of Mathematics at Oxford.

I only seriously transgressed regulations once, and fortunately did not get found out. Late one night, someone observed that the clocks were about to

---

[1] See my father's story about his bar exams in his own account of his early life.

be put forward, so the next hour did not exist. We were in a top floor room on E staircase, which projects into the centre of New Court. From the window it was possible to jump across the angle onto the roof, someone producing a climbers rope to improve the safety of this enterprise. Several of us then made our way at midnight along the roof of New Court, Third Court, Second Court and Chapel Court until we reach the base of the Chapel Tower, where remarkably there was an open spiral staircase leading upwards. Reaching the roof of the tower, we were not able to do as choir-boys do there, sing an anthem, owing to the porters beneath, so we marked out territory in the way that wild animals do, and returned.

I did try deliberately getting drunk once, to see what it was like, taking the opportunity of Derek Batey's 21st Birthday. Not being habituated to this I was sick during the night and felt awful the next morning. In the afternoon I had to play a College table-tennis match and had the experience commonly reported of the intoxicated: that whilst you could, or at least believed you could, hit a good shot, the thought, "Oh, what the Hell" was dominant. Later as a post-graduate, taking a field course, I tried the same exercise with beer, with only slightly less unpleasant results. On an academic visit to Poland there was no intent but I was given so many schnapps on the farewell evening that my head felt like a rock for the flight home next morning.

David Mackenzie

In the second year I shared a room with David Mackenzie. He came from Darlington and was one of a group of poor boys awarded scholarships to public schools, in his case Durham. He once said that the example of himself showed, "That this system did not work". Academically it must have been OK for him to get to Cambridge to read Maths.

Mac was the school fat boy, not at all as common then as it was to become in the 21st century. Like me he was something of an oddball, socially awkward, very friendly, but not 'one of the boys'. After graduating he took the education diploma but was quite unsuited to teaching, and rather unusu-ally failed to complete his diploma during the first year's trial period.

However, he got a job with the Oxford University Examinations Board, pleasing to the Board in recruiting such an able mathematician, and to

David in getting a job that did not involve keeping children in order. Mac remained in this post throughout his career, living in a flat in Oxford and not marrying. After retirement he went back to Darlington.

His congenital tendency to put on weight, allied to an appreciation of good food, led to a diagnosis of diabetes, and when this got worse he had to go into a care home. As happens with some diabetics, ultimately he had to have both legs amputated. When we last went to seem him he was in a wheel-chair, which did not stop him taking a weekly treat going down the road to a Chinese meal. He never lost his habitual cheerfulness and affability – that's the right word, it describes the way he talked.

So as with my school friend Leon, Mac's life was not without its difficulties, but he was able to make his contribution to the community in accordance with his abilities and limitations.

Graduation; with Mum, Doreen and David Mackenzie

7

THE START OF A LIFETIME OF BLISS

Thus far, my achievement at Cambridge had been satisfactory in the academic line but pedestrian in other respects. An event in the vacation before the final year was to change this.

There were four Options for the final year, Part II, of the Geographical Tripos: Physical, Economic, and Historical Geography, and Survey. From these, you selected two. In the first instance I opted for Physical Geography and Survey, which meant attending a Survey field course during the summer vacation. This was held under canvas on an estate at Blythburgh, near Southwold, in Suffolk, 10th-30th July 1953, led by two ex-Ordnance Survey types, Bill Williams, very military ("This place is getting like a midden!"), and 'Jackie' Jackson.

The reason that it still survived in the syllabus was to supply staff to the Directorate of Overseas Surveys (DOS), which was engaged in surveying the colonies. Old-style surveying, based on field triangulation, plane tabling, slotted and pinned layouts of air photographs, and the like, was in its last throes, soon to be replaced by telemetry (electronic distance measurement) and later, satellite imagery. We climbed to the top of church towers (this time with official blessing) and the like, took sightings on other trig points, and did horrendous calculation adjustments using logarithms and slide rules – no pocket calculators nor computers then. Considered as a field course, this was a more intelligent and constructive activity than many.

Cambridge survey field course
Front row right, Doreen (with my hand on her shoulder), Diana

There were 14 of us, in the nature of survey mostly men (in its early years the DOS would not employ women, nor even permit wives to accompany). This meant that these busily occupied and house-clumsy male students needed someone to cook for them. In earlier years, women from Girton or Newnham had been recruited but this proved not wholly satisfactory, with too much flirting when they should be cooking. However, during the War years, Bedford College for Women (Bedford College, London[1]) had been evacuated to Cambridge. Vaughan Lewis, one of the Cambridge lecturers, had got to know a formidable lady geographer from Bedford, Dora Smee.

---

[1] Now no more. It was merged with Royal Holloway and moved out of its Regent's Park buildings; but Royal Holloway now ignore the "…and Bedford College" title so Bedford College, the great pioneer of women's education, has all but disappeared.

On being told of Cambridge's dilemma, Dora announced, "I'll find you cooks!" One day two first-year Bedford geography students, Diana Johnson and Doreen Rolfe, found themselves summoned into Dr Smee's room, where the following exchange took place. "Can you cook?" "Well, yes, a little." "Can you behave yourselves with young men?" "Yes, we think so." "Right, you are the cooks on the Cambridge Survey Camp."

My courtship of Doreen started in this wise. We were sitting at supper and she said, "I need some water". I pushed an enamel mug across the table and said, "Share mine". Then one evening, most of the students had gone along to the pub. With my instinctive reaction of 'No' I was still in camp. The two girls apparently said to each other, "Oh, blow him", and went along also. I changed my mind, got on a bicycle, was overtaken by a fellow student in a car from whom I got a tow, holding onto the back (there's that safety theme again). When we got to the pub, darts was in progress. Here was a chance to make use of the skill I had acquired solitary in the bedroom in Letchworth. Somehow or other two locals, one of whom used tiny thin darts, challenged Doreen and me, so to show off to her called for all my skill. I don't suppose we won, but we put up a good fight. I guess we might have had the occasional moonlight stroll together.

Doreen's first visit to Letchworth, garden of 27 Field Lane

From then on, well, there wasn't that much doubt. Then I invited Doreen to stay – it was indicative of changing mores of those times that her mother, on being informed, remarked that the invitation should properly have reached her from my mother. One day when we were on our own in Letchworth, before Christmas 1953, I proposed, in the following romantic words:

"I've applied for a year of study in America after graduation. If I get it, do you think we might get engaged before I go?" The reply was wordless, a warm hug. That was our private engagement. The official one came more than a year later, when down in Bath I asked Doreen's mother whether she would be happy if we were to get married. The reply was, "Yes, but not yet".

After that, Doreen became part of the floozy express, the London-Cambridge train at weekends. In those days the girls really dressed up for this, and folk lore has it that the first time I walked right past her on the station platform. The end of the year should have been marked by the St Johns' College May Ball, but this was held the night before one of Doreen's second-year exams which we agreed should prevail.

There is a postscript to this story. On returning for my third year, I decided to abandon the Survey option and take Economic Geography instead. It was the right decision, the older methods of surveying being on their way out. How fortunate that I did not realize this a few months earlier.

My graduation was in June 1954, attended by Mum and Doreen but regrettably not by Dad. The morning before, an Austin 7 appeared on the roof of Senate House. I had nothing to do with this, but 50 years later at the College Golfing Society I met someone who was one of a group of engineering students who decided to demonstrate their skill with pulleys to achieve this difficult feat.

Glacial interlude

I was set on doing research, and one way to make a start appeared to be to go on a student jaunt to a Norwegian glacier, grandly entitled the Cambridge University Austerdalsbre Expedition. Doreen came with me, the first of our many joint travels in far-flung regions. We travelled from Newcastle to Bergen by ship, third class, dinner being thick pieces of bread and jam. A smaller boat took us up the coast and through the spectacular scenery of the fjords, the sort of trip tourists now do at great expense as a cruise.

Landing, we spent the night at what might be called a bed and breakfast, where the host spoke no English. After supper, he was seen to be thumbing through a book 'Sprekken Engelsk' (or similar), summoned up courage and approached us, book in hand, with the words, "You, you, bedroom?" We enthusiastically accepted. It was the first time we had encountered what was then unknown in England, the duvet, so thick that you alternated with spells sweating and freezing. We never did find the bathroom, making do with plant pots on the verandah. The next morning by boat up a lake to reach a village, Tungasaeta, which had no road connection with the outside world. The only vehicle to have been shipped there was a 1924 Chevrolet which ran a taxi service. Where the road ended there was nothing for it but to shoulder rucksacks (not well designed in those days) and walk up the valley to the camp.

To return to the object of the expedition (well, not really – the object of student expeditions is to go on expeditions). My erstwhile lecturer Vaughan Lewis had a theory about the movement of glaciers. Those which are fed from an ice sheet, up on the plateau, tumble down and become valley glaciers by way of an icefall, a spectacular sight, full of crevasses. Now there is a certain type of landslide called rotational slip, in which a chunk of rock breaks away and slides into a valley with the bottom travelling faster than the top, thereby rotating backwards. Vaughan had the notion that at the bottom of an icefall the glacier moves that way. A group of students were therefore set the energetic task of hacking a tunnel though the ice; a large plastic pipe would then be laid more or less horizontally into the tunnel, the snows of winter would bury it, and hey presto, if the theory was right it would appear next summer pointing diagonally upwards. Being known as a genius at survey (so that field course wasn't wasted!) my task was to survey the pipe as it was laid, as a baseline and in the hope of detecting some late summer movement. In the early stages this expectation was graphically fulfilled, the inner part of the tunnel moving downwards faster than the outer. This, however, made it too dangerous to continue in case of encountering a water pocket. So a halt was called to excavation and the pipe laid in the tunnel. It has never been found since.

Whilst others were hacking away with ice picks there was plenty of time to survey whatever offered itself, such as the moraines marking stages of retreat of the glacier. In my Final Year we had had a few lectures on scree slopes, and here they were in abundance. With nothing more than two poles, a tape and an Abney Level (a simple instrument for measuring angles)

Doreen and I staggered up and down these steep and irregular screes obtaining slope profiles, that is, their angles. In the short term this was to lead to my first published paper, the abstract of which was:

> Screes that are actively undercut at the base by glaciers are steeper and have the same slope all the way down, the angle of sliding friction. Those formed by rocks falling down from the cliffs above and coming to rest are not so steep, standing at the angle of repose; they are also concave, because the larger rocks tumble to the bottom.

Scientists nowadays are quite unable to write informative abstracts like that.

The Norwegian guide with our party, Olaf Sopp, had a wry sense of humour. One day he took Doreen and me up across the icecap, wearing crampons and roped together some 10 meters apart in case one fell through a snow bridge into a crevasse. Olaf, leading, did not, nor Doreen, but bringing up the rear, and thus responsible for the safety of the party, I fell through. After pulling me up, Olaf commented, "How do you say it? Qvis custodiet custodies"?[1] We reached an isolated rock outcrop, recently revealed by melting ice, and he thought we should establish a rock cache there. After writing a note recording when we had established it, Olaf asked if I had a container. I produced some elastoplast, removed the contents and handed him the tin. Gazing around at the vast snowy expanse of the icecap he read from the tin, "Keep in a cool place". On descending the valley side, Olaf was sufficiently skilled to ski down sloping ice on his boots, the rope pulling Doreen and me over so that we slid down on our bottoms, to be rescued by his safe hands before reaching the rock below. Later, down at camp, we used to mix up powdered milk in a bucket. One day a young calf, straying from the village, wandered into the camp and quaffed the lot.

At times we took some tents up onto the glacier and camped on the ice surface. Being midsummer with bright sunshine, this had a spectacular result. The exposed ice melted a foot or more each day whilst the area shaded by the tent did not, so you found yourself perched on an ice pedestal.

Shortly before leaving I really did fall down a crevasse and injured my arm. This meant that for the journey home, Doreen had to hoik my rucksack up

[1] Who shall guard the guardians? Plato.

onto the other arm every time. Stopping over in Bergen we went to a music hall, where I can remember only one act. In the middle of the stage was a ladies handbag. A tramp circled around this, gradually approaching, wondering if he dare pick it up. Just as he reached out to do so the micro-phone produced a loud, "Hrrpm, hrrhm!" and he jumped back, looking to see who had spoken. The approach was repeated, this time to be frustrated by, "Ay, ay!". This is my ideal of clowning.

I becomes We 1957

Doreen's degree course, Geography at Bedford College London, ran 1952-55, a year later than mine. It was followed by a year's Diploma of Education at King's College, London, 1955-56. This meant that she would meet me in Cambridge during my last year and in Sheffield for my first two years there. Reverse visits by me were mostly not to London but to see her in vacations at her home in Bath.

Once in Sheffield I had bought by first car, a 1936 Morris 8, for £50, but when collecting it, it kept stalling on a steep junction. I started to back down the hill, and spotted where I thought I could turn round part way down. Some boys helped to push, and unfortunately between us we tipped it over the edge, rolling over twice before coming to rest on its wheels. It started and ran OK, but none of the doors would shut. I proudly met Doreen in this vehicle, who pointed out that the interior was saturated with dust, spoiling her outfit. Soon afterwards I replaced this by buying from my mother the family Morris 12, also 1936 (DGY 901).

Doreen having passed the Dip. Ed. examination, there seemed too me to be no further obstacle to our getting wed in the summer of 1956. Oh no! She wished first to consolidate the qualification during the first year's teaching, so applied for posts in and around Sheffield. On at least one occasion the fact that she was wearing an engagement ring at interview put paid to her chances – that sort of thing could be done in those days. She succeeded, however, in getting a post at Sheffield's City Grammar, situated in the city centre. So for the first year there we both lived in Sheffield in separate digs – again something that later generations would regard with surprise.

Wedding bells

After these years of abstinence we were married at St John Baptist church, Bathwick, the family church for the Rolfes, on 3rd August 1957. It was Anglo-Catholic, meaning a certain formality, robes, chants, etc., in the services, but I do not recall any incense at our wedding. I remember a minor panic when it was found that my white shirt, newly bought for the occasion, had a collar that was substantially too large. The hymns, chosen by Doreen as she had had a long period of churchgoing, were *Now thank we all our God* and *Love divine all loves excelling*. Sister Pat and Doreen's best friend from school, Ann Hawker, were the bridesmaids. I chose as Best Man a mathematician from Cambridge, Tim Murphy.[1]

Wedding, St John Baptist, Bath

Unlike the modern practice, the reception was held in the afternoon, at Fortt's, Milsom Street. Tim, replying on behalf of the bridesmaids, said that

---

[1]   Tim became a university mathematician at Trinity College Dublin, but we lost touch with him.

in preparation for the occasion he had consulted a book on the duties of the Best Man, which included, "See that the horses are fed". We, however, set off by car on our honeymoon – turning back after a short distance when we realised the priest had forgotten to give us Doreen's passport in her new name (as required at the time). By then we had a Volkswagen beetle, passed on by my father (TKT 471, 'Tickety').

The next day we crossed the channel, not on the ferry but by what in retrospect turned out to be a very unusual manner: flying the car, using an air ferry service from Lydd to Le Touquet. It took just two cars, loaded into the front of the plane. The honeymoon was to be spent at two music festivals, Menton and Salzburg, hotels and concert tickets being arranged by an agent specializing in festivals (he went bust soon afterwards). Stopped over in Paris on the way, just drove into the centre, leaving by the périphérique. The journey to the south of France is still a substantial effort today, but more so by routes nationales (no autoroutes then), and we must have stopped one or two nights. Records of this trip are hazy, however, since two reels of 35mm film were not turning on in the camera, so the photographic record has large gaps. Furthermore, what remains is mostly geography, slopes and the like.

VW on plane, Lydd-Le Touquet

Montreux, on the Mediterranean coast of France near to Italy, is smaller and less crowded than Nice or Cannes. We stayed at the Prince de Galles. The recitals were held in the evenings in an open square, giving occasional unscored additions from motorbikes. Through northern Italy and across the Alps to Salzburg, seeing two operas, Strauss's *Elektra* and Verdi's *Falstaff*.

The audience was very smart for the former, perhaps it was a première, but not so much the following evening because the performance was intended to be in the open air but had been moved into the opera house because of the weather.

Once we were walking along the street in Salzburg and a Volkswagen drew up, the driver asking us in hesitant German the way to the Mozarteum. It happened that I knew this, and took advantage of my PhD-learnt language to reply, "Ach, ya, sie fahren sofort, nehmen die zweite Strasse am links, und es ist da". Walking away, we overheard, "Well, I think he said you go…".

The return journey, via Strasbourg, included a stretch of one of the early autobahns, with so little traffic that sometimes we were almost the only car in sight. The return crossing was by more conventional means, the ferry from Calais. Then post-haste by the winding A272 to Doreen's family home in Bath.

Home

With my own parents leading separate lives, I did not any longer have a home. True, my mother was still living in 27 Field Lane, Letchworth where I had spent my schooldays; but subsequent visits were to give her some brief periods of company. Likewise visits to my father and Peggy, in the various places where they lived, were to keep in touch with Dad. In neither case were they to 'home'.

But we were always welcomed by Doreen's parents, Arthur and Hilda Rolfe and sister Patricia, in 12 Henrietta Street, Bath. The house was surrounded by aunts and cousins. At base, it was somewhere we could store our possessions on return from Africa and during subsequent periods between jobs. They even tolerated our labrador, Mfumu, although stringent security measures were necessary to keep him away from their cat. On a number of occasions they looked after our children when we travelled, once when Chrysogon was a tiny baby. For some years Christmas consisted of three evenings of parties at Number 12 and the aunts' houses in Johnstone Street and Pulteney Street. So 'Number 12' became for me a wonderful new home.

Subsequently our visits to Bath continued, to see Doreen's sister Pat and her husband Michael Fair. Pat and Michael lived not in Georgian 'Jane Austen'

Bath but on Bloomfield Park, up on the slope overlooking the city. Both were teachers, Pat as Headmistress of a primary school. Like us they have two children, both with families. From my point of view that meant a big addition to my own somewhat slender and scattered family life.

8

DOCTOR IN THE NORTH:
SHEFFIELD 1954-58

To resume my academic career, I had failed to get a First, and applied for but did not get a BTA ('Been To America'), the year in a US university that was a common career step at the time. Being still set on a research career, I determined to become a teacher, do some research in the holidays, and use this as a mode of entry. I therefore got a place to read for the Diploma of Education at Cambridge. Unlike most institutes of education, they liked you do to teaching practice first, so that the lectures would be meaningful. This consisted of a short period at the end of the Summer Term in a school of a type different from that in which you intended to teach, followed by the whole of the Autumn Term in the chosen type. I started with three weeks in a Secondary Modern, Norton Road School, Letchworth. Sec. Mods were for 11+ failures, those who had not passed the intelligence tests sufficiently well to get into grammar school. Their pupils were destined for blue collar jobs, and such was my social background, ignorance of the working classes, and ineptitude in personal contacts that this was a fairly dismal experience. In the Autumn I started at Watford Grammar School, Head of which was the well-known educationalist Harry Rea. Had I been a rugby player, refereeing would have been my outside activity, but what constitutes a foul will forever remain a mystery to the non-player, so my outside activity was determined to be the scout troop.

I must have taught a bit of geography but not for long. Early in the term an advertisement appeared in the *Times Higher Education Supplement* for two Research Demonstrators in Geography at Sheffield University. I applied, was presumably reported upon favourably by my tutor Benny Farmer, and was invited to meet them. This, my first interview, I remember well. As might be expected I was asked about my undergraduate dissertation (which Benny had suggested I might submit for the Royal Geographical Society prize, though I declined). Describing it, the combination of a certain obtuse individuality with some genuine original thought went down well. The fact that I pronounced the soil type 'rendzina' wrongly made it clear that this was all my own work. The post called for its holder to work for a PhD, so they asked me what topic I proposed. I had read an article by Ronnie Savigear, who was on the interview board, about slopes in the cliffs of South Wales, knew the few basic texts on slope form and processes, so said I would work on some aspect of these.

I was offered the post, accepted, and told Watford G.S. and the Cambridge Institute of Education that they would not be seeing me any more, which unsurprisingly was not very popular. The duties of a Research Demonstrator in Geography were to assist at practical classes for six hours a week, the salary being £450 a year (2016: £11 000). It wasn't really a job, just support for a PhD student, a less common but better way of doing so than by a government grant. The second Demonstrator appointed at the same time was Allan Straw, who also chose to work in physical geography, on glacial deposits. We worked in the same room for three years, and for the year after marriage, rented the upstairs (Allan and Beryl) and downstairs (Doreen and me) of the same Sheffield flat. Allan remained an academic geographer, glacial geomorphologist, for the whole of his career, ending up as Professor at Exeter.

The Sheffield Geography Department was small, like most at that time, just seven staff, headed by Professor David Linton. He had begun his career working on the glacial geomorphology of the Scottish Highlands, later joining one of Doreen's professors at London University, S. W. Wooldridge, in working out the denudation chronology of the Thames Basin. Linton had a distinguished manner, immediately commanding respect. He strengthened my determination to follow an academic career, and directed it towards the tropics. At a Geographical Society Christmas dinner there was, he remarked, "A built-in snowstorm" hanging from the ceiling. His speech might be paraphrased as, "Go West, young man" or rather, go West, East, North or South, widen your horizons when you graduate. One of the research students, 'Fritz' (Roy) Koerner joined Wally Herbert's Transarctic expedition in 1969, then followed a notable career in polar research. As

Linton had also drawn attention to the geographic problems of developing countries, I went South.

We now move into a period in Sheffield which does not stay in my mind as prominently, nor in such detail, as the years before and after. I lived in digs (4 guineas a week including breakfast and dinner (2016: £100), scrupulously prepared the practical classes, but as was the intention of the post, spent long hours at my research. The summer vacations in 1955 and 1956 were mostly devoted to fieldwork, although that of 1957 was to be more note-worthy. Edison's statement that research was one percent inspiration and ninety-nine percent perspiration is about right. Having had an original idea you spend hours and hours doing the donkey work necessary to substantiate it, or more often, fail to do so and abandon it.

My research was even more boring because of the way I did it. You are supposed to work by deduction, which means that you have an hypothesis, then take the observations needed to prove it – OK you philosophers of science, one can never prove anything, you take observations which might disprove the hypothesis, and if they don't you might be right. I tended to work by induction, meaning that you make lots of observations and hope that analysis of them will reveal some kind of order. You could call this the Micawber hypothesis, that something might turn up. I spent days and days surveying the form of hill slopes, digging pits in them, and setting up rather amateurish field experiments to measure processes. One of these was later to become the world's longest continuous record of soil creep.

Fieldwork for my PhD was based on surveying slope profiles and digging soil pits along them in three areas: the Upper Derwent, west of Sheffield;[1] north Devon, not far from Clovelly; and Wales east of Aberystwyth. This meant a lot of digging, and subsequent soil analysis. Once I was told that in Devon a boy came across one of my infilled pits and dug it up to see what was buried there.

A story about the Aberystwyth area is worth putting on record. I saw on the map a remote farm at the head of the valley, and asked the farmer if this was still inhabited. "Two brothers live there" was the reply, "And one of them has a very remarkable head". Some time after this I heard a lecture by

---

[1] The reservoirs there were used during World War II for practice for the 'bouncing bomb'.

a (very) Welsh Professor of Geography, who related the fact that before the First World War and anthropologist had gone around Wales measuring cephalic indices (the shapes of people's heads). He found that in the central mountain areas there were people with unusually round heads, contrasting with the narrower heads nearer the coasts. He interpreted these as remnants of the original iron age inhabitants who had been driven inland by Celtic invaders. Many years later it was confirmed that a rare blood group was common in the central area. What is remarkable is that having been told to local residents prior to 1913, oral tradition preserved the story of this "very remarkable head" for 50 years.

In my third year at Sheffield Ronnie Savigear took a sabbatical year away in Pakistan. I was made Temporary Assistant Lecturer, and the Demonstratorship extended for a fourth year to allow for completion of the PhD. Its title is hardly inspiring: *Some considerations of slope form and development, regolith, and denudational processes* (regolith is soil and the weathered rock beneath it).

What was accomplished by this research, and did it change the world of geography, geomorphology, or anything else? The external examiner remarked that he would have like to award the thesis a star for special merit but the Sheffield regulations did not provide for this. Out of it came a book and some 12 articles, so journal referees at least thought there was something worth publishing. To find out if there was any impact I need to find a modern geomorphology textbook and see if the slightest effect is detectable. Soon after this time geomorphology went all applied, and you could not get a research grant without demonstrating practical applications, e.g. landslides, flooding. Slope evolution taking place over millions of years did not count. Yet the knowledge about landforms and that it gave me was to prove valuable in the very different work, directed at practical matters, that was to follow.

Return to Sheffield 1962-63 – and an important arrival

Let four years in Africa pass (see next chapter) and there we were, unemployed, living with Doreen's family in Henrietta Street for the time being, with visits to my mother in Letchworth and my father in Petersfield. I had no job, although the leave pay would support us for six months. I was set upon using my African experience, plus a very limited number of publications, as means to get a university post. Scanning advertisements in *The Times Higher Education Supplement* yielded openings for geographers in an African Studies Centre in Edinburgh and at the University of Galway. The Edinburgh application did not lead to an interview, and they obviously wanted a human geographer. It seemed somewhat attractive to go across the sea to Ireland but their reply stipulated first, that candidates should submit 200 copies of their application (did they not possess a photocopier?); and secondly, that on a specified date, candidates must attend an examination to prove their competence to teach in the Irish language, and the university would *not* be responsible for expenses. So that was the end of watching the sun go down on Galway Bay.

Leave pay came to an end and I could have claimed unemployment benefit, but Sheffield came to the rescue. My former professor, David Linton, was taking a sabbatical year, so would I for the second time take a Temporary Assistant Lectureship? This gave me a further year to look around for a permanent post. I don't have many recollections of the work, I suppose preparing lectures, many of which would only be given once, and working on some more publications from my thesis. I had gone into soil science by then, but the world at large continued for some years to treat me as a geomorphologist.

It was the coldest year of the 20th century and, fresh from the tropics, we had taken a flat on the western outskirts of Sheffield at 1300 feet altitude. The freeze-up lasted through the whole of February and into March.

More importantly, Doreen was expecting our first child. In Sheffield, if there were no complications she would be expected to have the baby at home. So in good time she went off to live with her family in Bath, where births in hospital were available. One afternoon I received a phone call to say the great event had taken place and set off by car, getting a police warning for overtaking a lorry on the outside of a bend. The next day, there was this lovely baby girl. I think Doreen was able to remain in a hospital bed for the better part of two weeks, very different from the situation nowadays.

We had researched names for a girl and a boy in advance, seeking something distinctive to go with my commonplace surname. Chrysogon, Greek for 'born of gold' seemed attractive, a 4th century (male) saint but which had subsequently been given to girls. I went to a Lecturer in Classics to ask whether the G should be hard or soft, being told that the Greek would be hard (as in 'gone') but oxygen and hydrogen (born of air and water) were soft, but we settled for the hard G. Many years later Chrys found the church of Saint Chrysogonos in the Trastevere area across the river in Rome. More interestingly, she discovered that she appears earlier than the saint on a Roman coin, and as a female name. Chrysogone was the wife of the Roman Emperor Gallienus, she had two sons and one daughter, and they were both killed by troops of the Goths at Milan in A.D. 268. Her middle name, Rosamond, came from the overture of our favourite composer, Schubert.

Bringing the baby back from Bath to Sheffield was hazardous, driving through banks of snow lining the road. Another chancy moment was introducing the baby to our labrador dog Mfumu, whom we had flown back from Africa. After an exploratory sniff he fortunately decided that she was acceptable and they became great friends. So somewhat late in life, at 32, our wonderful family had been started.

9

INTO AFRICA: NYASALAND 1958-62

Viewed in retrospect, this was it! The work carried out in Nyasaland (now Malawi) during these three and a half years was to prove a springboard for the rest of my career, whether in universities, research institutions or consultancy.

I suspect that in the manner of my appointment there was an element of the old boy system. Towards the end of my PhD a former lecturer at Cambridge, Dick Grove, got in touch to say he had learnt of a post of Soil Surveyor, Nyasaland, for which he thought I might be suitable, and would I like to apply? This was one of those "glorious elements of chance which guide our lives".

Why did the Colonial Office approach Grove? A speculative reason was found many years later when I was writing a book on the history of Colonial soil survey. In 1951 a forceful individual, C. F. Charter, was appointed Head of Soil Survey in the Gold Coast (now Ghana), and came to England seeking staff. The first keen young man he appointed was from the Cambridge Geography Department, Hugh Brammer, who proved to be knowledgeable, totally dedicated, and a workaholic.[1] So impressed was he that Charter subsequently displayed a strong bias towards Geography graduates from Oxford and Cambridge, an attitude which may have spread to the Colonial Office.

Events leading to this appointment display how circumstances were very different then from what they would become. I was interviewed and offered the post on a 'permanent and pensionable' basis; but mindful of my univer-

---

[1] In 2015, after a career of more than 50 years, Brammer was still active in research and writing.

sity career ambitions I said I would only accept it as a three-year contract. This was reported to the Director of Agriculture, Nyasaland, who sought the opinion of George Jackson, his Ecologist; George advised that it was unacceptable, since the need for experience of the local environment was so important that any new appointee would be of little use for the first three years! Less than five years later, all overseas posts were on short-term contracts.

This impasse having arisen, Sheffield came back and said they needed a Temporary Assistant Lecturer for a year, so that rescued me from impending unemployment. Near the end of that time I contacted the Colonial Office and asked if any similar work in soil survey was available, only to find that circumstances had changed: the Nyasaland post had not been filled and I could have it on a three-year contract basis.

At interview I got by on the basis of having spent my PhD years digging soil pits, not stressing that these were for geomorphological rather than pedological purposes. To put the candidate at ease they also asked what was my golf handicap, the reply to which I suspect was a white lie. But they had spotted a gap in my experience, namely that I knew little or nothing about soils, so asked whether I would be agreeable to a period of training at the Imperial College of Tropical Agriculture, Trinidad. I replied that I most certainly would. For some reason, however, this fell through, and they decided I should train with the Soil Survey of England and Wales; as I was going to the African Rift Valley, they selected the Vale of York as an appropriate venue.

This was a period of six weeks with the Yorkshire office of the Soil Survey, in the person of Alan Crompton. Alan was an amiable fellow, not a hard taskmaster, and we spent leisurely periods putting augers down in farmers' fields. Most usefully for me there was also air photograph interpretation, which brought the excitement of seeing landforms in three-dimensional view from above. Alan's favourite joke was that to keep his stereoscope clean he would use materials which clearly belonged to his colleague, Len Curtis, since the box was labelled 'Lens Cleaners'.

My lodgings in Leeds were back-to-back housing. Adjacent streets were called Albert Road, Albert Terrace, Albert Drive...Back Albert Road, Back Albert Terrace...Bertram Road...you get the idea. Once widespread, this type of workers' housing, high on neighbourliness but low on space and hygiene, has been almost completely demolished.

The journey out

The normal passage for Colonial officers was then by sea. My wife would not be allowed to accompany me as there was no house available – I would live in the Government Hostel. I was to ship all my household possessions. So we put all our worldly goods at the time into 13 wooden packing cases, two tin trunks and two barrels, these last being advised for china as they could be rolled and not turned over with a sudden impact. This brought to mind a passage from Lewis Carroll's *The Hunting of the Snark*:

> He had 42 cases, all carefully packed
> With his name painted clearly on each
> But since he omitted to mention the fact
> They were all left behind on the beach.

A short time before departure the Colonial Office reported that a house had been found so my wife could accompany me. This called for urgent action. First, a visit to Somerset House to get her passport in order. Secondly, a trip to London Docks to find those packing cases and open one or two, so that she would have tropical wear for the voyage. Doreen's powers of persuasion, which she has never lost, overcame all obstacles to these efforts.

So we sailed from London docks in the *Braemar Castle* on November 18th 1958 for a voyage of 30 days. What a civilized way to do things! There was a small swimming pool, deck tennis and shuffleboard, a competition for the last of which I won. At a fancy dress ball we joined another young couple to represent North, South, East and West, Doreen North as an eskimo in a fur coat (the Colonial Office advised bringing such, 'for the chilly evenings'), me as East, an Indian fakir, wearing only a sheet/loincloth, possessing a suitable build but with ribs painted on and my clarinet for snake charming. On the crossing-the-line ceremony I was selected, presumably as a fit young man, to be tried at the court of King Neptune and sentenced to be cast into the pool. Walking between my jailers, two crew members, the one in front whispered, "Throw me in", whereupon the other cried, "Here's a lively one" and some ducking followed. Obviously, all good preparation for what was conceived to be Colonial life.

The ship's practice was to put the same eight passengers on a table for all meals, nice enough people but which over a month limited the conversation. The oldest was Dr Brydon, who said he had been a doctor to Queen Victoria and had heard Gladstone speak in parliament; naturally for an elderly person one heard his stories more than once. We don't know his age but say it was 82 he would have been 25 when the Queen died, so as a junior assistant the first claim is just possible; unfortunately there is an article giving a comprehensive list of doctors attending Queen Victoria during her lifetime, 220 of them, and his name is not among them. He would also need to have been in The House when he was about 20, but let us not cast doubt on the veracity of his report of how Gladstone described a speech by one of his opponents: "Wilful exaggeration, persistent misconstruction, and copious, arbitrary and baseless verbiage!"

There were stopovers in Gran Canaria, Capetown, Port Elizabeth, East London and Durban before reaching Beira in Portuguese East Africa (now Mozambique). In Capetown there was time to visit the top of Table Mountain, which as true geographers we started to walk up, only to find that the steep cliffs of the upper part necessitated a return to take the cable car. In Beira Dr Brydon treated our group to an evening at a night club restaurant.

The next stage was a train up to Blantyre, not the capital but the chief commercial centre of Nyasaland, and site of the earliest mission. We arrived 19th December 1958, exactly a month after leaving London. Spending a night or two in Ryall's hotel we learnt that you should not completely finish the food on the plate until you were ready for the next course, as it would be instantly seized by waiters hovering behind. This same precaution is mentioned in Sir Harry Johnston's book of 1898,[1] except that he refers to the Government Hostel where each diner brought his own bearer as waiter.

So on to Zomba, the capital and administrative centre, where I would be working in the Department of Agriculture. Our first night there was in the Government Hostel, not in the main building but one of the wooden cottages in the Botanical Gardens. After dark – which is always 6.00-6.30 in the tropics – being a bit nervous we went to the bathroom together.

---

[1]   *British Central Africa.*

Returning, on opening the door the room was swarming thick with flying ants – we had left a window open and the light on. Retreating we discussed what to do. After a short time, gingerly opening the door again the air had cleared. The ants had cast off their wings but the floor was thick with them, in pairs, copulating. Swarming in this way only happens on one day of the year. Looking out of the glass door we saw a land crab, which did not improve our view of tropical fauna.

I was to work in the Headquarters of the Department of Agriculture as a member of the Research Branch. That may sound grand, but in HQ this consisted of an Entomologist, a Plant Pathologist, an Ecologist, and on my arrival a Soil Surveyor, overseen by the Chief Agricultural Research Officer, Stephen Hoyle. There were further staff, agronomists and plant breeders, at the principal agricultural research station Chitedze, near Lilongwe in Central Province. Given the population of Nyasaland at that time of 3½ million, you can see that staffing in the Colonial Service was on a relatively small scale.

My first contribution to the welfare of the country was of a different nature from that for which I had been recruited. Arriving only a few days before Christmas, it was found that there was no organist in the Anglican church for midnight mass, and somehow or other it was known that I could play the piano (although had never touched an organ). I tried it out in the after-noon. In the evening there was a dinner and by 10.30 I was dog tired, so we went to bed for a kip. Doreen woke with, "It's twenty to twelve!" Rushed down, arriving at the church when the procession was already entering. Reaching the organ I pressed a few keys – silence. Madly mimed to a pew several rows ahead, "Th-r-s an el-ctr-c plg down by you, switch it on!" Sound was restored, and I got through the service. Writing to my father about this, he produced a wonderful Victorian postcard, "The volunteer organist" with a picture and poem, "…Our organist is ill today, can someone take his place?" A tramp from the back of the church comes up, to the consternation of the congregation… "And the sounds that came forth were the sweetest ever heard".

State of emergency

So there was a job to be done: a reconnaissance agro-ecological survey of the entire country. But before this trivial task was begun, political affairs caused an interruption. In November 1958, exactly one month before my arrival, Dr Hastings Banda had returned from a long exile, to be welcomed as the leader and saviour of his people. In 1953 the country had been linked with Northern and Southern Rhodesia as the Federation of Rhodesia and Nyasaland, a development strongly opposed by the Africans of Nyasaland who saw it as a vehicle leading to domination by the much larger white population of Southern Rhodesia. The first report of anti-Federation activity was a report on stone-throwing in Blantyre on the day we sailed from London. By the time of our arrival rioting was common, and the police used tear gas (I got caught in it once, most unpleasant).

During this time, however, we went on a local village soil survey to Kachere in Central Province with the Ecologist, a Sheffield man called George Jackson. "Don't camp out in the bush", he said, "They'll think you are up to something sinister", so we set up camp in the middle of the village, and the small boys who watched us, fascinated, reported to their elders that we seemed to be harmless. Doreen was wearing slacks (later to be banned by Dr Banda), and a remark was translated to us as, "Is that a woman?"

George showed me how, in the absence of a Soil Surveyor for the nine years of his service, he had learnt to do his own. Given my non-tropical training, this was of the highest value. However, speaking fluent Chinyanja he was disturbed by what he heard from the villagers about the feelings of the people. Needless to say in these circumstances this soil survey was never put to its intended use, rationalization of fragmented land holdings.

The situation was getting worse, and I was called into the Director of Agri-culture, Dick Kettlewell, and informed first, that a State of Emergency was to be declared at midnight, and secondly, that I was seconded to the Police. The situation was that the regular police needed to go around the country arresting trouble-makers, so gash civil servants were needed to undertake routine police duties. They must have looked around the small Colonial staff for those whose presence seemed inessential. "Soil Surveyor? What does he do? Well, he's only just arrived so we can spare him." So at 6.00 a.m. on 3rd March 1959 I was told to take out a patrol round a residential suburb, my first experience of driving a Landrover; it dated from many years before, with no synchromesh in either first or second gear.

State of Emergency

Memories of a month or two spent in the Police are hazy, mostly sitting in the Station with a colleague, passing the time by such idle activities as throwing knives into the door. When the State of Emergency was lifted I returned to the Department of Agriculture, where the Director called me in and said, "I understand you have not been a very good policeman", to which I did not attempt the sort of reply which Doreen would have phrased.

Meanwhile Doreen was taken on by the Security Service. One task was to assemble records of detainees, such as items taken from them on arrest – which often included a biro, invariably described as, "and a Parker 51 pen". One day the BBC Overseas Service announced the number of detainees, "according to a usually reliable source", which Doreen was proud to be described as.

Work: a reconnaissance agro-ecological survey of Nyasaland

So my job was to carry out a survey of the whole of Nyasaland, 90 percent the size of England. "Think nothing of it, old chap, you're in Her Majesty's Overseas Civil Service so you do your duty." It was basically a soil survey, but when working at the reconnaissance scale you don't just map soils but the whole of the physical environment: geology, landforms, climate, hydrology, vegetation, soils, together with existing land use. Geology and climate were obviously taken from work by other departments. The objective was to assess and map the potential for agricultural development. The name 'agro-ecological survey' may have been taken from a similar study in Southern Rhodesia (Zimbabwe), possibly by George Jackson the Ecologist.

The Soil Survey of Nyasaland 1959-62

So what I was doing was basically to take air photographs and draw boundaries around areas which looked similar in one way or another – what you can see are the landforms, vegetation and land use. Then you go into the field and make Landrover traverses along every motorable track (and a good many that were not), and identify the soil types, vegetation and present land use that were found in the provisionally mapped areas. Standing in soil pits formed a good proportion of the fieldwork, although as George had left the country by that time I had to do my own ecology. I had had sufficient overlap with him to learn the value of indicator plants, which are trees which indicate the presence of, say, shallow or wet soils – except when you find them on deep or dry ones.

Stereoscopic air photo interpretation

Listening to the soil
The reaction to acid indicates the soil's alkalinity

It was at this time that I made a contribution to methods of soil survey. Many surveys at the time would map the soils first, then scratch their heads over what their agricultural potential and problems were. What I did, and subsequently spread the word, was to go to places where there was performance data (e.g. crop variety and fertilizer trial sites) and identify the soils present. This I did in collaboration with an experienced agronomist, Peter Brown, who put together all the agronomic data on each soil type.

Hence the books supporting the maps were published jointly, as 'Young and Brown'.

You may find yourself asking, as many do, "What use was made of this survey?" This is difficult to determine, but in retrospect I believe it served a purpose, to provide a starting point, including definitions of soil types and map units, which could later be used by the local, Malawian, staff who were to take over. Visiting the country many years later, Agricultural Department staff spoke with great respect when they found I was Young of 'Young and Brown'; but as has been famously said in a very different context, "They would, wouldn't they?" Soil scientist readers can find much more in my book, *Thin on the Ground: Land Resource Survey in British Overseas Territories*, which includes a chapter on Malawi.

Dr Hastings Kamuzu Banda
Life President of the Malawi Congress Party
visits the Soil Survey office

By the time I arrived George Jackson had been in the country for nine years, and hence was fluent in the local language, Chinyanja (with a Yorkshire accent). Besides his professional work he was head of the local Boy Scouts, and needed some camp fire songs.

His Chinyanja version of 'The Grand Old Duke of York' is a model of translation, retaining the meaning and with perfect scansion. The Duke became a warlike local chief:

Kawinga wapita	Kawinga has gone
Wapita ku nkhondo	Has gone to war
Wapita kumwamba phiri	Has gone to the top of the hill
Wabwera munsi nso	Has returned to the bottom again
Pa nthawi pamwamba	At times on the top
Pa nthawi pa munsi	At times at the bottom
Pa nthawi ali pakati	At times he was in the middle
Si mwamba, si munsi.	Not on the top, not at the bottom.

Lacking such proficiency in language I composed an ecological verse. In the local savanna there is an inconspicuous tree locally called *msolo* but with a very much longer botanical name:

> He went a-plant collecting, but came back on the dole-O
> All that he could find was the specimen *msolo*.
> What was it eased his troubles, and left him feeling holier?
> *Pseudolachnostylis maprouneifolia.*

Life: on ulendo and in Zomba

Doreen kept a journal during our time in Zomba, and you will find considerably more detail in this. There is also an archive of letters to our parents.

The great thing about the work was that it involved going on ulendo (Chinyanja for safari). On being authorized to begin the survey I decided to start at the very farthest north of the country, Fort Hill, and work southwards. By the end of the tour of service I had covered the whole of Northern and Central Provinces.[1] Doreen came on some of the ulendos, so we got the most wonderful view of the country and its people, far better than any tourist visit could give.

Where to start? Well, there are districts strung along the lake shore, Lake Nyasa then, but as this means 'Lake Lake' it is just as well they later changed it to Lake Malawi. In the north there is Livingstonia Mission, with a stained glass window of him. From there you descend the Livingstonia scarp, which is the side of the African Rift Valley, by a road (earth of course) with 18 hairpin bends; in a short wheelbase Landrover you only have to reverse on four of them, but more in a long wheelbase. The descent brings you to

---

[1]   The provinces subsequently became regions. The Southern Region was later mapped by Alan Stobbs, though he never produced an accompanying memoir.

Young's Bay, but I cannot claim credit for this, it was a military man some time near the turn of the century.

We stayed where possible in Rest Houses, an excellent system for government officers on ulendo. You took your own food but there was a cook to prepare it. One District Commissioner, at Mzimba, invited us to a pyjama party at his house, pyjamas or nightdresses to be worn, all jolly expat British stuff.

The Nyika Plateau is one of the country's greatest attractions, a high-altitude plateau at about 8000 feet/2500 metres. I went there twice, once on soil survey then again with Doreen on local leave. Laurens van der Post's well-known book *Venture to the Interior* implies that considerable effort was required to climb up to it. He must have started from the east side, the Rift Valley, as from the west it can be reached by a gently graded motorable track.

The highest point in the country is Mlanje Mountain, in Southern Province. The altitude is given on the map of the time as 9847 feet which, suspiciously, converts to 3001 metres ("Oh, call it 3000 metres"?). Porters carry your kit (sleeping bag, food, etc.) but the path up is still strenuous. The night is spent in a Forestry Department rest hut. Van der Post was there too, "dark, brooding and mysterious", and gave himself a bad name in the country by dramatising an unfortunate accident in a fast-flowing stream, and referring to books of dubious character on the shelves of a couple who kindly gave him accommodation. There is a grassy plateau with peaks rising above it. Given clear weather the views are wonderful, including across the plain to Zomba Mountain.

Far below this, at 200 feet altitude, is the 'lower river', the lower Shire Valley, almost the southernmost part of the African Rift Valley. There had been an earlier attempt to drain the Elephant Marsh and grow rice, explored through a survey by Hunting Technical Services. The temperatures there are formidable for much of the year, so it is fortunate that this was never implemented. You descended the rift valley scarp from Blantyre, then at that time crossed the Shire by a ferry, like entering Hades across the River Styx (a bridge has since been built). This was powered in an ingenious way, not by motor nor by men hauling it across. There was a cable, to which the front and rear of the ferry were attached by adjustable ropes; one of these was made shorter than the other so that the ferry lay at an angle and the current drove it across. To return, one rope was lengthened and the other shortened.

The administrative centre was Chikwawa, with eight government officers. To escape the fierce heat, in the evening the DC would take a deck chair, puffing his pipe to keep off some of the mosquitoes, and travel gently to and fro.

Back to the capital. Zomba Club was the centre of sporting, social and drinking activity. When we first arrived there were no African members but at an early date, an emergency general meeting was called to draw attention to a club rule that, "No African, other than employees of the Club, shall enter the Club premises", which we promptly rescinded. This rule had been intended to stop children's amahs coming in, and the fact that it effectively debarred Africans from membership was an accidental consequence. By the time we left I do not recall many Africans joining, but later return visits showed that their own government officers had taken it over as their social club.

The Queen Mother at Zomba races (put on for her benefit)
Security: one unarmed police officer

We played quite a lot of social tennis there, me less often than some on account of absences on ulendo. I entered the Nyasaland championship once, playing doubles with Dick Isaccs (Veterinarian), but we ran into Conforzi and Vetteroni, Italian bakers from Blantyre, who had been to the same tennis school as their top players; they would let you hit some drives, then place a drop shot or angled cross-court stroke unreachably.

We both played a little golf on the 9-hole Zomba course, which occupied the middle of the town, the capital at the time. Various government departments were located around its periphery, so to get in your round after work and before it got dark, geologists would start on the 3rd tee, foresters on the 4th, and so on. The course is still there but crossed by 'public footpaths', i.e. anyone walking to where they want to get to.

Organized activities included a choir before Christmas. I recall a South African reading out the title of one carol, "Whence is that goodly fragrance, man". There was a play-reading group for a time.

Livingstone's positively last journey

But apart from the bar at the Club, most social activity consisted of private dinner parties. A few had a theme, such as fancy dress or an art competition. There had been news coverage given to a sculpture, 'The unknown political prisoner', so I went to the PWD scrapyard and constructed a version, 'The unknown hypocritical prisoner' using bits of chain, angle iron, cog wheels and the like.

There would also be official cocktail parties at the homes of Directors. Dick Kettlewell, Director of Agriculture, had the Zomba staff of the Department round to his house. Word got around that his wife Margaret, circulating, reached Charles Sweeney towards the end of the evening and asked what he did. On being informed that he was the Entomologist, her reaction was, "Oh, I'm so sorry [to meet you so late], I thought you were an Agricultural Supervisor".[1]

The most formal event was tea in the grounds of Government House. Soon after arriving in the country you went to the gate and signed the book, which meant that in due course you would receive an invitation. The ladies could put on their best dresses, although Indians in their colourful saris looked finer. Following independence this became the first residence of Dr Banda, before he built his Presidential Palace.

There were local leaves. We saw the Victoria Falls at the end of the dry season, one of the lowest flows on record, which meant you could see the rock cliffs, normally hidden by spray. On to Salisbury (now Harare), crossing the Zambezi on a tiny ferry which held only a handful of cars. Met a soils colleague Philip Watson, then at the University; he was later to go to Fort Hare, the university for Africans under apartheid. Went to a fashion show in Meikles Hotel, the only time I have seen a dress on a model, called her across, and bought it for Doreen. It was purple, the best she has ever possessed.

Another local leave was to drive down to the coast at Beira in Portuguese East Africa (now Mozambique), where one became lost in acres of flat, uniform coconut plantations. We lacked the Portuguese for beach, and had to ascertain it by sign language (praia). When we found it, there was a vast stretch of idyllic sand with absolutely no-one on it. We also drove north to Nairobi, the Tanganyika section made easy by a new road constructed with Russian communist aid, and not yet deteriorated into potholes – there is sidekick money in construction but not in maintenance.

[1] European staff with an agricultural diploma, unlike Agricultural Officers with a degree.

Homeward bound 24th February to 24th April 1962

My tour of service was due to end after three years but was extended two months. I did not intend to return for a second tour, having the objective of using this overseas experience as a springboard to a university career. There was the added fact of Malawi gaining independence – their first general election had taken place, leading to a Malawi Congress Party landslide (which is an understatement) – with the accompanying uncertainty.

During our time there the normal passage for colonial officers was changed from sea to air. We did not take up this opportunity, but one member of the family did: Mfumu, our labrador ("Have the Youngs got any children?" "No, but they've got a dog"). In retrospect, having been used to the open spaces of Africa it would have been far better not to bring him to England, and Doreen said so, but I would not hear of it. So I went to the timber yard and constructed a box to British Airways specifications. For a few days we would give him his food in the box and leave him in it, to get used to it. Then off he went by air, to be met at the airport by a staff member from kennels, and kept for six months quarantine. My mother visited him, taking for an introduction a handkerchief which I had carried under my armpit, assuming that was how dogs recognize people. He was never happy in England, becoming aggressive to other dogs, but I kept him for some years, exercised him, even took him to dog-training classes to get him used to others. Only when he started to go blind did I have him put down. I remain very fond of dogs – other people's dogs.

Doreen and I, on the other hand, chose to drive home. The original idea was to cross to West Africa, calling in at the Tropical Soils Research Centre in Yangambi, Belgian Congo, where my former colleague in Sussex, Ron Paton, now was. We would then cross the Sahara. This was in any case an over-ambitious plan, and the Congo emergency put paid to it – Ron got out to Uganda with a toothbrush.[1]

So we settled for the classic Cape-to-Cairo route. After spending a last night with Angus and Anne Macdonald (Angus was to become a judge) on 24th February 1962 we set off northwards in our Volkswagen Beetle, which already had 70 000 miles on the clock. The first part of the journey, north

---

[1]   He was to spend the rest of his career with the Australian soils research organization, CSIRO.

through Nyasaland, was already familiar through soil survey. At one point the road passes into Northern Rhodesia (now Zambia) and back again, and the Young Pioneers, the youth wing of the Malawi Congress Party, had set up their own "customs and immigration post"; but after satisfying themselves that powdered milk was not drugs we were allowed to proceed, I think without passage of money.

Setting off to cross Africa

During this journey, as on many subsequent trips, Doreen kept a journal. It is one of nineteen such journals in which she continued to write daily accounts of our trips. These contain considerably more detail of daily happenings, and are also more accurate (see Sources).

Through Tanganyika (now Tanzania) was more of a problem. The middle of the country is flat, the road earth, and February was the end of the rainy season. With the help of a spade we got as far as Tabora, right in the centre, but then the road became impassable and we had to put the car on a train. It left at 4.00 a.m. so we took turns to keep awake. The journey was an unusual experience. The car was fixed onto an open railway truck and we were required to travel in it, to stop locals from jumping up and removing spare parts. Our truck had something wrong with the bearings and gave a repetitive sideways lurch. Naturally after a time I wished to relieve myself, could not risk getting out, so had to make use of the only container to hand, our thermos flask.

Digging out the VW, Tanzania

This got us to Mwanza, on Lake Victoria, then it was by road again round the west side of lake and into Uganda. The very long-horned Ankole cattle are a striking sight, although after photographing them one had to make away fast as their owners came running up to demand a royalty payment. Many years later I was to return to this same area when our agroforestry centre set up a research station there. Kampala provided an urban break. The African women wore a Victorian style of dress in which they had seen when the British first arrived in the 1890s. Going on north the car suffered one of only two mechanical problems on our journey, not surprisingly a broken shock absorber, but we found a Sikh garage mechanic to repair it.

From Gulu in northern Uganda we reached Juba in southern Sudan, beyond which only four-wheel drive vehicles were permitted. The route was now by Nile steamer through the swamps of the Sudd, to Kosti. The steamer, the SS Hurriyah, was of an economical if navigationally cumbersome design. The powered vessel is flanked by two others, first class on the left, second on the right. These push (not pull) two more barges, with third class passengers, with chickens, stoves and other means of sustenance, together with the cars. All are lashed together. This left very little opportunity to steer, so the way to get round the numerous bends found in a swamp was to bump against the reeds and bounce off.

Of course we were among the 14 first class passengers. One of them was a Sudanese army officer who had to kneel down to say prayers five times a day facing Mecca, no easy task as the boat snaked along the broadly meandering bends. In second class was an English couple called Cotton, also in a VW. When the crew were not looking they would come across to our cabin for a bath; she then retired into her VW, and somehow emerged looking like a bandbox. Cotton gave an impression of competence, military style, and their company during the next stage of the journey was welcome. What was thought to be suitable food was inherited from British Colonial days, including steamed puddings. There may have been beer available, but at 3/6d a bottle we were hard put to afford it, and drank a sweet pink concoction. There were intermittent stops at villages; if at night you were woken by a blast on the hooter. By day some trading with our passengers took place, against regulations so we hid purchases from the crew. This section of the journey took six days, covering a sizeable chunk of Africa: 650 miles as the crow flies, but more than double that following the meanders of the White Nile through the swamp.

Now onto rail, with the cars, from Kosti through Khartoum to Wadi Halfa, still in Sudan but close to the border with Egypt. Construction of the Aswan Dam was only just beginning, after which it would take years to fill Lake Nasser, as the reservoir was to be called. So now it was another boat journey on the Nile, passing the Abu Simbel temple in its original location, before the UNESCO project to move it stone by stone above the level of the lake. We saw it to the west with the setting sun behind, so had to buy a postcard to supplement our photograph.

Disembarking at Shellal, it was back to the cars again, the Cottons and ourselves in convoy. The first need was to find an hotel in the nearest settlement of any size, Aswan. Setting off northward it became dark. Several times lights appeared, only to pass away to the left or right. Some 20 miles on we found a village, and enquired of a storekeeper how much further it was to Aswan. "20 miles", he replied – pointing back the way we had come! Apparently Aswan was where we had landed, and we found the Grand Hotel. The status of Shellal is questionable: it is listed neither in *The Times Atlas* nor on Google Earth, so if it ever existed, it must have been flooded by the lake.

From here on we were dependent on our little car to traverse a still larger chunk of the Cape to Cairo route, and onward along the North African coast. This was tourism the way we have done it all our lives since, finding our own way to places and viewing them not in a tour party. First to Luxor, spending two days there, overawed by the massive pillars of the temple. A ferry across the Nile to the Valley of the Kings, where one was required to go into the tombs with a guided party. At one point I chose to drop back and go down a branch of the tunnel where we had not been taken, coming across a man with a pot of paint and a brush, busily putting Egyptian hiero-glyphics on the wall – one may charitably assume that he was touching up what was already there in more shadowy form.

VW crossing the desert

On to Cairo, although not Shepheard's Hotel in which Grannie Young had wintered. Visits to the pyramids and the sphinx, getting to the centre of the Great Pyramid for an amount which I believe was the equivalent of 3/6d.

Then to Alexandria, where we were entertained to dinner by a former Geography research student at Sheffield, Ali Shahin. The meal consisted of a large spread of dips, delicious so we ate our fill – only to find that this was the first of several courses.

Westward along the North African coast, where one is advised not to stray from the road owing to land mines left from the wartime fighting in the early 1940s. Passed names familiar in radio broadcasts and newsreels of that time such as Mersah Matruh, Sidi Barrani and the turning point of World War II, El Alamein. We also saw the war cemeteries. The British ones were in the dignified style and impeccable maintenance of the Imperial War Graves Commission. The German and Italian had tanks and guns on show at the entrance – some might think this distasteful, as if to show pride in them, but if the message is that the deaths were the result of war, then it can be thought appropriate.

Across the border into Libya, doubtless with some modest payments to secure visas. Passed the ruins of the city of Cyrene, first Greek then Roman. At one point, outside the boundaries we drew up the car and found ourselves right beside the ornamental top of a Corinthian pillar. I hesitated at the temptation to put this in the boot, but decided against for fear of the trouble this could cause at customs.

From there to Benghazi, the Berenice Hotel. In the dining hall there was a stage framed, appropriately, by palm fronds, onto which at dinner came a Palm Court Trio. The music they struck up, possibly Kreisler's *Caprice Viennois*, was so perfectly appropriate to the setting that we could not refrain from bursting out with laughter.

By boat from Benghazi to Malta. The Mediterranean can get rough and it certainly did so. This was the worst sea sickness either of us have ever had, we ate nothing and never left our beds in the cabin. A bus (very cramped) around the countryside of Malta, and then a calmer crossing to Syracuse in Sicily. On the road again, then from Messina to Reggio di Calabria in Italy by a recently introduced form of marine transport. The Accountant in Nyasaland had asked me to send details of the trip to justify payment of the equivalent of the air fare, and at this point I was able to write, "Scylla to Charybdis: hovercraft".

Up through Italy, first stop Naples. A somewhat affected couple in Zomba were wont to say, "Dear old Napoli", and many years later we were to find out what a fine spot it indeed it is for the tourist. On this occasion, however, on first reaching the outskirts we drew up outside a bar for a coffee and, we intended, a rest, being unaware at the time of the Italian practice of standing up in bars. On discovering this, I thought blow this for a lark, and we drove straight on – so much for Dear Old Napoli.

In Rome we did stop. The traffic by then was already pretty manic, the hotel had no parking, so I dropped Doreen and set off to find the nearest spot to park. Round a block, no luck, every place taken; round a wider block, same result. On the third try, found myself in the city's substantial road tunnel, on emerging from which I was far from the hotel with no idea how to get back to it. Because of many subsequent visits to Rome I cannot recall what sights we saw on that occasion. It was cold and Doreen needed her overcoat, only to find that the maxi-coats which had been de rigeur when we left four years earlier now looked out of fashion; she found a seamstress to shorten it.

One more stop in Italy, Milan. Knowing the fame of La Scala opera house we found our way there and headed for the box office with no great hopes of a ticket for that evening. Crossing the square we were approached by a man in a raincoat with, "You wanna da tickets?", and doubtless paying appreciably over the odds we bought them. This was a most serendipitous day to have arrived, for we saw one of the greatest moments in a long life of watching opera, Bellini's *La Somnambula* with Joan Sutherland, 'La Stupenda', in the name part, including the Mad Scene. To get tickets for such a star name nowadays one would have to book months ahead.

Now impatient to get home, there were long days of driving, across the Alps with a road tunnel and at least one high pass, the Simplon could it have been?

Memory of the route now fails me. For details go to Doreen's journal – as, indeed, for the whole of this journey. After a night in Calais came travel to Dover by a more conventional type of ferry, and we set foot in England. A phone call to tell Doreen's mother that we had arrived, then it was off to Bath along the A272, not the greatest of motorways even now, but 30-40 mph driving then. Doreen asked to pull up to buy a bunch of flowers so as she could arrive with them in her hand. So by evening we reached 12 Henrietta Street and her family.

We had been away – no home leave, no telephone calls, only letters – for three years and four months, the last two on this trip. But in retrospect, the experience gained there was to become the foundation for the rest of my career.

10

NEW UNIVERSITY: SUSSEX (AND TRAVELS!)
1963-1968

With Nyasaland achieving independence as Malawi, prospects for completing a second tour of Colonial service became dubious. In any case, all along the African experience was intended to be a springboard for a university career. So I resigned, and for the second time in life found myself on the dole. Rescue from this came in the form of the universities established 1961-65, including Sussex, Keele, York, Lancaster, Kent and Warwick. Sometimes dubbed plateglass universities, as a play on redbrick for the civic universities of pre-war days, they more often became known simply as the 'new universities'. Based (in principle) on Schools of Studies, within which could be found Departments, Sussex set up a Geography Department in the School of Social Studies with a Professor, Tom Elkins, and two supporting staff in social geography. Tom was not a very dynamic person to have chosen for a new venture, but he needed a physical geographer to give a broader base. That was me, aided by my African experience which helped him expand the Department into the School of African and Asian Studies. Appointed in the Spring of 1963, I took up the post in September. I was asked, however, to come and meet the first cohort of geography students, four of them, in the Summer Term, which meant that I saw the University in its second year.

So there I was in charge of the whole of physical geography: meteorology, geomorphology, biogeography, soils. I must have given a foundation course, though have no recollection of it. I focused on developing a third-year option in Soil Survey and Land Evaluation. My first overseas students came at this time: Gottfried Ageypong was from Ghana; he returned there, and after discovering he had a lectureship in Nigeria and was growing rice to make money when his salary wasn't paid, I lost touch. Jayanthi Perera was a refined Sinhalese lady, who on returning to her country married someone from the administration of the University of Peredeniya. We called in on them on one of our later trips, were invited to dinner, and had the somewhat embarrassing experience of eating our dinner whilst they looked on, saying they only dined later. The fact that there was a waterfall in the dining room, falling into a mosquito-breeding pool below, did not add to our ease.

Bernard Swan was also from Ceylon but from the burger community, descendants of the Portuguese and Dutch who occupied the country before the British. He had been teaching in England, and completed a PhD at Sussex. He was married to a Sinhalese lady and had four children, one of them handicapped. The family were deeply devoted Catholics. Returning to his country he found that Sinhalese nationalism was rife and he was required to teach in that language, which he couldn't. Rather surprisingly he managed to score sufficient immigration points to be admitted to Australia,[1] and spent the rest of is career as a lecturer at the University of Armidale, initially in Geomorphology but subsequently founding a Department of Peace Studies.

The greatest enthusiast for the soil survey course was an English mature student, David Parry, who looked like a rugby player, and indeed had played for Harlequins. He went into soil survey with Hunting Technical Services, and rose to Project Manager with them and later another consultant company, one of the few soils specialists to do so – project managers are apt to be economists.

Whilst at Sussex I wrote my first book, *Slopes,* arising out of the PhD work at Sheffield. As was to happen on another occasion in the future I was racing to compete with another book on the same subject, Carson and Kirkby's *Hillslope Form and Process.* Together these helped to establish slopes as a distinct branch of geomorphology. (Credit for this should go also to my PhD supervisor, Ronnie Savigear, who also moved out of geomorphology, in his case into remote sensing.) Mike Kirkby stayed in geomorphology whilst I moved into soils, and his book was more focused on processes (landslides, erosion, etc.) which became the fashionable aspect. My work

---

[1] I once tried the entry qualifications for New Zealand in a Wellington museum; they wouldn't let me in.

centred on slope evolution, the change in form over time. As this takes place over time scales of 1-10 million years it has almost no practical applications, and hence does not attract research grants.

I must have been very busy writing at that time, as my publications list shows 17 articles dated 1963-70. Some were still on slope geomorphology, but I was moving into soils, tropical land resources and land evaluation.

As I was just back from Africa and a member of the School of African and Asia Studies, soon after arrival I was invited as a staff member to a party to welcome overseas students. One of these was a mathematics student who was later to achieve fame in a very different field. Virginia Wade was British born but when she was one year old her father became Archbishop of Durban. She spent 15 years there and learnt to play a mean game of tennis. On reaching Sussex she retained a strong South African accent, although now we know her as having a rather good class British voice.

Sussex had a system of Arts-Science Dissertations, whereby science students wrote a short dissertation on an arts subject, and vice versa. Virginia chose to write on African Music, and as there was no Music Department at the time I was asked to supervise her. She completed her Maths degree (getting a II.2 I think) as a fallback in case the envisaged tennis career didn't work out. It did. She won Wimbledon in its centenary year 1977 (the last British grand slam singles winner until Andy Murray in 2013), and became the only woman to have won titles in all four grand slams, three singles and the French with Margaret Court.

Life in Sussex

We had a lovely house in Kingston-near-Lewes, a village between Brighton and Lewes, situated on a Chalk slope. Right by the house was a high Chalk Down. Chrysogon went to her first English school. Doreen was able to resume her teaching career, as Geography Mistress at a small private school. Next door, by which is meant 100 yards along a track, lived Chuck and Nora Reid, and Nora would look after the children when we were both at work. We also had a babysitter who was the sister of Max Bygraves. In our last year in Sussex, Doreen was invited to buy the school and become its headmistress.

Darryl was born whilst we were there, and Doreen followed the same procedure for the birth of Darryl as she had for Chrysogon's, taking up temporary residence with her parents in Bath in order to go into the hospital maternity ward there. Future genealogists may puzzle over the fact that both childrens' birth certificates show that they were born in Bath, although they have never lived there. For his name, Darryl Anthony Rolf Young, Darryl was mainly just because we liked it, although there was a link with a geography/anthropology book by Daryll Forde which both of us had studied. Anthony was from me, and Rolf from Doreen's family surname before her grandmother insisted that her grandfather add an "e" before she would marry him, as 'Rolf' sounded too Germanic.

First consultancy: Pakistan 1964

From the point of view of my career, the most important events took place when I wasn't at the University at all, but on unpaid leave. This was to set a pattern: universities, having taken me on, seemed highly desirous of getting rid of me. These were not sabbaticals, in which the university continues to pay your salary – I have never had one of those – but unpaid, self-financed, leave.

It all began in 1964 when one of the consultancy companies in land resource development, Hunting Technical Services,[1] asked me to go to Pakistan. This must have been on the basis of my Nyasaland experience, although curiously no soil survey expertise was needed in the job. Probably the old boy network via Cambridge was responsible. The Managing Director of Huntings, Vernon Robertson, was a Cambridge Agriculture graduate who joined Huntings as a one-man natural resources department and built it up to become a leader in land development planning. Their early bread-and-butter projects were on irrigation schemes in the Middle East, particularly Iran; as this was at the instigation of the Shah of Persia, for political reasons these projects were abruptly terminated. This was not before one of their soil surveyors had been invited to marry a rich princess; he declined, and joined the Soil Survey of England and Wales, something of a comedown. I guess Vernon looked first to the Cambridge Geography Department for someone versed in natural resources.

---

[1]   They changed their name several times, and I will henceforth call them Huntings.

Mine was a six-week posting with the Upper Indus Project, in the Lahore region of Pakistan. The irrigation schemes developed by the British in India from 1932 onwards were huge. To give some idea of the scale, when water is first taken off a reservoir this is into a Major Canal. These divide into Minor Canals, then Major and Minor Distributaries, before passing onto farmers' land via a nakkar, when it is again distributed through the fields by his own system of ditches, the whole a vast inverse dendritic system of water channels. A nakkar is vertical slot maybe six inches wide (if made of concrete it is a pukka nakkar). It is where the quantity of water the farmer takes from the system, and pays for, is measured. I was told there were at least five known ways of circumventing a nakkar.

Pukka nakkar

The tributaries of the Indus and Ganges emerge from the Himalayas onto the alluvial plains where these huge irrigation systems were in place. Partition of India and Pakistan in 1947 led to much contention over which country gets the water. India alone has the Ganges, but the tributaries of the Indus cross the newly-established boundary. They all start in India, which therefore has the whip hand and could deprive Pakistan of the water on which nearly all its agriculture depends. There are five major tributaries: Punjab = paunch ab, five waters. A Commission settled that Pakistan should have be water of the main Indus, the Jhelum and the Chenab, whilst India cut off and diverted the Ravi and the Sutlej. The biggest dam of all is the Tarbela (pronounced 'Tarbvela') on the Indus.

The ever-rising population meant that Pakistan had to greatly extend its area under irrigation. This was done through the Lower Indus Project (Karachi area) and the Upper Indus Project, based on Lahore. To find out if desert or semi-desert land is irrigable there are two requirements. First, is the land 'under command', that is, does it lie at a lower altitude than the outlet, existing or planned, from the reservoir? Secondly, is the soil suited to irrigation?

However, soil survey on flat alluvial land is a boring task, and thank goodness Huntings already had staff doing it. At about that time development agencies had begun to realise that the fact that a soil is suitable for a particular use doesn't mean that it will miraculously be put under that use. This has to be done by farmers, and a starting point was to find out what the farmers were currently doing, called farm system studies.

This was where I came in – at the time knowing nothing about farm system studies. The task was to recruit Pakistani graduates in Agriculture, mostly from the Agricultural University of Lyallpur, and dump them in villages with charts and questionnaires. In developing countries the most able students do not read Agriculture, but we had to do our best. In due course the Upper Indus Project went ahead, turning large areas of desert into fertile farmland – until rising water tables led to soil salinization, but that is another story.

> Man with his hydroelectric power
> Has learnt to make the desert flower
> A sight beloved of every mammal
> Except the desert-loving camel.
>
> He views with mounting indignation
> The ravages of irrigation
> And water as it flows and squirts
> Robs him of his just deserts.

Punjab, discussion with farmers

So what can I remember of this first consultancy? The only time I have come close to being airsick as the plane from Karachi to Lahore bucketed around on approaching landing. The Administrator giving me a per diem allowance in local currency remarking, "That much would keep one of these chappies going for a year". The Project Manager was much respected, and by no means handicapped by having only one arm; but occasionally he would get some detail wrong, and having with this arm seized the wrong end of the stick it was difficult to wrest it from him. And of course, the experience of everyone the first time in the Indian subcontinent, a spell of runny tummy. I believe I coped by eating in the evening and going off for the day's work without any breakfast, quite a sacrifice for me.

The British had set up a system of canal rest houses where government officers could stay, similar to those in Africa but found along canals. We arrived at one, two Huntings staff and a couple of Pakistan officials, and went in for drinks. Immediately, without being asked, the punkah was started up to keep us cool. A punkah is a long slab of wood with grass beneath, suspended at both ends; in the middle a rope goes through a hole in the wall outside which sits the punkah wallah, pulling it to and fro with his toe – just as he (or quite possibly his father) had been doing since days of British rule.

There was a touching moment. Outside in the garden was a stone memorial to a little girl, six years old, who had died there, quite likely from malaria. One thinks of her parents, far from medical help, giving her all that love and care could offer, but in vain.

Many years later, some time in the 1980s, I was in Pakistan again, and there was the usual 'cocktail party' to meet other consultants and local staff. A tubby little man with glasses came up to me and said, "Professor Young, you will not remember me, but you gave me my first job". Now I did remember him, for among the graduates whom we recruited in 1964 he stood out from the other 15 in intelligence and ability. "Yes, I do remember you. What are you doing now?" "Director of Lyallpur Agricultural Research Station" – the leading centre in the country. So that was another of those very satisfying cases, like Reginald Mwangala in Nyasaland, of local staff who made good. There were to be more.

It would appear that Huntings were satisfied with my services, as they took me on twice more, for projects in Malaya whilst I was still at Sussex, and in the Niger Republic, West Africa, many years later.

Malaya and into the jungle 1965-66

With only a small cohort of Geography students, most of them with a focus on social or economic studies, Sussex then found it academically (and no doubt financially) desirable to get rid of me for a whole year, which including two summer vacations became 15 months. This was again with Huntings, on the Jengka Triangle Settlement Project, right in the centre of Malaya, a contract they held jointly with an American engineering firm, TAMS.

We travelled out via Sri Lanka, as Ceylon had become by then. When in the former Empire, try to stay in the old British colonial hotels, Faletti's in Lahore, the Norfolk in Nairobi. In Colombo this is the Galle Face, on the sea front but not with the objective of being a beach hotel; the original building was the Governor's residence. Colombo isn't great, so we were soon up into the central hill area, Kandy. We stayed not in an hotel but a guest house, run as a sideline by a rich lawyer, Da Souza, which indicates Portuguese descent. We learnt there was to be a dance performance in the garden, at the behest of a reporter and a photographer from the National

Geographic Magazine. We were welcome to take our own photos. Their way of doing so was to take a reel of 36 Kodachromes, all of the same dance, then call for another. I asked whether ordinary geographers like ourselves were likely to get an article into the National Geographic, when most came from professional reporters. The reply was certainly in principle, although, "It would help if you did something that we can't, like walk across the Antarctic".

We met the Professor of Geography at the University of Peredeniya, Chris Panabokke, an amiable man who was to remain a friend for life. He told a story of when the incoming Sinhalese government, under Bandaranaike, demanded a massive and immediate increase in their student intake. Lacking a large enough lecture theatre, he had lectured to them through a micro-phone in the grandstand of the racecourse, producing a photograph to prove this.

Travel there was by hiring a car with driver, a procedure not without its dangers, as they are apt to take the numerous blind corners on the outside, requiring a nail-biting slalom skid if an oncoming vehicle appeared. You may have noticed that Sinhalese names appear to be something of a mouthful, like Malalasekera. Thus the focus of the tea-growing area is Nuwara Eliya, which is not really as bad as it appears, some of the syllables are essentially consonants, so it is pronounced more or less Nu-rail-ya. Tea-growing country produces wonderful scenery since the crop calls for high rainfall but freely drained soil, and hence long, sloping valley sides. A colonial relic was the Nuwara Eliya Club, oak panelling, leather armchairs, and a notice half way along the corridor, "Ladies are asked not to proceed beyond this point". The club was built of Scottish granite, despite the fact that much of Ceylon is underlain by granite.

Then on to Malaya (soon to become Malaysia) and the Jengka Triangle Project. The objective of this was to take Malay farmers from the over-crowded coastal areas and settle them on a area 40 miles by 20 in the almost unoccupied centre of the country. "But isn't this covered by primary Dipterocarp forest, some of the finest rain forest in the world?" Yes. "So they will have to cut this down?" Yes. "Who is financing the project?" The World Bank. "I assume these magnificent hardwoods will at least be harvested?" The best species were, but most of them were burnt. Attitudes to forest clearance were very different then.

Soil survey team, Jengka Triangle
Malay settler's house behind

The objective of the soil survey was to divide up the land so that the best soils were to be planted with the (then) most profitable crop, oil palm, and the less good soils with rubber, leaving only some steep rocky ridges under forest. We were a team of three. Bill Verboom, the leader, was a weather-beaten Dutchman who before the war had been manager of a plantation in the Dutch East Indies. He was captured by the Japanese, spent time in the terrible conditions of their prisoner of war camps and was in Japan when the atomic bombs were dropped, which saved his life. The third team member was John Bennett, later to follow a career with the UK Land Resources Division.

Early in the survey Bill took the view that if you were living in jungle you needed to get support from above. On enquiring which was the best reli-gious establishment in the area he found it to be a Hindu temple patronised by the Tamil community. He went there and for a small donation received the priest's blessing. This proved a wise precaution. Later in the survey I went down with dengue fever, whilst a large tree fell right across John Bennett's landrover.

Soil survey in the jungle

We had a flat in Kuala Lumpur but much of the time, when on field survey, was spent living a wooden hut built for the first of the incoming settlers. As normal for Malay houses it was up on stilts to reduce, somewhat, the animal and insect life. Travel from the project office in Kuala Lumpur was via a continually twisting road across the central mountain range, facing the hazard of heavily loaded and mechanically insecure logging lorries.

Soil survey in rain forest is somewhat repetitive. You cannot base the boundaries on air photo interpretation because the forest canopy obscures everything. You have to walk along paths cut through the undergrowth, called rentises. A herringbone pattern was cut, with a central north-south main rentis and east-west lines extending either side of it. You went into the jungle with 5 Malay labourers, made soil observations at intervals, then camped for the night and continued the next day. Back at base people would say, "He went in on Tuesday" or "We think he will come out before the weekend". On the final map there are a few suspiciously straight east-west lines where two of us, on adjacent rentises, took different views as to the classification into soil series.

Crossing the River Pahang
Limited freeboard

Camping in rainforest is not like with the Boy Scouts, nor British colonial safari camping. A tent would be far too hot, so all you have is a tarpaulin stretched across a roof pole and held at a fairly gentle angle by guy ropes to nearby trees, which allows any breeze to flow through. A normal camp bed is out of the question because of leeches, so the labourers construct beds consisting of four posts with a Y at the top, two lateral poles which go through loops in the canvas bed, with two stretchers at the ends with reverse grooves, to hold the sides apart. The labourers construct this setup nightly with remarkable speed, cutting green understorey trees with their very sharp parangs (Malay for panga, machete).[1] During thunderstorms, which typically occur at night, you remain dry with the torrential rain all around, but the noise is such that when Doreen and our infant daughter

---

[1] I retain one to this day, invaluable for garden work, though nowadays not to be carried in public unless in Scouting uniform.

Chrysogon came once, you could not make yourself heard between adjacent beds.

Camping in the jungle

I was supposed to know something about land evaluation, so was asked to prepare a system of evaluation for oil palm and rubber – mostly based on the soil, since the climate was uniformly hot and wet over the whole area. Having selected criteria – soil depth, fertility and the like – I prepared maps showing where the land was suitable, or not suitable, for these crops. When Bill saw the one for oil palm he begged to differ for some of the area. "I have been manager of an oil palm plantation. If I say the land is suitable, then it is suitable, isn't it?" One could not dispute this unorthodox but doubtless superior system of classification.

Besides the soil surveyors, who always appear at the beginning of land settlement projects, there were a range of specialists such as foresters, who did a forest inventory, agriculturalists, and of course economists who inevitably, in World Bank projects, make the decisions. As at the time the price of oil palm was high and of rubber relatively low, oil palm was the recommended crop for most of the area – a somewhat short-term approach, since oil palm takes four years before it is ready to harvest, and rubber seven years, by which time the relative prices might be very different.

Our work won some US prize for a consultancy report. Moreover, the project went ahead, and in a World Bank follow-up study twenty years later, the map of the completed development scheme bore a strong resemblance to our original soil and land suitability maps.

What did we do out of work time? Well, in that climate there is a strong disincentive to do anything other than laze around the pool at the Club in Kuala Lumpur. We didn't play golf nor tennis there, but I learnt to play squash, quick on my feet but lacking stamina. I have heard of players there weighing themselves before and after the game to measure the loss in sweat. There were some bridge evenings, with air conditioning set so low that the ladies were offered fur wraps. Once at a bridge evening in a private house I found myself in the supper break sitting with a man and we got talking. I generally ask people's profession, and he proved to be a tax lawyer. "That's interesting," I replied, "So was my father". "You don't mean to tell me that you are the son of S. M. Young?" When I agreed to this, he continued, "He borrowed a book from me in 1936 and I never got it back". Confronting Dad with this later, he denied it.

Chrysogon, aged 3, went to her first school in Kuala Lumpur. Another pupil was the granddaughter of the Prime Minister, Tunku Abdul Rahman. Once on a parents' social evening at which he was present, worried about asking for alcoholic drinks, we were advised to say to the waiter, "I'll have the Tunku's drink" which was lemonade – with a liberal admixture of gin. Our cook-housekeeper was Yoke, highly efficient and a good cook. Chrys was cared for by his wife, whom we knew simply as Amah.

The company had rented flats for staff in the suburb of Kenny Selatan. Ours was on the ground floor, which gave easy access to the garden. Unfortunately it also meant easy entry. One evening we had returned from a party having drunk too much and fallen into a sound sleep. The next thing I knew was Doreen shaking me to say that something was wrong. Burglars had forced the door, putting cotton wool with chloroform across her mouth; I was too soundly off to need this treatment. They took her jewellery and also a small black case of mine which might have been supposed to contain the same, but in fact held my clarinet. It may have been for this reason that I bought a guitar, and subsequently composed the accompanying ditty (mandor=foreman).

THE BALLAD OF THE JENGKA TRIANGLE PROJECT
To be sung to the tune of "Too-ra-li-oo-ra-li-oo-ra-li-ay"

Of a project in Malaysia a story I'll tell
A fine tale of Hunting (and of TAMS as well)
They completed their project upon the right date
And all of them met, their experiences to relate.

Chorus: Singing Too-ra-li-oo-ra-li-oo-ra-li-ay.

The Forester said, "I have counted the trees
But an unusual dry spell put me ill at ease,
And on visiting Jengka last Tuesday I found
That the whole of the forest had burnt to the ground".

Chorus

The Agronomist had a sad tale to relate
He had visited every oil palm estate
But an urgent recall sent him hurrying back
All the oil palms were killed by a fungus attack.

Chorus

Said the Soils man, "In order my map to refine
I returned to the site at JE 2/29
But re-digging the pit to examine its face
I discovered my mandor interred in the base".

Chorus

The Project Director was looking unwell.
He said, "There is something I really must tell
When drawing up the contract with FLDA
We omitted the clause which required them to pay".

Chorus (mournfully)

Weekends and some local leave allowed us to zoom around Malaya. Malacca with its historic ruins, and the Cameron Highlands, altitude being the only means of getting away from the heat. We spent Christmas on Penang Island, visited by the Chinese Salvation Army singing carols. But best was the east coast. Ulu Jempol, our base in the Jengka Triangle, was already half way across the central mountain range, so it remained to continue eastward to the coast at Penang. Then one travelled up the coast, past magnificent beaches with almost no tourists. Once I took a plastic ball that Chrys had and threw it laughingly as far as I could into ocean, hoping to watch the waves wash it ashore. Unfortunately the ball being light floated mainly out of the water, and an offshore wind carried it away, to her great distress; to avoid this I was last seen disappearing into the South China Sea.

As it turned out the days of land settlement schemes were largely over. By 1970 most good agricultural land in the tropics had been occupied. What remained was largely rainforest, and there was a strong lobby against further forest clearance.

Homeward bound

The Jengka project had given me experience of the humid tropical zone, to add to that of the subhumid, savanna, environment gained in Malawi. Having taken in Sri Lanka on the journey out, we planned to see something of Thailand and Nepal on the return. Burma would have been great, but political conditions there did not favour tourism. Bangkok is a crowded city (though not as severely congested as when I worked there many years later). A day's stopover in Calcutta allowed a visit to the Tollygunge Club, still frightfully British although of course largely Indian membership by then. The next day we were surprised to be told to take the coach to the airport at 4.00 a.m., the reason being the likelihood of delays. One drove along street after street covered with bodies sleeping on the pavement. An anna or two of 'rent' would be exacted from them by protection gangs.

The flight to Kathmandu by Air Nepal produced unusual in-flight refreshments, plastic bags full of cold, soggy potato chips. On the approach to Kathmandu, suddenly mountains appeared above us on both sides. Some temple viewing was of interest, one did not feel at all threatened nor badgered for money, and the days of hippy tourism had not got under way.

A change of flights in Tehran gave time to walk around the streets, seeing the range of breads available. At the airport we were then told we would have to travel to following day as the flight was full. This was the result of overbooking, which airlines do because there are normally no-shows. On this occasion this had not happened because the greater number of seats had been filled by the Israel Symphony Orchestra, who were naturally either all missing or all there. In one of the finest ever demonstrations of her powers of persuasion, Doreen talked us onto the plane.

Up the Amazon 1968

Back in Sussex, more overseas trips turned up. The Brazilian government was building a road northwards from the new capital, Brasilia, into the Amazon rainforest, with the objective of opening up new land for agriculture – the so-called 'frontier of settlement' which had been a phalanx of the country's economy since the days of expansion for coffee. They knew that this would wreck the natural environment, so invited the Royal Geographical Society to send scientists there to record this before it went. The RGS lacked sufficient funds so asked the Royal Society to mount the expedition jointly. Invited to form part of the RGS contribution, I wanted to do the soils but was informed that this had been appropriated by the University of Newcastle, so would I stick to geomorphology. Agreeable to anything to get there, I planned a rather turgid exercise based on slope profiling.

Flights were to Rio di Janeiro and from there to Brasilia, then onward by landrover. The road became earth and gravel, and at one point there had been a storm and water was flowing fast across it. Our wheels started to spin, dislodged stones, and we just managed to cross before a full breach had been made, so we were cut off from civilization.

The expedition was to survey, scientifically, a square of land ten by ten kilometres, diagonally across which ran the boundary between cerrado, the South American version of savanna, and the beginning of the Amazon rainforest. The grass and short open trees of the cerrado don't conserve moisture, the forest does, so this boundary is relatively sharp and stable.[1] We had a camp set up there, with a rotating population of scientists – botanists, zoologists, soil scientists, geographers, entomologists, together with Brazilian labourers.

We were in ex-army tents, but beds were hammocks, essential to keep insects off – you had to dust the ropes at the ends with insecticide. There were food stores, including a paraffin frig, though much of the meat was

---

[1] OK, some of you know, there's a halfway formation of tall woodland, the cerradào (pronounced -don).

cured as pemmican. One day the leader went off to a ranch to acquire meat, asking if he might buy a steer. "Certainly, they're out there, shoot whichever one you wish."

South America is known as a biologically rich continent, and this soon became apparent from the insect life. Prominent among these were leaf-cutting ants, who would gnaw out a chunk of leaf, several times the size of their body, and carry it back to the nest. They had not learnt to distinguish books from leaves, which was apt to destroy our scientific records. Worst in the field were some insects locally called pumes, very tiny flies which did not bite but settled all over your face and neck the moment you stood still (as when slope profiling). These could be checked by netting over your hat and tucked into your shirt. A retired Professor of Entomology, Owen Richards, one of the doyens of the subject, was there to identify species of wasp, a dangerous task as if disturbed they could swarm and very seriously sting. He approached them with something like a butterfly net but long and narrow, had to take the whole nest in one swipe and immediately twirl it round to close the exit.

There was disappointingly little animal life, but the camp possessed a tame capybara, possibly orphaned. Now the capybara is the world's largest rodent, bigger than a beaver. Its mouth does not have teeth but several hard ridges. On land Capy was quite slow moving, but in water he moved more like a penguin. A camp game was to take a newcomer to a nearby pond, offer them a swim to relieve the heat, then push in Capy and wait for reactions to a (fairly harmless) nip.

I cannot say that my scientific contribution to this expedition was great. It was mostly a model of slope evolution, not comparable with work by the biologists. Almost by accident, however, there was a serendipitous discovery. The landscape was formed by a gently-undulating plateau, into which were cut valleys, the upper part of which was formed by laterite scarps. One finds this type of landscape commonly in Africa, e.g. in Uganda. The standard explanation was that a sheet of laterite (hard ironstone) had been formed when the area was nearly level. Then when valleys started to cut back into it, the laterite formed steep-sided scarps. During an idle moment eating lunch sandwiches, I started to wonder how the depth of soil overlying the laterite varied as one went back from the scarp. In research you are meant to have an hypothesis but I didn't, just curiosity. With an auger I started taking bores through the soil along a line back from the scarp, getting a gradual, expected, and uninteresting increase in soil depth. Then all of a sudden whoof! No laterite! The auger just went down through soft, very red soil.

More or less at once I realized what was the true situation. Water falling on the plateau picked up iron compounds as it passed through the soil. When it reached impervious rock it seeped sideways to the valleys. It only hardened into laterite when exposed to air close to the developing valley side. So it was not a case of a sheet of laterite underlying the whole plateau; there were only rims of it which maintained themselves as the valley sides were cut back. I don't think this discovery, buried along with those of other geographers in *Geographical Journal*, ever reached the scientific world. It was of use to me once: at interview for my Chair, I was asked, "What is the most exciting finding in your research, and what is the most important?" I was able to cite this as the former.

Into the Sahel 1968

Sussex had one more gift for me, or rather two, one academic, the other of a medical nature. My job there finished at the end of the Summer Term 1968, and a new life one was about to begin. In the interim, Huntings came up with a request to do a soil survey in the French territory of République du Niger. This was the Dallol Maouri project in the semi-arid or Sahel belt of Africa; Sahel is Arabic for shore, meaning the land which borders the Sahara Desert. The academic gift of this job was to add field experience of the semi-arid environment.

Huntings were engaged on a survey for an irrigation project, although at this distance in time I am far from clear where the water was to come from – if you are a consultant you don't ask awkward questions. One day, driving along in the sand, we were approached by another cloud of dust and as one does, stopped to exchange greetings. I explained that I was doing a soil survey for an irrigation project. A Dutch accent replied, "That is very strange for I, too, am doing a soil survey for an irrigation project".

But to go back a bit, I didn't fly out to the capital of Niger, Niamey, but to Accra in Ghana. The task there was to pick up two of Huntings' landrovers, recruit two drivers, get documentation for them, and drive across Togo and Dahomey to Niger. This was to be with the assistance of the FAO representative in Accra, who turned out to be Odo Cherik, the Pole who had entertained Doreen to African maize beer when in the remotest northern part of Nyasaland. The international clout of FAO accomplished what would otherwise have been a well-nigh impossible task. When sorting it out my eye caught an ornamental screed in traditional German script on the wall behind him. I could get the start, "Jedes Tag es kommt in meinem Bureau…" but then there was something which I thought might be doctor, Arzt, and the verb lecken which I didn't know at all, so asked for a transla-tion. "Every day someone comes into my office who tries to lick my arse."

Heigh-ho, off we go, starting across Togo (before 1914 a German colony), which stretches inland from a coastal strip only 50 miles wide. Waiting at the border with Benin was, improbably, a young lady hitchhiker who proved to be a London University research student in Anthropology. This enlivened the trip, notably on an overnight stop at a beach hotel. Probably she was heading for Nigeria so dropped off when we turned north. This part of the journey was a practical geography lesson, driving through the successive climatic and vegetation zones of West Africa: forest, savanna, Sahel.

The capacity of Africans to learn languages is impressive. They do it like a child, by listening and copying, not by the book as we do. My drivers spoke respectively Ga and Twi, the two local languages of Ghana, plus good English. It was only a few days into Niger when I overheard one of them in the market, "Non, c'est trop cher".

The soil survey was not very complex, since all the usable land was covered by sand. When it came to practical development planning I thought of suggesting taking on seven maids with seven mops for a half-year consultancy, but realised with regret that the allusion might not be under-stood by the clients. Rising above these valley floors were spectacular cliffs, 200 metres high, formed by what could be the deepest soil profile in the world: a capping of solid laterite (ironstone) 20 m thick, below which was a soft white totally-weathered rock. Above the cliffs there was a rocky plateau, partly covered with gravel, with scattered hardy bushes, a vegetation cover of much interest to ecologists but no use to man nor beast.[1]

---

[1] I returned for a week in 1969, to help in writing up the Project Report.

Soil survey, Niger, Foreign Legion style

So the work was not really soil survey but landform mapping. All the people lived in the valleys, where they grew bulrush millet, each stalk planted several feet apart to give the roots more chance to take up water from occasional rains.

We stayed in a the Hotel Terminus in Niamey, wonderful French food (but more of that later). Breakfast as usual was coffee and bread. One day I was struggling to make the best of this when at 6.30 a young French engineer came in, dressed in T-shirt, shorts and sandals. He went up to the bar, asked for a coffee, and stood there talking with the barman. Five minutes later he was off to start work – simple, no time wasted. He would break midday for an extended lunch. Entertainment consisted of the Centre Cultural Francaise, which was showing a Fernandel film.

Another recollection was coming across someone with a camel and, for the experience, asking if I might ride on it, expecting he would lead it gently as if I were a child. He misunderstood this purpose and handed me the control rope, expecting that I would appraise the merits of his fine camel as compared with others less worthy. At market day in an up-country town, Dogondoutchi, there was a substantial parking problem – but all the vehicles were camels.

The job lasted for five weeks, before I flew back via Paris. The next day Doreen and I set off in the VW for a holiday in a caravan which her Aunt Lil possessed on the Somerset coast. Stopping at lunchtime to visit a friend in Hampshire I felt poorly and asked Doreen to drive. Arrived at the caravan and spent the night being repeatedly sick, so back to Bath next morning. Was given chicken fricassee as being suitable when one is ill, which proved not to be the ideal food. The next morning found a doctor who happened to be an Indian lady. She took one look at me and said, "Hepat-itis". That was the second gift from this project.

The treatment was total bed rest, no milk products, and no alcohol for six months. I persuaded her that we needed to get home to Sussex, so was required to sit very still whilst Doreen drove. The Sussex doctor confirmed that up to three months in bed was essential, otherwise you might lose your liver. To keep me occupied I luckily had some computer output from a project done the previous term which I could analyse. This was a principal components analysis of the environment of Africa. The results came out very well, with such striking findings as component #2 the Sahara desert. What could component #1 have been? The Ethiopian highlands, much less extensive but totally distinct from the rest of the continent. I never submitted this exercise for publication. To keep me happy Darryl, then 16 months old, would come and sit on the bed and play. This episode meant that I was on sick leave for a whole term.

But not from Sussex.

INTERLUDE: MUSIC AND FILMS

FAVOURITE MUSIC

Desert Island Discs is the longest running BBC radio programme, created 1942 and still broadcast. "What eight gramophone records would you take with you to a desert island?" is used as a basis to get the week's guest to talk about their life. The constraint of getting eight recordings into half an hour means that the records are short, when the programme was started as 78rpm discs.

More recently Radio Three started Private Passions based on the same formula, pieces of music which are most liked by the guest of the week or which played a part in their life, but an hour long and without the artificiality of the desert island situation. The guests are often more up-market, though the pieces chosen are by no means all classical.

With no time constraint, here are my chosen items, in some cases pieces of music in general, in others specific recordings.

> *Bach: St Matthew Passion, the opening chorus* Whatever my views on Christianity, it has given rise to a large corpus of magnificent music. The orchestral introduction to this chorus, with its long pedal points, sets the huge scale and depth of feeling of the work.

> *Mozart: Sonata 8 in A minor* Performed by Dinu Lipatti when he was so ill with cancer that he could not leave the stage during the interval. His take on the last movement is ethereal.

> *Beethoven: Sonata 32 in C minor Opus 111, the second movement, variations on an adagio theme.* As we understand, never heard by Beethoven.

> *Schubert:* I cannot choose between:

- *Piano trios 1 in Bb and 2 in Eb* Recorded by Cortot, Thibaud and Casals in 1926. It has been said, "When you have heard Casals' phrasing, you never want to hear another."

- *Cello sonata, "Arpeggione"* On Desert Island Discs, this could be the "Take one record only".

Schumann: Fantasia in C An outpouring of his love for Clara, at a time when her father refused permission for him to marry her.

Richard Strauss: Trio from the last act of Der Rosenkavalier. Often chosen on Desert Discs, Private Passions, and Classic FM, but rightly so. A very moving situation – the ageing Marchioness realises she must give up her lover to a young man, played as a breeches part – matched by idyllic music for three sopranos.

Britten:

- *Viloin Concerto* played by Janine Jansen.

- *Chorus of trees: once in a lifetime the moon turns blue* from the opera Paul Bunyan.

- *Chorus of fairies, On the ground, sleep sound* from Midsummer night's dream. Having fairies in the plot allowed Britten to indulge in his (purely platonic) passion for boys. On the BBC Overseas Service record request programme 'Anything Goes' Doreen got the presenter, Bob Holness, to play this, "For her husband who is leaving Kenya", and to broadcast to the whole world, "Mrs Young doesn't want to leave Kenya".

William Walton: Belshazzar's Feast.

James P. Johnson: Harlem strut / Make me a pallet on the floor Early on I collected 78rpm records of traditional jazz, which I have recently given to the Norwich Jazz Club.

Songs

The choice is hard because these are so short and so many. Let us settle for:

Granados: el mirar de la maja; sung by Victoria de los Angeles accompanied by Gerald Moore.

Bernstein: the aria *Glitter and be gay* from *Candide,* sung by Natalie Dessay.

Schubert: How can one choose from among the best of 600 odd? I would go along with a popular choice, *Der Erlkönig* (The Erl King); then two slow and quiet ones, *Der Leiermann* (The organ-grinder) and *Der Doppelgänger* (The Double).

Schumann The greater number of the best songs for men are written for tenor, a voice which most men do not possess. Schumann often wrote for the lower men's voice. Let us choose *Die Alten bösen Lieder* (The old wicked songs). In the *Dichterliebe* cycle, after 15 songs in which a young man expresses his love, usually frustrated, on strides Schumann in one of his two personae, the impetuous extrovert Florestan. "Let us bury the old, wicked songs. Bring me a huge coffin. Why so large? Because I have put into it my loves, and my sorrows."

Samuel Barber likewise set the originals for lower voices. Let us pick *Sure on this shining night* and *I hear an army,* the last of which I learnt but never sang because my teacher could not manage the fiendish accompaniment.

Malashkin: *Oh, could I but express in song.* An example of that feature sometimes found, an unknown composer who wrote one magnificent piece. Doubters listen to it on YouTube, preferably sung by Chaliapin.

Virtuosity

I am a sucker for virtuosity. Once in South Africa I went to a recital by a fat young German flautist, who could play two-octave runs at glissando speed, and produce two notes at once, the lower and upper register; but I have failed to identify him.

Le Rossignol sung by Mado Robin. The French soprano Mado Robin had an ultra-high coloratura voice. At her first appearance at the Met, New York, she didn't tell the conductor what she was going to do, didn't do it at rehearsal, but in the performance finished on her speciality, the Bb *above* top C. You get this in the last verse of *Le Rossignol.*

La ronde des lutins (Dance of the Gobelins) played by Heifitz. The story goes that as a boy he played this at a competition for violinists, upon which the judges announced immediately that he was the winner, since it was impossible for any of the subsequent competitors to reach this standard.

Chopin's study in Gb (black notes study) adapted by Godowsky to be more difficult, with comments by the performer, Vladimir de Pachmann. Description is impossible; a very crackly version is on YouTube.

A story about virtuosity. Two violinists were discussing who was the greatest ever. They reached the point of agreeing that several were top in one way or another, so there could be no 'greatest ever', violinist or any other musician. "But you are wrong", said one one of them, "There is Horowitz. Not only is he the greatest ever pianist, he is the greatest ever musician – and he is not human!"

FAVOURITE OPERAS

Doreen and I are opera buffs in an amateur kind of way, going to English National Opera, the Royal Opera, English Touring Opera, occasionally Glyndebourne, and a range of European houses, plus New York and Sydney. I just couldn't reduce the list any more.

Purcell: Dido and Aeneas The story moves through funny witches and sailors, to finish with Dido's lament and the chorus which follows it, taken together the most moving moment in all music.

But other pre-Mozart, including Handel's many operas, don't make this list.

Mozart Almost all of them, but I have to include *Die Entführung aus dem Serail, The marriage of Figaro, Cosi fan tutti, Don Giovanni,* and *The magic flute.*

What to select from Donizetti, Bellini and Rossini? *Donizetti: La fille du regiment,* A top for humour, especially if sung by Natalie Dessay. *Rossini: La Cenerentola* gets its place for Cinderella's final aria.

And then there's *Rossini's Il viaggio a Reims,* which needs ten good soloists. Infrequently performed, seek it out!

Again a selection problem for Verdi and Puccini:

Verdi: Rigoletto. Puccini: La bohème, Turandot (But I am happy to walk out after Act I, with its two great climaxes), and *Tosca.*

Wagner: Has to be from The Ring, *Die Walküre,* if possible tacking on Brunnhilde's Farewell at the end of *Götterdämmerung.*

After leaving Purcell a long time ago, we reach British operas again:

Britten: Peter Grimes Masterly in the true tradition of opera. He never equalled this. But before it, *Paul Bunyan*, wonderful humour from the W. H. Auden libretto and from the music, including the moving *Chorus of Trees*. Infrequently performed, seek it out.

Twenty, all except two from the standard repertoire.

FAVOURITE FILMS

Some are recognized as 'great', others definitely not. Most are 1930-1960, but that was the golden age of cinema, like the nineteenth century for the novel. The first three are one picked from examples of their genre.

> *Genevieve* (UK 1953, director Henry Cornelius; Kay Kendall, Kenneth More). One of the set of classic British comedies.

> *North by Northwest* (USA 1959, director Alfred Hitchcock; Cary Grant). Likewise there has to be one of the Hitchcock's, and this runs close with *Rear Window* and *Vertigo*. Besides the perfect thriller technique, his idea of female glamour coincides with mine.

> *Die Dreigroschen Oper* (Germany 1931; director G. W. Pabst; Lotte Lenya). What?! The video I have is grainy and noisy, but no matter. Quite apart from the gravelly singing of Lottie Lenya, the atmosphere of low-life Victorian London is magnificent – few directors successfully manage to show dirt, squalor and poverty because, of course, the actors don't want to suffer.

> *Amelie* (France, 1991, director Jean-Pierre Jeunet, star Audrey Tatou). We nearly ended up with nothing post-1960, but the French are still able to make films which are charming and natural, so this whimsical, somewhat surreal fantasy is included.

> *Shadows and Fog* (USA 1992, director and star Woody Allen). Another 'recent' film to find a place. It was made as a homage to German expres-sionist film-makers. I saw it dubbed in French, which may have added to its distinctive, hard to describe, aura.

> *Jour de Fête* (France 1948; director and 'star' Jacques Tati). Selected with difficulty from Tati's *Monsieur Hulot's Holiday*, *Traffic* and *Playtime*.

Citizen Kane (USA 1941, director and starring Orson Wells). I'll go along with received opinion on this one. Besides the camera techniques, Wells' acting of Kane when elderly is extraordinary.

La Belle et la Bête (France 1946, director Jean Cocteau). Grips you in a magical way, as when jewels turn to dust in the hand.

A Matter of Life and Death (UK 1946, directors Powell and Pressburger; David Niven). Wonderful use of film techniques, including black--and-white for the dream sequences, and the way that Niven's dream interacts with real-life events.

The Blue Angel (Germany 1939, director Emil Pommer; Marlene Dietrich, Emil Jannings. Here I go along with popular opinion.

High Society (USA 1956; Bing Crosby, Frank Sinatra, Grace Kelly, Louis Armstrong, who cares about the director). Halliwell slates it, but the main function of films is to be entertaining, and this is superbly so.

Mamma Mia (director Phylidda Lloyd, 2008 – yes, 2008!). I said that films are meant to be entertaining and this is wonderfully so, from beginning to end.

The River (India, 1951; director Jean Renoir). Seen in the Washington DC connoisseur's Bioscope, still waiting to see again. Set on the Ganges, an early film in colour. Indescribably beautiful, and with a ultimately sad but perfect story, nothing overdone. If asked to name a best film ever, this is it.

AND WHAT ABOUT DANCE?

I enjoy ballet, but modern dance less so. However, I have a passion for tap dancing, and enjoy the expressive dancing found in film musicals. Let's settle for:

Gene Kelly Yes, there's the much chosen sequence from *Singin' in the rain;* but I'll go for *I got rhythm* from *An American in Paris*, with French kids putting in the 'I got's.

Fred Astaire The sequence with Ginger Rogers, Dancing cheek to cheek from *Top Hat*. Astaire insisted that the dances were filmed without cuts and editing. It's a lousy film, but this sequence is, as the lyric says, the nearest thing I can think of to Heaven.

11

ENVIRONMENTAL SCIENCES: UEA 1968-82

Sussex was a nice place to live, the family liked it, but academically it wasn't getting anywhere. The Geography Department was not strong, and I didn't get research grants. I suspect that the next move came not from perusing the adverts in the *Times Higher Education Supplement* but from a personal contact. The University of East Anglia (UEA) was another of the new universities, founded in 1963 with two Schools of Studies: Social Sciences and Biological Sciences. The founding Vice Chancellor was an historian, Frank Thistlethwaite, previously fellow of St John's, Cambridge.[1] To advise on the science side he co-opted Sir Solly Zuckerman FRS, an anatomist, originally South African, a former Chief Scientific Adviser to the government on science.

Besides FRS, Solly was Knight Commander of the Order of the Bath, Order of Merit, and goodness knows what else. Had he been given these honours for his anatomy? No, for bombing. During the war he was Scientific Director of the BBSU which, as we all know, was the British Bombing Survey Unit. By the 1960s he was an important guy, not least in his own estimation. Someone who went to an open lecture which he gave in the university reported that it was lacking in content and very dull.

Solly suggested to the university authorities a School of Environmental Sciences. He probably had in mind a high-level scientific set-up in which physicists, chemists and biologists applied themselves to problems of the environment. However, when the University interviewed for a founding Dean their committee were split between two candidates, Brian Funnell, a

---

[1] He was to become the only serving Vice Chancellor to perform a piano concerto in public, playing Mozart's double concerto with the Professor of Music, Philip Ledger.

geologist and Keith Clayton, a geographer/geomorphologist. They called them both back in and asked them to go out, and come back with ideas for the new School. In half an hour they did so. The committee liked these and they were jointly appointed Deans, Clayton for three years to be followed by Funnell. They were to given 12 lectureship posts from September 1968. The new School was probably very different from what Solly had envisaged. In particular, Clayton knew that here would be a demand from students who had previously chosen geography. This was important because at that time, a mainstay of finance was the government grant for undergraduates.

Given a hint to apply, I was enthusiastic. My line in geography was not centred on regional differentiation but on its other focus, man-environment interactions. I said this at interview, and was given a lectureship. The new School spanned a gamut between geophysics and town planning, with the following founding staff:

Geology/geophysics area:

> Brian Funnell, marine geology; Professor and second Dean
> Neil Chroston, geophysics
> Joe Cann, hard rock geology (paleoenvironments)
> Geoffrey Boulton, soft rock geology
> Nick McCave, sedimentology

Geography area:

> Keith Clayton, geomorphology; Professor and first Dean
> Richard Hey, river hydrology
> John Harvey, marine hydrology
> Athol Binns, meteorology
> Anthony Young, soils and tropical development
> John Tarrant, regional geography
> David Hauser, economic geography

(Oh dear, where were the ladies?)

Missing from that range of subjects was ecology, to be filled by the early recruitment of John Barkham. Binns left after about one year and was replaced by Trevor Davies.

Another early appointment was Fred Vine, geophysics, which was hard luck on the career prospects of Neil Chroston. Fred had made major discovery in his PhD, that the magnetic stripes on either side of the mid-Atlantic ridge originated from ocean floor spreading, for which he had been made FRS. He spent the rest of his career looking for something remotely comparable in importance, and never found it.

Cann, Boulton and McCave later became professors elsewhere. Tarrant got nowhere with research (hedgerow clearance in East Anglia does not hit the headlines) but was an excellent administrator, becoming Dean ENV, Deputy Vice Chancellor UEA, Chancellor of the University of Huddersfield for ten years, then Secretary General of the Association of Commonwealth Universities. If you add Fred Vine to the foundation twelve, their subsequent careers encompass eight professorships, three Fellows of the Royal Society, an OBE and a CBE, not bad for a start.

UEA was not the first university to establish a department of environmental sciences – Lancaster opened one a year earlier – but it quickly became the largest and, without question, the best. It grew to an undergraduate intake of 60 students a year. International and national awareness of environment was growing, to be boosted by the UN Conference on the Human Environment in 1972, which led to the setting up of UNEP.

So we were in at the beginning, and quickly set up a strong research basis. Funding came from NERC, the National Environment Research Council, and when the government preferentially supported 'centres of excellence', there we were. Nine of those first 12 appointments produced a strong record of research. With four books, two monographs and 37 articles, I may have been the most prolific staff member in terms of number of publications.

ENV went from strength to strength. When they took on a chemist, Peter Liss, to begin with he had to put on a course in elementary chemistry for those students who had come up without this (I went to it). Soon they were in a position to ask for three science A-levels, getting the environmental enthusiasm by letting one of them be geography. By the time I left it was becoming more like Zuckerman's initial concept, the study of environmental questions from a strong scientific base, but not omitting the policy aspects.

Methods of soil survey and land evaluation

A rare, nay unique, event took place at this time: I got a research grant. For most academics this is the major basis of their research. In environmental sciences, grants came mainly from the Natural Environment Research Council with some from the Social Sciences Research Council (NERC and SERC) and other grant-giving bodies in biology, agriculture, etc. A problem is that to get these grants you have to do what they want done, preferably including a buzzword, like desertification, sustainability, or recently, climatic change.

I prefer to do what I think needs doing, which gets you nowhere. I wanted to look into how the length of time that land has been cultivated affects its soil properties, and in Malawi we had sets of air photographs from 1948 (RAF flights[1]), 1963 and more recently, so you could map the intensification of cultivation. There was a spinoff, how the transition from shifting cultivation to permanent agriculture took place, a wonderful opportunity for historical geography. All this cut no ice with grant-giving councils.

Soil survey research, Malawi
with Peter Goldsmith and Darryl

But almost without me trying my Dean at the time, Keith Clayton, got me a grant to apply and compare methods of land evaluation in Malawi. This

---

[1]   They navigated by keeping a constant distance from a central beacon, so unlike most sets of air photos, which are in parallel straight lines, the print lay-downs for these were in concentric circles.

carried a three-year support for a research associate, who would get a PhD out of it. It also got me flights out to supervise him in the field, and a ropy old vehicle. The chosen area was Dedza District, the southern end of Central Province, with a good variety of landforms, soils and agriculture. I recruited Peter Goldsmith, who proved to be an excellent choice. We did some soil survey along the lines I had formulated: go to where there are data on performance (crop yields, forest plantation growth) and identify the soils there.

We presented the results to the Royal Geographical Society and published them in *Geographical Journal* (1977). Peter got his PhD and went on to a career in soils, particularly in Asia (Nepal, Laos) at a time when the golden age of soil survey was coming to an end.

Which soils produce the best crops?
Agricultural show, Dedza, with Peter Goldsmith, Chrysogon and Darryl

On one of my supervisory visits a disaster was narrowly averted. The Forestry Department had kindly let us stay in a house in Dedza Mountain Forest Reserve, which of course was built of wood. There was no electric supply. I like to start early, and one morning was shaving before sunrise, using not a tilley lamp, which you pressure pump, but an Aladdin lamp, the sort which has a tall glass tube above the flame. Ablutions finished, off we went into the field. When we returned in the afternoon there was a smell of burning. The rising heat from the lamp had ignited a spot above it, which was visibly creeping outwards across the ceiling as a burning circle three feet across. Had we not come back in time, it would have been embarrassing to explain to the Forestry Office that I had burnt their house down.

CSERGE, CRU and DEV (what?)

I played a small part in three developments which strengthened ENV and UEA as a whole. In 1973 I was interviewed as an internal candidate for a Professorship. One of the questions asked was, "If appointed to this post, what would be the next staff member whom you would recruit?" Having recently returned from a consultancy at the World Bank I was in no doubt as to the answer, and the exchange proceeded thus:

> "An Economist. Without an Economist, no-one will listen to us when it comes to making decisions."
> "What sort of an Economist?"
> "An Environmental Economist."
> "What's that?" [!]

In due course I was appointed, we advertised for an economist and appointed a young man called Kerry Turner. Some years later he was to establish, and head, CSERGE, the Centre for Social and Economic Research on the Global Environment, a leading institution in the large field of environmental economics.

Also while I was there, negotiations were undertaken with Hubert Lamb, who held responsibility for long-range weather forecasting at the Met Office. This led to the foundation of CRU, the Climatic Research Unit, with Lamb as its first Director.[1] When Hubert retired his position was taken by Trevor Davies, who had joined ENV as an Assistant Lecturer; he was later to become Professor and Dean of ENV.[2]

I was also an obvious choice for the ENV representative on the committee set up to establish a School of Development Studies (DEV). This was the brainchild of Athol Mackintosh, an economist. His concept was for a teaching unit for development studies, whose staff would increase their

---

[1]   He was the grandson of a mathematician, Horace Lamb. Hubert's son was Norman Lamb, sometime Liberal Democrat MP for North Norfolk (and resident in Claremont Road).

[2]   Trevor's successor, Phil Jones, became headline news when some emails of CRU were leaked which were thought, wrongly, to suggest rigging of data.

experience by spending one third of their time on practical development consultancies, either individually or by DEV bidding against commercial consultant firms to secure contracts. They would correspondingly only get two thirds of their salaries from the university. Athol's way of getting things through committees was to make the position more and more complicated until only he understood what was being proposed, whereupon he would say, "Are we all agreed then?" He achieved his dream.

As my basic science was weaker than that of most ENV staff, and my experience of development projects greater that most in DEV, it was obvious to consider asking to transfer. I was put off doing this by two things. First, I have never been good at asking for money. Secondly, I sensed a whiff of left-wing attitudes in DEV, something which I have to confess put me off. As their soil scientist they appointed Michael Stocking, a known figure in soil conservation (and also a rarity among university staff, a Seventh Day Adventist) with whom I got on fine.

Proctorial Episode

One day a phone call arrived from the Pro Vice Chancellor: would I take on the duties of Disciplinary Officer (what Cambridge calls Proctor)? Previously, discipline in the university had been handled by the Dean of Students, but as his main responsibility was student welfare, it was observed that he could find himself in the position of being both prosecution and defence councils. You can appreciate that this was far from being my wish, but as I had just been made professor I could hardly refuse. Fortunately I was joined by Paul Ashbee, eminent archaeologist, a member of the Historical Monuments Commission, and more importantly, someone who instantly commands respect.[1] Most of the time we saw students who had transgressed the university's disciplinary code in minor respects, such as causing damage when drunk. Paul rightly considered that fooling around with fire extinguishers in residences was a more serious offence.

There was one noteworthy occasion. The 1960s was the period of the student protest movement, with marches, occupations of university build-

---

[1]　Funding for Paul's research may possibly have been assisted by the fact that he was married to Richmal, niece and literary executor of Richmal Crompton, author of the *Just William* books.

ings, and the like.[1] What they were protesting about is epitomised in the aphorism, "You ask what is the demand. There is no demand. The demand is the demand!" At UEA this blew up in 1969 with some brief lockouts from teaching buildings, and night-time spray painting. On the entrance to the School of English and American Studies was sprayed the immortal phrase, "UEA IS A BOURGUEOISE ORGASM". The porters thought they knew who had done this, and the Dean of Students certainly did, so some students were brought before a Disciplinary Committee hearing. In the end the Committee's finding was, "We think you had something to do with this but we cannot find you guilty. We therefore return the Scottish verdict of not proven". The night before this hearing, another slogan appeared in the wall of Senate House: "DEATH TO YOUNG AND ASHBEE", the only time I have achieved such notoriety.

Gongs

Whilst at UEA a couple of awards arrived. The first was in 1972 when I was given the Cuthbert Peek Award of the Royal Geographical Society. This is given for, "Advancing geographical Knowledge of human impact on the environment…through earth observation", so I suppose it was intended for my work in improving methods of soil survey. I certainly never applied for it, although I had spoken on this topic at two meetings of the RGS.

I did, however, put in for a Doctor of Science (DSc) degree. This is awarded on the basis of a string of publications on some topic, in my case tropical land resources. There were two hiccups in this process. First, one of their referees spent over a year sitting on the heap of papers and books before he reported. Secondly, at the degree ceremony when this was eventually to be awarded I was Dean of the School, hence 'presenting' to the University Pro-Chancellor all the undergraduates and postgraduates for their degrees. When my turn came I stepped back and the previous Dean said, "I present to you my colleague Anthony Young for the degree of Doctor of Science". Now the Pro-Chancellor at the time was Sir Edmond Bacon who had a few gongs himself: Lieutenant Colonel, 13th *and* 14th Baronet (isn't that overdoing it?), KG, KBE and Lord Lieutenant of Norfolk. Maybe the multiplicity of these titles had used up his short-term

---

[1] One of its leaders, 'Danny the Red', had spent a term as visiting student at St Christopher School.

memory, for he replied, "By the authority of the University I hereby confer on you the degree of Master of Science". This wasn't exactly what I had expected, as MSc is typically given when a PhD student isn't up to the mark. Anyway, the certificate says Doctor.

Life in Norwich

As already noted, part of my first term was spent on sick leave. This didn't matter as there were only first-year students being taught Prelims, and it was easy for them to shunt the soils into Term 2. Doreen had to drive up to Norwich on her own to find us a house. So that I wouldn't have to do alterations she chose a modern town house, 29 The Walnuts, terraces facing a common central garden.

We also needed to find a school for Chrysogon. We had been advised that schools in the City were better than those in the County, which ruled out the over-the-river area of Cringleford, and gave Colman Road School for her, although this proved to be less than optimal. This was solved by her move to Norwich High School, giving her a period of stability in the senior school, after being shunted around to six schools previously. Darryl likewise began at a state school, Fairways, although from its catchment area around Cringleford it had a distinctly above average intake. Fairways built a swimming pool, and when the great day of its opening came, the children were being tentatively persuaded into the shallow end. Darryl, aged about four, had spent a term in Singapore by then so, unable to understand what the problem was, he dived in and swam a length with a fast crawl.

I became active at UEA at the beginning of November, my diary showing interviews with the students who had been allotted to me advisees. Teaching duties during the Prelims-only year were light, and wise colleagues spent the greater part of their time preparing lectures, seminars and practicals for their coming special options. I have never been good at getting my teaching all tied up in advance, leading to panic at the last minute.

All this time—school, university, Sheffield, Sussex, UEA—there was the bane of hayfever. In May and June my nose was running, eyes itching, mild asthma. Any outdoor activity, like camping, was anathema. Courses of 22 graded anti-histamine injections produced little result, and the more recently available sniffers were not much better. I can remember chairing an Examiners' Meeting with a machine behind me which was supposed to extract pollen from the air. There we go again, social activities were a 'no' for two months every year.[1] Miraculously, this allergy disappeared when I went to Kenya at the age of 51, and did not resume on return.

Singapore interlude 1970-71

I am not clear how this arose but UEA let me know that I could have the Autumn Term 1970 off if I could find a salary. I went to the British Council in London to enquire if there was an opportunity at some university in the tropics, and it happened that the Vice Chancellor of Nanyang University, Singapore was visiting. One or other of these bodies found the cash, so in July the family were off, taking a week's holiday in Cyprus on the way out and a stopover in Beirut, one of many world trouble spots which I was to visit.

It has to be said that this was not a very successful adventure, although it was the first time that I held the title of Professor. Nowadays Nanyang University of Technology is one of the world's leading universities. Things were very different then. It had been founded privately by Chinese businessmen during Colonial days, when they considered that the University of Singapore was neglecting their community. Quite likely the British favoured happy-go-lucky Malays, the original inhabitants of Malaya, and viewed with suspicion the inscrutable Chinese newcomers, who doubtless greatly outscored them in School Cert and entrance examinations (as American universities were to discover). When Singapore broke away from Malaya to become independent in 1965 they inherited its two universities.

Nanyang was situated at the western tip of Singapore island, 16 miles from the city, and in 1970 was still an all-Chinese university (visiting staff could be accepted because English was compulsory for all students). We were allotted a house on a hill in the centre of the compound, close to that of the VC. There was air conditioning in the living room but the only way to cool down Chrys and Darryl's bedroom was to leave the door to the living room open.

There were nine students doing my Soil Science course. Whilst able, hard-working and with adequate English, I soon found there was a problem.

---

[1] Chrysogon has regrettably inherited this problem.

Their upbringing was to cultivate respect for elders, in this case me. A basic concept to the British way of teaching, "It might be this, or it might be that. Discuss" was alien to them. I tried something straightforward, the origin of laterite, to which there are several well-defined theories. Going through these I saw them looking at me and realised what they were thinking: "He knows which one is right; or if he doesn't, he is not as good a teacher as someone who does". It was difficult to get reasoned essays. However, the brightest student, Leow Kwek Siew (Albert) came on to UEA to do a PhD.

The university seized upon Doreen to teach English, TEFL, Teaching English as a Foreign Language. The previous tutor had been Pakistani, which would have had a strange effect on Chinese accents. Doreen was faced with a class of forty, all in identical white shirts, many with horn-rimmed spectacles, and mostly called Mr Yang, Mr Song, Mr... It was quite a challenge, which of course she was up to.

Singapore is an authoritative society, and rather old-fashioned in a Victorian kind of way. We were invited to a student party. The boys sat along the right, the girls along the left. Honourable staff members, occupying the end of the room, were applauded as they came in. The students played games, like trying to pop balloons attached to a couple's ankles until only one was left. At Chinese New Year it is the custom to let off strings of firecrackers, adjacent business premises competing to see who was rich enough to go on for longest. But you had to follow regulations: newspapers announced that, "Fireworks could only be let off by authorized persons, in designated places, between permitted hours". So lets all have a wild time of it.

For social life, after earlier experience abroad we said to ourselves, "This time let's not plunge into British expatriate life. We are on the campus, there are links through my colleagues in the Geography Department, so let us live the life of a Chinese university".

This was not successful. First, through inability to read posters in Chinese we didn't always know what was going on (e.g. a piano recital). But more substantially, we found that their social life involved Chinese dinners to which Doreen was invited because they knew that this was our custom, but at which their own wives were not present. So we called it a day to that and joined the Tanglin Club, spending time mostly sitting around the pool.

For Chrysogon there was a school run by a Scottish headmistress, 17 miles from Nanyang. Her teacher was shocked that at her English school she had not learnt her times tables, so when driving to school it was, "Seven eights are fifty-six, eight eights are...". Two remarks by Chrys are indicative of the contrast in educational levels. First day at Singapore school: "It's terrible! We work all day". First day back in Norwich: "Oh, we just play most of the time". Darryl went to a playgroup of Indian boys, who would pull his hair on the school bus.

We had two good friends in Singapore, 'Y. S' and Dorothy Lau. Y. S. was a soil mechanics engineer, and had met and married Dorothy when she was a geography student at Nottingham University. They were strongly Christian (there you go again, why do we so often link up with such folk?). How did we get to know them? Well, one of my publications was a book for schools, *World Vegetation* (1966). This was written jointly with a Sheffield schoolmaster, Dennis Riley, who had approached me when I was lecturing to the local geography society. Dennis had taught Dorothy, kept in touch with her, and learnt that we were going to Singapore – what a chain of links! One of their daughters, Meilan, became a good friend of Chrysogon.[1] The Lau's belonged to the Singapore Swimming Club, whose pool was larger than that at Tanglin, and the day before we left they invited us there. Chrys slipped on the pool steps and knocked out two of her front teeth. Meilan dived to the bottom of the pool and retrieved them! They then took us to their dentist who replaced the teeth, and on learning of the circumstances absolutely refused to accept a fee. What a happy end to our stay!

Hush-hush: lecture tour of South Africa 1977

UEA also let me go on a lecture tour of South Africa, although this was all very hushed up because at the time British institutions were supposed to be boycotting apartheid. It never appeared on my CV and indeed, such was the lack of documentation about this trip that when writing this chapter about my time at ENV I initially finished without including it. The invitation came from an English geomorphologist, Bernie Moon, on behalf of the South African Geographical Society; there was no fee but they paid all my expenses, I guess from a gold or diamond-mining grant. Bernie invited me

---

[1]   Meilan is now a doctor in the US – as are her three brothers.

as a slopes geomorphologist, but when they found I was going to speak on tropical land resource survey they were pleased.

The tour took in Transvaal, Orange Free State, Natal, Transkei (African), Western and Eastern Cape Province, with short incursions into the margins of Lesotho and Botswana. I lectured in 14 of the country's 17 universities, including the one for Indians, Pietermaritzburg, and the Afrikaans language one, Bloemfontein. I did not go to the university for Africans, Fort Hare, but their students came to Grahamstown.

Some stories. The Vice Chancellor of Fort Hare rang his opposite number in Grahamstown, saying his students would have a long bus ride and on arrival would need some refreshment, but the law forbade them from eating in Grahamstown refectory. The reply was, "They eat in our refectory". This kind of getting around apartheid regulations was common at the time. At Bloemfontein I stayed the night with an Afrikaans geographer (only just not starting on dinner before grace). He took me to a new house he was having built, with a swimming pool and tennis court. "Oh, so you play tennis?" "No, I don't – but you have to have a tennis court." In the main square was a statue to a very holy man who had translated the bible into Afrikaans. One night, students painted footsteps coming from the statue into the liquor store and back again. At Capetown they took me on a long excursion to reach the margins of the Karroo Desert. On arrival it rained, the first time for a year, so my photos of desert plants are in rain. Altogether a most successful visit, although I had to keep it under wraps until the ending of apartheid in 1994.

That wasn't the end of the trip. Doreen, Chrysogon and Darryl flew out to join me and we hired a truck camper (not quite so cramped as the one we had in Canada). Our holiday took in two national parks, Umfulozi and the huge Kruger, the Drakensburg mountains, and Swaziland, this last completing my visits to what had been the three 'High Commission Territories': Bechuanaland/Botswana, Basutoland/Lesotho, and Swaziland (unchanged).

South African joke. A visitor is taken to a remote farm managed by an Afrikaner. Everything is neat and orderly. "What a wonderful place you – and the Good Lord – have created here". "You should have seen what it was like when I arrived."

Back to Norwich

We returned to UK in February 1971. For me, this was to carry on as before. For Doreen, however, there was something fresh. Backtracking, through someone in the History Department at Sussex, a contact had been made with Norwich High School for Girls. When their Geography mistress reported that she would have to leave to have a baby, the School contracted Doreen. This was shortly before we went to Singapore, so Doreen replied that she was not immediately available but would get in touch on return. On doing so, she was told that the present incumbent would be *very* pleased to learn this. So Doreen began teaching, initially for two days part time, on 5th March, less than three weeks later. This was subsequently to expand into a full-time position, by 1982 Head of Geography and Head of Sixth Form.

By 1983 Doreen had a prospect of applying for the post of Deputy Head-mistress, but selfishness on my part for my career prospects prevented this. After the deanship has passed through Clayton, Funnell, Vine and Tarrant, I was no longer able to avoid it and in 1980 began a three-year term. In the first year colleagues seemed broadly satisfied with my open way of running things. Then came an unanticipated circumstance, Mrs Thatcher's economy cuts. The university had its grant reduced, so each School was asked to put in a bid saying why this should not apply to them. 'Centres of excellence' came to be used, and if you were not one of these you were in for the chop. Confident that ENV was indeed the leading centre of its kind in the country, I coordinated our bid. The outcome was that our support was cut by 7% (£65 000 – 2016: £200 000), good compared with most other schools, such as 15% for Social Studies.

That left implementation, and meant that all decisions had to be made against a background of saving money, a situation which I did not fancy. About this time I learnt of a World Bank job on land use planning in Nigeria. Putting two and two together I came up with a solution: why not cut the Dean? I applied for this job and when it was offered, put in for three years' leave of absence – that's unpaid leave, not a sabbatical, something which I have never had. Somewhat unexpectedly this was granted (it was reported that the Vice Chancellor had remarked that staff who go off for three years generally do not come back). A colleague was happy to go off to Hong Kong and advise them on landslides, and together these two savings in salary accounted for most of our cut. I dare say words were spoken between colleagues when I ducked out like this, but no ill-feeling was openly expressed.

So ended the university career upon which I had embarked upon some 30 years earlier. If a somewhat inglorious departure it did mean that throughout my life, past and to come, all changes of job were my own decisions.

12

VISITING FIREMAN: CONSULTANCIES 1972-84

I was never any good at getting research grants. Indeed, up until retirement I only even received one, to work on methods of land evaluation in Malawi. For someone with about 150 published papers, this must be something of a record, and certainly gave the university good value for money.

Instead, most of my research was based on consultancies, paid for by those who requested them. In the field of international aid, consultants are known rather portentously as experts, or more disparagingly as visiting firemen. I did about 55 consultancies of one sort or another, taking me to 38 countries, mostly in the less-developed world. These include many of what were to become trouble spots in the years that followed: Afghanistan, Somalia, Haiti, Ethiopia, Viet Nam, Northern Nigeria.

Consultant companies

It was Britain's leading company in the field of land development consultancy, Hunting Technical Services, which got me started in the commercial world. There were three jobs with them, two in dry places, Pakistan and the Niger Republic, and one of more than a year in a very wet one, Malaysia, which served to get consultancies on my CV. As they were undertaken whilst I was supposed to be working for the University of Sussex they have been described in Chapter 10. Three more jobs for consultants followed, before I was to divert my services to international organizations.

Murdoch Macdonald, the Shemankar Irrigation Project, Nigeria 1972 Yes, it's Nigeria this time, and no it's not, as is usually the case with irrigation projects, making the desert bloom. Murdoch Macdonald was an engineering firm, well versed in the water management side of irrigation. They knew that a soil survey was also needed, otherwise the water would be put on all sorts of unsuitable land. Shemankar is in the Plateau Province, south of Jos in the centre of Nigeria. It gets plenty of rain, some 55 inches (1400 mm), but I was told they had a Pakistani Irrigation Officer who thought that if other, drier provinces were having irrigation schemes, why shouldn't his too, and commissioned a survey. Consultants try to please the client, pointing out that dry spells would come along, and a little supplementary irrigation might improve the crops.

Two geographical facts added to the strangeness of the survey. First, it was carried out in September, towards the end of the rainy season. Secondly, large areas were covered with vertisols, often known as black cotton soils. These have the most difficult physical properties: they expand to a heavy impermeable clay when wet, and become rock-hard when dry; if you can keep the water content in-between they are fertile. On some days we were walking across plains ankle-deep in water. To add to my geographical know-ledge there is a feature called gilgai, consisting of deep hollows formed where dry-season cracks meet. As these were hidden by the surface water your legs would sometimes sink down into them. In an earlier book I had written that gilgai was "the only term in soil science derived from the Australian aboriginal language"; a reviewer pointed out that there were 57 aboriginal languages.

I guess the Company wrote up a report on irrigation potential as per the contract, but cannot believe that it went ahead.

The ODG of UEA, Village Relocation Assessment, Iringa, Tanzania, 1975 This cumbersome heading calls for a tedious explanation. One of the sections of UEA was the School of Development Studies, DEV (I helped to found it). Staff of this were members also of the ODG, the Overseas Development Group, a consultant company. They were expected to spend one third of their time on outside-financed work, hence the teaching School could appointed extra staff.

The socialist government of Tanzania under Julius Nyerere had embarked on a programme, *uhuru na ujamaa,* 'freedom through unity' – ujamaa was Swahili for the extended family – but Nyerere used it to mean village consolidation. The idea was to bring scattered farmers together into compact villages. This made it easier to provide them with services: education, medical clinics, access tracks, markets, etc. It also meant that party officials could keep an eye on potential trouble-makers. This programme had gone ahead in Iringa District, and ODG obtained a contract (World Bank financed?) to assess the viability of the consolidated villages, and took me on as an outside consultant.

By this time I had moved on from soil survey into land evaluation, the assessment of the potential of land for agriculture and other uses, and this was my role in the survey. I was able to draw on a method developed many years previously by the Colonial Service in Northern Rhodesia. You took the area of agricultural land, soil types, potential crop yields and the need to restore fertility by fallows, and by some arithmetic worked out how many people could be provided with food. I don't recall very much of this, but I expect came up with the conclusion yes, they'll be OK – without at that stage pointing out that this would be far from the case after population increase.

As usual when on overseas trips my diary goes blank but for two entries, the first, "July 14 brakes failed". Surprisingly the ODG did not take on local drivers but elected to drive a minibus themselves. Gilroy Coleman usually took the wheel. I was very much aware that on dry earth roads he took corners too fast, and sent a letter to Doreen, "Before long Gilroy is going to turn this bus over". The second entry was, "July 19 bus tipped over". Rounding a corner he tipped it over and it slid gracefully along on it's side. I was in the front seat and, aware of this likelihood, on corners braced my feet against the front, with the result that I remained unhurt, hanging above the driver. I remember Gilroy started to say, "I'm terribly sorry..." to which Ian, the Project Manager, responded, "Don't worry, these things happen to all of us". Gilroy was later to become Dean of DEV.

Passing through Dar es Salaam, I stayed at a 'four star' hotel, but services had by now become fairly primitive – no hot water, for example, and indeed no piped water in the rooms most of the time. The breakfast was noteworthy. In a large square dining hall a scattering of guests, mostly international consultants, were sat at tables around the perimeter. In one corner was a buffet table, but with no food on it. A waiter appeared at the diagonally opposite corner carrying on his shoulder a tray loaded with bread. Some nearby guests who had been there several days jumped up and helped themselves from the tray. This action precipitated a rush, as we all realised the situation and followed. By the time the man had reached the buffet table, the tray was empty.

After this job I went on from Iringa to Malawi, to check up on some research. Then the family joined us for a super holiday. This included going up Mlanje, the highest point in the country, and with 8-year old Darryl very nearly reaching the peak having to turn back, amid some enormous boulders, owing to mist, time and safety.

Mobil North Sea Oil: geomorphological analysis for oil reserves 1976 The next short consultancy was a one-off, first through harking back to my earlier work on slopes, and secondly through taking place in darkest London. Mobil took on the British Geomorphological Research Group (BGRG) on the long shot (but at negligible cost by their standards) that we could help them in oil exploration beneath the North Sea. There is a major geological uncon- formity, if I am right between the Jurassic and Cretaceous, which they had mapped, as contours, using seismic soundings. This would once have been a land surface, with hills, ridges and river valleys, and their geologists must have told them that geomorphologists were the people who knew about landscapes, so was there any chance this could help them to find oil reserves?

My role was to take some of the main slopes, as shown by the contours, and subject them to a computer program of slope profile analysis which I had developed. This didn't lead to anything. Others in the group spotted what they believed to be a case of river capture – one river cuts back into the basin of another and captures its upper tributaries. We made an immediate presentation of our findings, excitedly highlighting this discovery. The deflating response was yes, they had noticed this too.

FAO Rome, 1975 onwards

Looking back over all the varied kinds of work I've done, the most enjoy- able have been the jobs of one kind or another with FAO: the Food and Agriculture Organization of the United Nations, Rome. Including consultancies and what FAO calls 'expert consultations', meaning confer- ences; these numbered about 30, stretching from 1975 to 2000.

But it all began not with an invited consultancy but as a visit on my own initiative. UEA had a small amount of money for study travel, and I had heard that FAO was active in studies of soils and land resources in developing countries. I went to Rome, no doubt on some cheap flight, and asked to see the Director who happened to be an Englishman, Tony Smyth, and learnt about their work on completing the first *Soil Map of the World*, to be followed by a project on land evaluation.

Some time after coming back, I was pleasantly surprised to be invited to their Expert Consultation on a framework for land evaluation. This is essentially the next stage after soil survey, assessing the suitability of different soils etc. for specified types of land use. FAO's starting point was a Dutch PhD study. I made only one substantive contribution, to suggest changing a class 'Unsuitable' to 'Not Suitable', on grounds that 'N' in most European languages means 'Not'. (I now realise that this remark might not have pleased the French.)

A few weeks later, again unexpectedly, I was asked to write, jointly with a Dutchman, an FAO handbook to be called *Framework for Land Evaluation*. At this point I will quote from my book *Thin on the Ground*:

> The *Framework* became one of the most widely used of all FAO publications. A note may be put on record about its origins. Robert Brinkman and I agreed that I should write an introductory chapter, outlining the method, and we would then meet to discuss who should draft the rest. When Brinkman saw the 'Introduction' he remarked, "Wait a minute. We don't need very much more. With a little bit of expansion, and the addition of examples which I will find, this will be adequate to put across the method". That is the reason it is such a compact document.

In succeeding years the *Framework* was followed by detailed handbooks of land evaluation for different types of land use, called 'Guidelines'. I wrote those for rainfed agriculture and for forestry, others tackled irrigated agriculture and the most difficult one, grazing – difficult because the land users, cattle, sheep and goats, could walk from one piece of land to another. As with soil surveys, one has to ask how much these guidelines were used. The one on rainfed agriculture was certainly taken up on a number of regional evaluations, such as a vast exercise in central Nigeria by the British Directorate of Overseas Surveys, and an evaluation by the Soil Survey of Jamaica.

Don't ask about the next stage, putting the results into practice in development.

I doubt, however, if the forestry guidelines were used; foresters had their own well-tried methods of deciding what trees to plant, where and how; in any case they didn't have much option over what land to use, it was the hilly and high-altitude areas that the agriculturalists didn't want. However, some years later I was asked to contribute a chapter on land evaluation for forestry to a massive (and costly) compendium, *Tropical Forestry Handbook* (1993); and more than 20 years after that I was requested to revise this for a second edition (2015), which could be taken to mean it has been some use – or that the publishers want to sell it to libraries. After no little work on this they sent me an illuminated certificate: "We are grateful to Prof. Dr. Dr. Anthony Young for his invaluable contribution on Land Evaluation and Forestry Management". As they are selling their book for some £1524 they might have added a Sainsbury's voucher.

So that was the start. FAO decided I was a useful link to the academic world, and between 1975 and 2000 invited me to 12 expert consultations. On all but one of these we, the invited outsiders, did what FAO expected, rubber-stamped what they had already intended to do. The exception was a 1978 meeting in which, having completed the *Soil Map of the World*, the Frenchman in charge of their soil erosion activities wished to follow it up with a world map of soil erosion. Now I knew there was a problem in this: no-one had actually measured erosion on a regional scale; the resulting map would therefore be a desk exercise, based on calculation from a well-known formula[1] for estimating erosion on small experimental plots from rainfall, slope and ground cover. So I led a posse which held that to apply this on a world scale would be wasted effort. We actually got them to reduce the proposal to a trial map of Africa, which was never followed up. Soil erosion on a world scale was not tackled until a project completed in 1990, which has been used ever since.[2]

Having found out that one thing I could do was to write well, FAO took me on for a succession of authorship consultancies. Having moved from survey to evaluation, the next step was land use planning, or putting the results into

[1]   The Universal Soil Loss Equation (USLE).
[2]   The Global Assessment of Soil Degradation (GLASOD).

practice in development. With help from my main contact and friend in FAO, Maurice Purnell, I attempted to draw up procedures for land use planning. This proved to be more difficult than land evaluation, since the purposes for which land use planning may be done are so varied. There had been a Dutch committee which drew up a list of 'identified activities' in regional land development: they identified 963 of them! I managed to squeeze the procedures down to 10 basic steps, and wrote the FAO handbook, *Guidelines on land use planning*. At this point Maurice retired and his place was taken by someone with very different ideas: he listed some 20 'basic sources of information' of which Soils was only one.

Going back a few years, there was a major FAO exercise on Population Carrying Capacities of Developing Countries, which meant would they be able to feed themselves. After allowing obviously for non-agricultural activities which allowed a country to import food (e.g. Singapore doesn't have to grow its own food) we looked at potential cropping areas (rainfed and irrigated), crop yields under three levels of inputs, and hence food production. My input was to determine 'fallow period requirements', needed to maintain soil fertility at the low-input level. Then the UN population people took national populations at the time of the study, 1975, and forecast the increases to the year 2000. Using dietary needs for satisfactory health, basically calories, this could be compared with actual and potential production. This project was done in the days when computer output consisted of wide rolls of paper with holes along the sides. These became so bulky that FAO had to allocate a room to their storage, shared with some young Dutch 'associate expert'.

The outcome of this project was a table showing countries at 'lower, higher, and highest risk' of food shortage in 2000. Now that we can look back on what happened that year, the highest risk countries show strong similarities with those in which there have been famines and food emergency programmes: Rwanda, Haiti, Somalia, Ethiopia, Malawi, etc. If you've noticed that these are also countries showing political instability (a euphemism for dictatorships, civil war and the like), you are absolutely right.

Then UNEP, the UN Environment Programme, asked FAO for an input on their review, *Global Environmental Output*. By this time another good man, Freddie Nachtergaele had replaced Maurice Purnell, and he set up for me this and one or two other writing jobs.

Why don't FAO staff do these projects themselves? Their own time is fully taken up with backstopping field projects. HQ personnel can't actually do any research and writing themselves so they take on consultants. Is this highly remunerative? No, the rates were always very modest.

FAO consultation on population carrying capacity

The 'Spare Land' saga

As part of the population carrying project, FAO got interested in the spare land question: how much land is there which is cultivable but not presently cultivated? FAO's logic was that you start with an inventory of climate, to find out what could be grown where, then overlay on this the Soil Map of the World, ruling out some clearly unsuitable land such as lithosols (bare rock or very stony soils); that gives you cultivable land. Next, every year FAO produces statistics on present land use, including agriculture, and also on areas under specific crops: wheat, rice, etc. That is (supposed to be) cultivated land. Subtract cultivated from cultivable land, make allowances for things like cities and nature reserves, and Bob's your uncle, they reason that you get 'spare land'.

The tables of spare land, by country, were to my eyes crazy. I started with Malawi, where they calculated that less than one third of cultivable land was under cultivation; if this were the case, why do farmers plant on very steep slopes, or in semi-arid regions subject to recurrent droughts? I first came into this debate in an ad libbed discussion contribution to a Royal Society symposium, saying that:

- The estimates of cultivable land taken from small-scale maps were too high.

- The estimates of present land use were too low (the statistics range from unreliable to ludicrous).

- The land requirements for uses other than cultivation were considerably higher.

Having nailed my colours to the mast in that way, I subsequently expanded the argument into four publications on the lines of, 'Is there spare land?', concluding that official (FAO) estimates were typically 50% too high. Some years later, in their review of world agricultural prospects, FAO conceded that their estimates had been challenged, "in some quarters". I was happy to be named as such.

Rome sweet Rome

A love-hate relationship would best describe my attitude to Rome. The touristic side, both ancient Rome and Renaissance/Christian, is of course marvellous. Indeed, it is sometimes difficult to decide whether what you are looking at is ancient, mediaeval or contemporary Rome. Only very occasionally would I visit one of the tourist sights. The walk from the hotel to FAO took one past the Colosseum, but Doreen was surprised when after maybe half a dozen visits, I said I had never been inside it. I did have a spare day once and decided to walk across to the Vatican, only to find St Peter's Square swarming with people waving palm fronds, green, silver or gold according to their piety and wealth, this being Palm Sunday. Edging my way through into the back of the church, there in the far distance were tiny little men with red hats doing things around a table. Just one had a white hat, and lo and behold, he was lifted onto a chair and carried down the aisle past us, casting blessings on all sides, which should have made an unforeseen improvement to my consultancy.

Whilst on this subject, there is Charles Lamb's story. Charles lived at No. 2 Claremont Road. I used to see him tending his garden. He was somewhat deaf, but through long experience visiting my father I knew how to talk to deaf people (face on, about a yard away, don't shout but make the consonants clear). One day I asked about his service in WWII and learnt he had fought all the way up Italy. "When we got to Rome – I'm a Catholic you know – some of us Catholic troops went to get a blessing from the Pope." I love the thought of Charles and his fellow soldiers getting a Papal blessing and then going back to carry on shooting Italians.

I always stayed in the Pensione Lancelot, soon to become the Hotel Lancelot. Its origin was that an English member of FAO, Mr Woodcock, had the task of getting accommodation for visiting consultants, finding this to be in short supply. When he retired he used his lump sum to purchase an apartment on the Via Capo d'Africa, in a block of roads adjacent to the Colosseum and 15 minutes walking distance from FAO, and converted it into the Pensione Woodcock. After a period he set himself up for a second retirement by selling out, all this before my first visit.

The purchasers were two ladies, Mrs Khan and Mrs Music, Helen Khan being a Canadian Pakistani. They needed a new name, and decided to call it by the first guest who registered under their ownership. This happened to be a Frenchman, Monsieur Lancelot, so it became the Pensione Lancelot. Their headed notepaper shows Sir Lancelot brandishing his sword.

In its early days the Lancelot was convenient and inexpensive, retaining Mr Woodcock's discount for FAO consultants, but certainly not luxurious. Reception was on the third floor, which could puzzle guests on first arrival. The dining room and sitting room were also up there. The other floors had bedrooms, accessed from the stone steps by a key. Each was served by one bathroom and one loo, no 'en suite' in those days. In the evening I would sometimes roam around in a dressing gown to see if any of the access doors had been left open, then commandeer their bathroom. The rooms contained distinguished furniture of some antiquity although unfortunately the desks, on which consultants naturally wish to work, usually had the fold-down writing area broken. To save electricity, light bulbs were 40 watt; I used to buy a 100-watt bulb and substitute it each evening.

But the ambience of the Lancelot was great. The dining room consisted of tables for eight, on which one would quickly get to know fellow guests. Dutch consultants were common, owing to support from their government

171

to gain experience. If you joined a Dutch table they would, of course, immediately switch to English. Tourists were welcome also, if at times surprised by dinner time conversations about fish stocks, soil erosion or forest clearance. Dinner began with bottles of red and white on the tables, and you could ask for more. Italian regulations required that on registration you hand in your passport, and not infrequently at the end of dinner Asti Spumante would be brought out to celebrate a birthday.

Once, just before Christmas when there were few guests, Helen Khan and three others were engaged in a game of bridge. Others came to stand behind the players and watch. I was inspired to remark, "Now we have a truly FAO situation: everyone who is actually doing anything has an expert adviser". Helen was delighted at this and asked for it to be put in the Visitors Book.

Over the years the dear old Lancelot had to be modernised in order to raise its star rating. Showers were installed in all rooms, reception went down to the ground floor where a porter was stationed, doubling as a barman. Mrs Music left, so Mrs Khan took control. Her daughter, Lubna, became the receptionist and her son, Faris, after training in Switzerland, returned as a first class chef. Doreen picked up quite a few tips from him. So comfort was much improved, without loss of the friendly ambience.

The walk to FAO went over a hill with optional diversion through a park. In winter one would pass small piles of ash, where the ladies of the street had lit fires to keep their very exposed legs warm. "It's Tuesday, Maria, your day to bring the firewood." The police got rid of this practice, so they resorted to adverts in the newspapers on the lines of, "A.A.A.A.A.A.A.A Swedish masseuse, tel…"; the more A's you paid for, the higher up the Personal Services column. I was told that in the early days of FAO there was a shrubbery outside the building but when the D-G heard what it was being used for he had it cleared.

A few FAO employees lived in the Lancelot. One was Mary Mudie, who worked in the filing room (yes, paper files in those days). I took her to the opera once. Mary was a refined lady, daughter of the Governor of Punjab. At the end of formal dinners there the ladies would of course retire, so the the gentlemen could enjoy port, cigars and bawdy conversation. From one end of the table to the other the ladies would get up in twos, go to the door, and turn and curtsy to the men before leaving. If you were near the far end of the table you were terrified there would turn out to be an odd number of ladies, such that the last would have to curtsy on her own, to loud cheers!

There were three faults of Italian organization: banks, post, and money. On the first day you got your lire per diem from the bank in FAO, on Mondays especially involving a long queue whilst to clerk searched for your papers in a leather compartmented bag. When this authorisation had been received you then had to queue again at a counter where a less prestigious employee counted out the money. A colleague who had spent many years as a consultant worked out he had spent two weeks queueing in the bank.

Overseas mail was so delayed that you took your letters to the office of Casa, the employee's union, and dropped it, already with British stamps, into bags marked UK, etc. Any consultant returning home was expected to pick up mail for his country.

Small change was a menace. The lira was running at about 2500 to the pound, so minor items would be in hundreds of lire. But the government had not minted anything like enough coins so small change, if you got it at all, might be given in sweets.

Why is FAO in Rome anyway, when for most of the war Mussolini's Italy was an ally of Hitler? Well, when they saw they were going to lose they swapped sides. The UN specialist agencies were scattered around the world, UNESCO in Paris, UNEP (later) in Nairobi, and so on. (Quiz question: What did London get? The National Maritime Agency.) Rome was able to offer a large empty building, Italy's former Colonial Office, it's colonies having been taken away. Such were the organizational problems that FAO once mooted leaving Italy. Munich offered to take them, paying the costs of the move.

I did very little tourism, other than belatedly going inside the Colosseum, generally at weekends going into the office to work. But sometimes Doreen came and joined me, when the Lancelot would give us one of its few superior rooms with its own bathroom. Doreen became an expert on the tourist sights of the city, Roman and Medieval. There is also the Doria Pamphilj collection, founded by an English-Italian couple. It includes Velasquez's savage portrait of Pope Innocent XI – the basis for Francis

Bacon's series of 'screaming popes' – reaching a position at the summit of their career but imprisoned by it. (Bacon never saw the original.)

I would occasionally head off to music, opera or dance, with varying success. Aida in the open-air Caracalla Baths, along the road from FAO, is worth seeing once, though the flow of the plot might be interrupted by cries of "Gelati" from itinerant sellers. At the start of a performance of Donizetti's *Lucia di Lammermoor* at the Opera House there was a long delay, "These Italians just can't organize things" one thought. After half an hour there was an announcement, which I could not follow but which ended by saying that the Management was "Senza responsibilitate". On came a gang of huntsmen in kilts. The soloists sang but the chorus were silent, just mouthing their words. It turned out that this was a strike, Italians having a habit of leaving these to the last moment. By the second act they had secured their increase in pay, or whatever was the grievance, and resumed singing.

Years later I went for interview for a permanent post with FAO, in a group which formed a liaison between the international agricultural research centres. It transpired that to get a full pension you needed to work for 10 years, which I didn't have available before retirement age. I would really have rather worked in Paris for UNESCO, and had begun to build up a few personal contacts (like taking an English lady attending a consultation out to dinner). But at that point Britain withdrew its support from them, on learning the degree of corruption of their incoming Director General, so that rather kyboshed any chances.

Another important arrival

It was probably at a land use classification project that I was working on in Rome (and Doreen doing the tourist sites) when a phone call from Chrysogon informed us that her second child, Oliver, had been born on 15th February 1994. Taking turns at the wheel we set off from Rome via Florence, Genoa and Turin, and into France by the Frejus Tunnel, covering 519 miles that day, all on autostrada. The next day covered the greater part of France to spend the night at Laon, after which the channel ferry and on to Coulsdon, to find Chrysogon and Oliver still at the hospital. What a journey, 1100 miles in all.

On safari for FAO: Ethiopia 1982

I've worked twice (three times if you count Julius Nyerere's Tanzania) in communist countries, the first in Ethiopia 1982. FAO with UNDP had an ongoing project, "Assistance to land use planning" (a typical FAO title) which sought to prepare a Master Land Use Plan for the whole country. This meant a land resource survey, followed by land evaluation – I guess the actual planning would be left to the national government. Now Ethiopia covers one and a quarter million square kilometres, five times the size of UK, so survey presented considerable problems. It would certainly have been impracticable to use the classic method of air photograph interpretation, so they based it on satellite imagery, which at the time meant Landsat images. Robert Ridgway was there, and was aware that I knew about land evaluation. (After I had once examined his PhD he had become something of a disciple of mine.)

By the time I was brought in they were well into land evaluation, and to the best of my somewhat hazy recollection my main task was to assist in writing up the report, the usual, "Send for Young, he knows how to write". The project manager was a Korean, Mr Choi, who for reasons of language had problems in supervising this; but he was a good project manager, not always the case with my bosses. It was a strange situation, as you rounded a corridor you would be confronted with posters such as, "Workers of the World, Unite!" In the main square was an enormous billboard showing drawings of Marx, Engels and Lenin, surely the only place in Africa where three white men were given such honour.

One of the hotels in Addis Abeba possessed an olympic-size swimming pool based on natural heated artesian water. Ethiopian food was another attraction. You sit at an hourglass-shaped basket the top of which is a large round tray, covered by a grey thin pancake, njera, made from the local cereal, teff. You break off pieces from the edge and use them to scoop up the various items of food placed on it. In fact for reasons of cost – I was unemployed at the time – I didn't eat there often, but found a Chinese restaurant where one noodle dish was enough to satisfy. The city is up at 8000 feet altitude, which means thin air, a very large diurnal range in temperature, and by day a great difference between being in sun and shade. As someone put it, you start the day well wrapped up in sweaters and as the morning goes on, progressively shed them like onion skins. The first experi-ence of tennis was alarming, as due to the low atmospheric pressure a normal ball bounces eight feet high. You buy special tropical balls.

We all know today that Ethiopians are exceedingly good at long-distance running. They are also, dare one say it, more intelligent than most Africans. One of our land use staff, called Sultan, joined as a trainee and I think became the next project manager.

The country is strongly Christian, their own Coptic variety, and the religious art is delightful. Painted on skins you get, in a kind of comic strip layout, all the bible stories. But in them every character, from Adam to Jesus, is brown and with bent noses like mine, very clearly Ethiopian.

13

WRONG TURNING:
OH DERIA, IT'S NIGERIA 1982

To return to my main career, we left this with ducking out of the Deanship at UEA. This was technically taking three years' leave of absence (unpaid leave), with a fallback that I could rejoin.

For once the new post wasn't obtained on the old boy network but by seeing an advert in *The Economist* and applying. This was for a Senior Land Use Planner in Sokoto, northern Nigeria, one of the World Bank's 17 Agricultural Development Projects (ADPs of course) in the country. Having recently written FAO's guidelines on land use planning I felt confident that I stood a chance. I didn't realise at the time that another major factor in my favour was willingness to go to Nigeria. The dollar-based salary was good, but what excited me was the prospect of adding World Bank employment to my record with FAO. The prospective project manager, Manohar Singh Gill, even came up to Norwich to vet me and was charm itself. I remember also a lunch at Brown's Hotel, London, probably when getting a medical exam from an expensive consultant.

So in March 1982 it was London-Amsterdam-Sokoto, once again to become one of the founding staff of a new institution, the Sokoto Agricultural Development Project. Besides the Project Manager there were four senior expatriate staff to begin with: Mechanical Engineer, Agricultural Engineer, Accountant, and Director of Planning. What about Senior Land Use Planner, the post to which I had been appointed? Oh well, they needed a Director of Planning, it sounded to the World Bank much the same thing, and as 'Director' carried a higher salary than 'Senior' I didn't complain.

There had been a previous project for part of the region, Gusau ADP, and Sokoto ADP was a statewide extension of this. What underlay all these ADPs was taking the money that Nigeria earned from oil, and with World Bank assistance using it to raise living standards of farmers. At its simplest they gave them fertilizer which of course raised crop yields, in the short term at any rate. But there was much else besides, and I was given the project document of an earlier ADP in a different climatic zone of the country, which was most impressive. "What a perceptive and comprehensive geographical and economic appraisal!" I thought. It was only when saw another of these for a different region, and found it to be almost exactly the same with substitution of names, that I began to have doubts on the Bank's attitude to natural resource development.

These suspicions were confirmed when I got hold of a confidential document, a post-project evaluation of the Gusau project. This had indeed raised crop yields and living standards of farmers within the area covered; but the improvements were just as great in surrounding zones which had not received the beneficence of World Bank advice and subsidies. In the spirit of self help much beloved of developers, the Gusau farmers had found it more profitable to sell their allocation to fertilizer-starved chaps in the surrounding areas. A quick buck could also be made by selling it across the border in the adjacent French territory of Niger.

We needed somewhere to set up HQ offices, and Gill took over a set of dilapidated prefabs, the former use of which escapes me. These were repaired after a fashion, cleaned, and equipped with desks and shelves, a big bonanza to local furniture makers (what a surprising number of these there turned out to be). A priority was air conditioners, and after a few days a craftsman arrived, bashed a hole in my wall and pushed one in, ignoring irregular large gaps around the margins; he was most angry when I declined to sign the job completion slip.

As mentioned already Gill, a turbaned Sikh, was a charming man but as a Project Manager he had one defect: he didn't manage. He never set up postal services (companies existed for this) nor any kind of social facilities. I don't recall there was ever a meeting with senior staff. It was rumoured that to make decisions he would take advice from his wife. How did he come to be appointed to an African project? A possible clue came when we had a visit from a very senior, bewhiskered, World Bank agricultural expert, who clearly was of the same religious affiliation.

To begin with the senior staff lived in a guest house. The electricity supply came in four "phases", any one (or three) of which could be cut to reduce the load. At one stage we had an electrical engineer from a company bidding for the lucrative borehole contract, and when a cut came he made some adjustments with 'hot wires' to improve our situation. When all four phases failed a noise sprang up and grew along the road as diesel generators were started. The water supply, if it may be called such, came for short periods mostly in the middle of the night. You filled the bath and other containers, waited until a thick layer of brown mud had settled to the bottom, then scooped off the water above. Being extremely hot, 40C or so, a cold bath was welcome, in which case you disturbed the mud and the sedimentation process had to start again. For food, the cook was given a sum in naira equal to about £40 a day, went off to market and came back with an itemized, priced, shopping list which might have been submitted for the Booker Prize for literature.

There was a Sokoto Club, ah, the old British Colonial institution of the club! This had as usual deteriorated somewhat, becoming mainly a bar. There was a small swimming pool, maybe ten metres long, which was filled from the club's own borehole. I arrived in the late dry season, however, and although we could technically have continued to fill it with artesian water, with the local women queueing at pumps to fill debbies and gourds, to continue to swim would have been unacceptable. There was also a usable squash court, but besides the effect of temperature there was another problem. The builder had been given the dimensions which he followed except that he made these the external dimensions, so the court was a breeze block smaller, making it even more difficult to hit a winning shot.

Thanks to Nigeria's oil reserves there was an adequate supply of petrol. This, however, was not available from petrol stations. The lorries bringing it up from the south were stopped by boys out in the country who had a supply of storage tanks and debbies, and who bought the petrol from the drivers at a price higher than was offered by the stations. You thus had to drive out and find one of these intermediaries where they sold it at a substantial mark-up, doubtless adjusted according to their estimate of the financial resources of the customer.

A few other souls had established their own social institutions. The expat community at Sokoto University would invite such as us to drinks on a Friday night. There was also an engineering company which had set up their own club, to which we welcome. Once, doubtless after a few drinks, we were talking about old films and "The magnificent men in their flying machines" came up. I recalled that the best moment was when the Prussian officer stood up in an aircraft, reading from a book, "How to Fly ze Flying Machine. Number Von: Sit Down!" A neighbour said to me, "Keep your voice down Tony, we're in the German engineering club".

There was one compensation. When you are in a Moslem region you are relatively safe. I think it is that the penalties for assault, burglary and the like are so severe as to deter potential criminals. *What, what, what!!! That was written ten years ago. The recent (2015) growth of extremism has led to this being very far from the case.*

What about the Sokoto ADP? Early on our beloved Project Manager decided that it would meet with World Bank approval if he purchased a large supply of fertilizer. This was imported and distributed to all the 17 ADPs. You might think that, Sokoto being so far away we would be low in priority for receiving it, like farmers at the bottom end of an irrigation distribution system. Far from it. The Sokoto contract was the most lucrative for the lorry drivers, and for all I know we got not only what was meant for us but some intended for other projects where the drivers reckoned they could get more. This massive supply needed to be stored, so Gill bought a house and stacked it floor to ceiling. Not surprisingly the floor collapsed.

On 23rd April my mother, who had been in a care home in Letchworth, died peacefully in her sleep. Such was our communications system that it took a week for news of this to reach me. I was given leave and flew home, leaving Kano on 3rd May, just too late for the funeral which was on the 4th, attended by Doreen and Chrysogon.

Returning to Nigeria on 12th May, two months after the start of the project, I still believed that obstacles might be overcome. When writing home the best I could do was to end with greetings from 'sunny Sokoto', which it certainly was. The Id el Fitr festival took place at this time, with a gathering based on horsemanship. In a previous year the Sultan had killed himself playing polo on a laterite (ironstone) pitch.

I guess I began to assemble such documents and maps as could be acquired, and made some field trips to view the agriculture. There were some World Bank studies of interest, although how things had transpired were often not exactly how the Bank expected. One I have already mentioned, that the supposed benefit from the preceding Gusau Project were shared equally by nearby non-project areas. Another referred to planting dates. It was gospel of the agriculturalists that the highest yields would be obtained if the crops were planted early, before the start of the rains. Farmers, however, showed a reluctance to do this. A follow-up study showed that they had a different strategy. If you planted all your crop early and the rains arrived late you would lose all your seed. So they would take the food crop, sorghum, and plant part of it very widely spaced in the field. If the rains arrived and this germinated, then they would fill in the rest of the plants. Only when this had secured their food supply would they turn to the cotton, which to the frustration of visiting experts didn't do very well when planted late.

There was another World Bank study which I got hold of later in Washington DC but which is of some relevance. It was marked Confidential, and was a study of the success of Bank agricultural projects, 'success' meaning a positive benefit/cost ratio. This contained a formula for an *un*successful project, this being one which would contain any or all of the following:

- An overall regional plan intended to reduce poverty, without a sectoral focus;

- A project to improve nomadic pastoralism;

- A project which depended to a significant extent on cooperation between two or more government agencies.

Back to Sokoto, with the family soon expected to come out to sunny Sokoto I was given a house of my own, together with a cook/houseboy. Having been unoccupied through the dry season, which included the harmattan, it was covered several inches deep in dust. I was starting to try and make it habitable for Doreen when the whole situation changed.

Staff on Nigerian World Bank ADPs were paid by recruitment agencies based on London. Mine routed my salary via an address, 39th floor, Hopewell Building, Hong Kong, and paid it into ABN Bank, Amsterdam.

This may seem a bit of a fairy story. Perhaps, when the postman had staggered up onto the roof, after 30 floors an inscrutable Chinaman was sitting cross-legged and passed communications to a junk out in the harbour. Anyway, it seemed to work.

But at that point the Nigerian government decided the recruitment agencies were ripping them off, sacked them, and said they would pay us themselves. Well, they might or might not have done but what about health insurance, education travel and other benefits? The whole senior staff could not trust to this, and we upped and offed, leaving Manohar Singh Gill seated at his post with $250 million of World Bank money and no-one to stop Nigerians dipping their hands into this lucrative bucket. I drove 100 miles or so into French West Africa to make a phone call home, telling Doreen to book a family holiday, pronto, anywhere she chose.

On 26th July I left from Kano for UK. Nigeria had one more reminder of how things were done there. To fly your possessions home, you didn't attempt to do this yourself but employed a facilitating agency. On their bill was listed at item: "Bribery $120".

A week later, on our Silver Wedding Anniversary, the four of us flew off for a fortnight in Crete.

What had I got out of sunny Sokoto? Some savings to tide me over coming unemployment; and more importantly, a World Bank job on my CV.

And a Union Bank of Nigeria paperknife.

On the weekend of 25th July, having just finished my half-year report, the following lines came to mind. These illustrate the admiration of the staff for our Project Manager, Manohar Singh Gill.

The Ballad of Dangerous Dan McGill

After Dangerous Dan McGrew (1907) by Robert W. Service

A bunch of the boys were downing some beers
        in a Sokoto saloon
A steward was shouting some orders,
        and the power had gone off at noon.
A dozen magadis were sleeping outside,
        and all of them ready to kill
When into the midst of this fearsome array
        strode Dangerous Dan McGill.

Said the bold CME, "I've 20 BDs
        and a scraper or two somewhere lurks
We're instructed to build half a dozen earth dams,
        but regrettably none of them works".
They glanced at each other but nobody spoke
        and the air held a terrible chill
As they thought of the wrath that would soon issue forth
        from Dangerous Dan McGill.

Around them were lying tarpaulins galore
        half-covering broken-down racks
Of ammonium sulphate and supa and CAN
        all done up in sinister sacks.
The DP suggested they sell off the lot,
        and they took up the task with a will
For they knew that the fraud would be kept from the Board
        by Dangerous Dan McGill

They had millions of dollars disbursed by the Bank
        to meet payments all long overdue
And the FC was ready to sign all the cheques
        for a dash of a fiver or two
But scarce could they pay for the first round of drinks,
        still less for the Guest House bill
When they found that the lot had been swiped for the pot
        of Dangerous Dan McGill

(sotto voce)

It's hot and its dry on the Sokoto plains
    and the boys have all left long ago
And the vultures are tearing out pieces of flesh
    from the corpse of the CEO.
But a figure appears riding out from the shade
    of a solitary laterite hill
For still to this day (and drawing his pay)
    rides Dangerous Dan McGill

Magadi: watchman. CME: Chief Mechanical Engineer. BD: bulldozer. supa: superphosphate. CAN: calcium ammonium nitrate. DP: Director of Planning. Bank: the World Bank. FC: Financial Controller. CEO: Chief Executive Officer.

14

INTO AFRICA AGAIN:
KENYA AND ICRAF 1983-91

How did this next job, my last post in full-time employment, come about? There I was, having resigned (in effect) from UEA, filling in with jobs for FAO both in Rome and Ethiopia, and even fitting in an opera holiday with Doreen in Vienna in October – that must have been half-term week, as she was by now in a senior post at Norwich High School. Yet somehow in the middle of all this the fledgling International Council for Research in Agro-forestry, ICRAF, got in touch.[1] It could have been from a staff member of the School of Development Studies, Mike Stocking or David Gibbon (inev-itably the funky gibbon), though how did ICRAF know about DEV?

In any event, ICRAF wanted land evaluation for agroforestry. Their method of recruitment was more than just an interview. They invited me out to Nairobi for a week from September 25th 1982, and during this time I talked with all the staff, in other words they gave me a going-over to see if I was acceptable. Not knowing a thing about agroforestry this called for some mental agility, but I found that they too had only hazy ideas of what it was. Their 'publications' to date consisted of a few short documents typed on green paper. At the end of this exercise I was invited to join them as a Senior Scientist, with responsibility for soils and land evaluation. So on 7th January 1983 I arrived in Nairobi to start work. In retrospect it is surprising that I had no worries about starting a new job overseas at the age of 51, but this thought never entered my head at the time. What mattered was that here was a research post, free of teaching duties apart from occasional training courses.

---

[1] 'Council' was to become 'Centre', and subsequently it became the World Agroforestry Centre.

There were some hiccups at the start. Doreen retained her post at Norwich High School until the end of the Summer Term, joining me, with Chrysogon and Darryl, for the Easter holiday. After a few days in an hotel I moved to a flat, then found a house in Lavington, a western suburb of Nairobi. I took on a lady as cook, but became worried that I could not find things, and when this included the camera, that was the end of her. Doreen came out for good in February 1984, but unfortunately she had at this time broken her Achilles tendon playing tennis, and had her leg in plaster. A week later the Fair family arrived and we went down to Mombasa for a camping holiday. Chrysogon by then had started Engineering at Leicester University. Darryl moved from being a day pupil at Norwich School to their small boarding house.

Agroforestry

What is agroforestry? You may well ask. So did its early staff when ICRAF was formed in 1978. Since it clearly means combining agriculture with forestry the first Director, Kenneth King, was keen on taungya.[1] This is a system in which foresters, when starting a new plantation, invite farmers to grow their crops in among the young trees, getting out after three or four years when the trees stifle the crops. This has been tried in several countries but not very successfully: the foresters don't like letting farmers onto 'their' land, and the farmers don't like being turned out.

However, there are many better ways of combining trees with crops, nearly all of them involving planting trees on farms. Besides timber, trees can provide fruit, fuelwood, and fodder for animals. There are also ways to use trees, shrubs and hedges to check soil erosion and also, if you choose nitrogen-fixing trees and spread the leaf litter, to improve soil fertility. After all, the oldest agroforestry system is shifting cultivation, in which tree fallows are used to restore soil fertility after a period of cropping. There are about 20 agroforestry systems, ways of combining herbaceous crops with woody plants. Rather than the tedious formal definition which takes four lines of text, a good way of describing it is:

Agroforestry = Planting trees on farms

---

[1] A Burmese word, from where it was first tried.

I even invented a crossword clue which nearly works (OK, you've got to delete a few letters): GROW A TREE YOURSELF? (12) ... AGRO-FORESTRY!

The task for which I was appointed was land evaluation for agroforestry. Those readers who didn't skip the earlier section on land evaluation will know that this means identifying and describing systems of land use, and specifying what kinds of land (climate, slope, soil) are most suited for it. To do this you need to have performance data: what are the inputs to the system – capital, materials (fertilizer, seed, etc.), labour – and what are the outputs – food, wood, cash from sales. It was soon apparent that quantitative data of this kind didn't exist for most agroforestry systems. I brought out a Working Paper, *Land evaluation for agroforestry*, which explained this trivial limitation to exact assessment. So if that's what he says, better sack Young?

Fortunately the Board of Directors noticed that I was a soil scientist and, advised by the new Swedish Director, Bjorn Lundgren, thought that there might be a potential for soil conservation using trees and shrubs, so I was commissioned to undertake a study of this. I'm pretty sure that by soil conservation they were thinking of erosion control – after all, that was a speciality of Bjorn's wife Lill. But I set about educating ICRAF that soil conservation meant conserving soil fertility, its capacity to grow crops. Checking erosion was one aspect of this, but equally or more important was to conserve the physical, chemical and biological condition of the soil: its structure, organic matter, nutrients. Hence my first book for them, *Agroforestry for Soil Conservation*, only had a quarter of the space devoted to erosion control, the greater part being on maintenance of soil fertility.

I was allotted a Dutch associate expert,[1] Paul Kiepe, who possessed all the qualities I lack for good scientific experimentation: a strong scientific base, attention to detail, careful measurement. We set up an experiment on ICRAF's field station at Machakos, an hour's drive from Nairobi, in which we tested the potential of hedgerow intercropping[2] to reduce erosion. This

---

[1] A system the Dutch government has for giving young people their first field experience, lack of which is the Catch-22 situation which makes it difficult for British graduates to get their first job.

[2] Often, misleadingly, called alley cropping.

means planting hedges parallel to the contours on the cropped land; if you make these hedges of nitrogen-fixing trees you can prune them and spread the litter to raise soil fertility for the adjacent crops. A weekly trip to Machakos to 'supervise' Paul provided a welcome break from the office.

Agroforestry trial at ICRAF Machakos field station
Contour hedgerows of *Leucaena* within maize

Measuring soil erosion
with apologies to Samuel Beckett's *Endgame*

We found that in one respect this is a very successful system in that it does greatly reduce erosion, although not in the way you might have first thought.[1] That was the good news. The bad news is that farmers have rarely been found willing to plant and maintain hedges across their land. ICRAF's early achievements were of the hunting, gathering and classification type. There was an inventory of existing (mostly indigenous) agroforestry systems – shifting cultivation was the first, the tree fallows restoring soil fertility. Then we coined the term "multipurpose trees", meaning trees people use for purposes other than wood, and started collecting data on these; but of course the forestry people had a lot of material, and it took time to integrate this. We set up, and practised, a method called 'diagnosis and design', which meant a team went to a farming system, diagnosed its problems, then designed a solution which would reduce these; needless to say this was always some kind of agroforestry, often hedgerow intercropping. Then there was my book, *Agroforestry for Soil conservation*, assembling what little was already known about trees and soils.

With that lot done, we were ready to go into practical work: field experiments, how to set up tree nurseries, and as time went on and we got more technical, detailed studies, e.g. of tree roots. A few of the experiments were done on our Machakos Field Station, but that had a very unusual climate, semi-arid but with two rainy seasons (if you're lucky), so it wasn't a good base for developing practical agroforestry systems.

Group visit to ICRAF Machakos Field Station

[1] It's not the barrier effect of the hedges which checks runoff and thus erosion; it's the fact that the roots of the hedges greatly increase infiltration. There, you've got the answer – which took some years to discover.

On one occasion when the Board of Governors were taken to the Machakos field station. The Director-General, Bjorn Lundgren, addressing them, included the following: "And on my right is Tony Young, who looks more like an Englishman in the tropics than anyone I know; and who is in fact an Englishman in the tropics".

An Englishman in the tropics

The development of agroforestry systems was done by a network (groans from professionals). The first time round we got the design of this wrong. An energetic but difficult to get on with Argentinian thought he could dash around the world telling local research staff what to do and how to do it. It didn't work. (Mind you, the centre for soils research, IBSRAM,[1] got their network design even more wrong, and collapsed when funding agencies withdrew their support.)

---

[1] Work it out! Hint: it's not a centre but a board.

The said individual left[1] and we worked out a better way of doing things: set up national field stations, on each of which there would be at least one permanent member of ICRAF staff. The research scientists at ICRAF HQ could conduct experiments at these local centres, greatly widening the range of environmental conditions available. The national centres were grouped into regional networks.

So if I didn't offer ICRAF very much experimental work, what did I do for them? What I do best, write. In the early years there was a need to spread the word about the potential of agroforestry to the world at large (government, aid agencies, research and training institutions). I was going to say that I produced about 20 publications for them, but on counting found it was 55! These included *Agroforestry for Soil Conservation,* which sold around 4000 copies, satisfactory for an academic publication, and was translated into French and Chinese.

On safari with ICRAF: Malawi 1983

Some of the International Agricultural Research Centres (IARCs!) have a regional as well as a sectoral mandate. Not so with ICRAF. Ours was the whole of the less-developed world. There was consequently much opportunity for travel. In the first instance this was to set up the networks and choose which national research centres would take part. I only took part in two such trips, not being either good at, nor desirous of, negotiations with governments.

The first was the Southern Africa network, comprising Zimbabwe, Zambia and Malawi, for which I was an obvious choice to join the planning team. In Malawi, they suggested we base our research at a place currently used as a tobacco research station, "…not far south of Zomba, called Makoka". This sounded familiar. When we got there I asked if there had ever been a soil survey of the site. "Yes, I think there might have been" was the reply, and leafing through a filing cabinet they pulled out – my own, hand-drawn, crayon-coloured survey, done when the station was set up 40 years ago. Southern Africa became our first, very successful, network on the new model.

---

[1]   To become Director of Research at CIP, the South American potato research centre.

Malaysia was another suggested collaborator, and with my previous experience I went along. However, I have only hazy recollections of the trip, didn't like the way the country was changing, and I don't think it came to anything. After that, ICRAF set up a separate division for the collaborative programme, so my organisational incompetence was not further called upon.

But like Sussex and East Anglia Universities, ICRAF, having obtained my services, showed a remarkable willingness to get rid of me, to workshops (euphemism for conferences), training courses, consultancies and responses to invitations. I suppose I could be relied upon to produce and present a paper, a kind of PR agent. Running through diaries for the ten years 1983-1992 shows a total of 41 working visits, covering 23 countries. Most frequent were five visits each to Malawi (how ever did I manage that?) and FAO Rome. In the light of subsequent political disturbances, the most way out were Somalia, where we gave a training course; Rwanda, part of our East African network; and Haiti.

Sri Lanka 1984

Land evaluation and two medical problems The first of these non-Rome jobs, in 1984, was certainly obtained by the old boy system. Robert Ridgway was a tall man, and he and his wife were very committed Christians. (Why does this happen? I am not a Christian, but all my life have been taken up as their friend, once even by a Seventh Day Adventist.) Robert was in Sri Lanka in charge of an FAO project, Assistance to Land Use Planning. Knowing I was a gen kiddie, he took me on to devise a computerised system of land evaluation for the country.

There was a slight interruption. One day I felt absolutely terrible and went to the doctor. He said I had dengue fever (which I had already had in Malaya, it doesn't confer immunity) and there were two reasons for this: the small hotel in which I was staying had an ornamental pool in the dining room, where mosquitoes bred; and there were a lot of tourists there harbouring dengue fever. Robert gave me cassettes of Beethoven string quartets to pass a week of sick leave. On ringing up Doreen to report this suffering, Chrysogon replied with, "Hard luck. Mum's broken her other Achilles tendon". The first time had been on the other foot in 1983.

Planning a forestry research network Also in 1984 the International Union of Forest Research Organizations, IUFRO (say "yew-fro") held a meeting in Kandy, the lovely high-altitude area of Ceylon where the tea plantations (and their leading university) are found. Organized by Jeff Burley of the Commonwealth Forestry Institute,[1] it was held to discuss the best way to design research networks. Jeff is amiable goodwill itself, and after an evening dinner produced the following gem of humour:

> *Jeff is standing holding a large net*
> *Colleague:* "I say, I say, I say, how do you make a net work?"
> *Jeff (hurling it across the room)* IUFRO it.

At a papers session a very handsome Chinaman from Taiwan, with a head of thick jet black hair, began: "Chairman introduce me as Dr Yang. With respect, I not doctor, I Mr Yang. I 62 years old [gasps]. Take my PhD next year. Is a lesson for us: we go on learning all our life."

We had an excursion to the Kandy Botanical Garden, notable particularly as the spot where the first rubber trees to be brought from the Amazon were planted and propagated, before being taken to Malaya where they formed the basis of their extensive rubber plantations. During lunch break I was sitting with two Dutchmen when we were approached by another Chinese (Malaysian) with, "You not mind if I take photograph. Is for memory". (With a glint in his eye) "To oriental, all Westerners look alike." During our tour around the garden we turned a corner and the leader said, "This is the bamboo avenue". Someone called to the back, "Jim, this will interest you" and his companion said, "I didn't know Jim was a bamboo researcher" to which a Chinese voice replied, "He not bamboo researcher. He donor funding bamboo research, want to see what bamboo look like".

The best moment came at our closing dinner, held in the open air seated around the hotel swimming pool. It was decided that after dinner, each delegation, in alphabetical order, should sing a national song. There were five Brits, joined by the representative of Papua Guinea who would have felt spare on his own. I suggested *I am a bachelor, I live...* as our contribution, which was accepted. However, whilst the other songs were in progress, Jeff Burley came round, advised each of us to put on old clothes, and handed

---

[1]   Later to become the Oxford Forestry Institute as they didn't want to be restricted to the Commonwealth.

out a new last verse he had written. We negotiated with the USA that they would come before us. So the six of us stood on the edge of the pool and sang our traditional song, "I am a bachelor, I live with my son" but with the last verse amended from "weaver's trade" to "forester's trade:

> I am a bachelor, I live with my son
>> and I work at the Forester's trade
> And every single time that I look into his eyes
>> he reminds me of that fair young maid
> He reminds me in the summertime
>> and in the winter too
> Of the many many times that I've leapt into the pool
>> 'cos we Brits just love to play the fool

whereupon we linked arms and stepped forward, disappearing into the pool with instructions to stay under water for as long as possible.

Vietnam 1985

In 1985 Vietnam was under communist rule. After countless years of war, first against the French and then North versus South Vietnam, the country was naturally in a state of dreadful poverty and destruction. The Swedes were sympathetic to their regime and had asked them what sort of aid they wanted. It is striking that they asked, not for food or roads or housing, but to establish a pulp and paper mill capable of producing 55 million school exercise books a year. Paper needs short and long staple timber, and the long staple was to be supplied by bamboo. Then the bamboo all simultaneously flowered and died, which it does every nine years or so. The mill was at Bai Bang, about 70 miles north of Hanoi, and included the whole sequence: timber to pulp, pulp to paper, and paper to exercise books.

My consultancy there was in this wise. A Vietnamese delegation had been on a visit to South America and seen fast-growing, fertilized plantations of eucalyptus (bluegum), which they reckoned could be planted on their unused hill country and would supply a more reliable source of long-fibre material. They asked Swedish aid to conduct a feasibility study, and the Swedes asked their leading soils-forestry expert, Bjorn Lundgren, to do this. Bjorn, however, was by this time Director of ICRAF, so he asked me to go instead.

We had a system in which staff could take along their wives (beg pardon, spouses) on a limited number of overseas trips, so Doreen came along. Whilst on leave at Christmas we had to go to the Vietnamese Embassy in London to obtain visas. This was a spooky building of small rooms and corridors, filled with polite but inscrutable orientals. Whilst we were waiting I asked to go to the toilet, a tortuous journey, and Doreen thought she might never see me again. But we got the visas. We also had to get a whole string of vaccinations, all the usual together with Japanese encephalitis.

All well and good so 19th January Nairobi-Hanoi. At immigration Doreen and I joined different queues. I was soon through but Doreen was turned back: there was no date stamp on her visa (nor had there been on mine, but I had a less eagle-eyed officer); so there we were on either side of the barrier. We were, however, being met by the Swedes and explained the situation, to which they said that locally there was a universal solution to such problems: a box of 500 Pall Mall cigarettes. So there was Doreen, in Viet Nam, without a passport.

The Swedes were set up in a camp at Bai Bang, surrounded by a high wire fence so that Vietnamese could not see the luxurious life of Westerners. Entertainment was mostly dinners. One was some Swedish special day, when the fare on offer included surströmming, fermented Baltic herring or in simpler terms, rotten fish. The smell has been described as like a gas leak, and the taste calls for some acclimatisation; I tackled it though Doreen kept to an alternative which was on offer.

On arrival we needed some local money, and asked to go to a bank. This suggestion was met with horror. I said that as an international consultant I did not want to risk prosecution for illegal currency trading, but was told that no-one ever changes at the official rate. We were taken to a small store selling linen and lace, and bought some table mats. Asked quietly if we wanted currency, we handed over an envelope enclosing a single $100 note, and were given in exchange a fat packet containing 300 000 dong, about 100 times the official exchange rate. I asked where this huge demand for dollars came from. "Oh, they employ Russian consultants, paid in dong, who are desperate to get hold of hard currency."

This meant that anything bought for local currency was extremely cheap. One Sunday we drove up to a hill viewpoint where there was a restaurant, got out our own picnic lunch and ate it there, finishing with a small glass of brandy. I asked what we were to pay the restaurant for using their facilities. "Oh, we leave them the rest of the bottle, they'll be very happy". It had been bought from the 'dip shop', the diplomatic store open only to foreigners, for the equivalent of about 60p.

We travelled around the north of the country, visiting government officials and sites that had been suggested for eucalyptus plantations. The work was done through interpreters. As a counterpart (aid jargon) I had a Vietnamese soil scientist with a PhD, who was being paid the equivalent of about £4 a week. When we travelled his overnight bag was about the size of a spongebag, possibly spare pants and a toothbrush. The government guaranteed its officers housing, which meant that the small rectangular room of a forestry officer had a desk at the front and his bed and possessions at the back.

Since all agricultural land was already in use, the sites suggested were mostly hillsides, and I was asked to advise on soil conservation if they were put to tree plantations. On one such, there were a few inches of soil overlying hard laterite. My first thought was to say you can't make a silk purse out of a sow's ear, but realising this would pose difficulties for the interpreter, I made it, "We have a saying in England: you cannot make a ladies handbag out of the ear of a pig".

We had been given privileged status, which meant that along the road our driver constantly hooted to get the mass of cyclists out of the way, if necessary into a ditch, and at ferry crossings we roared past the long queue to the front. One day we were driving north, close to the frontier with China. Despite both being communist, relations between the two countries were bad, with armed standoff along the border. A soldier stopped us on the road and said to the driver something on the lines of, "Dùng xe của bân, cho bân biët hành khách dẻ nhạn ra, và tay trên các phím…" which being translated was, "Tell your passengers to get out and hand over the keys. The army is commandeering your vehicle". Our driver replied with some emphasis, words to the effect, "My passengers have been given the official status of members of a provincial party committee. Get your backside out of our way, or when we inform your superiors the consequences for you will be distinctly unpleasant".

One Sunday we were given the honour of going to Hanoi to see the embalmed body of Ho Chi Minh. It had recently come back after a wash and brush-up by the Russians. With a Swedish colleague, Doreen and I were taken by taxi to a huge square, where we were met by an armed soldier. Doreen was told to leave her handbag with the taxi driver, and not surprisingly protested. She was told not to worry, the penalties to the driver if anything happened to it would be so severe that she could be fully assured it would be safe. So we set off across the square in single file behind the soldier, Doreen saying *sotto voce*, "If my father could see me now...". Approaching from the right was another soldier at the head of about 100 Vietnamese. On seeing that we were foreigners he came to a halt and waved us ahead. This took us to a small bamboo hut in which Ho Chi Minh had chosen to have his office, rejecting the large three-storey building from which the French Governor had operated. After paying due respect to his body we emerged into a large ornamental garden, with a carp pool and the like. The route was now a yellow line which we were meant to follow, and when I stepped off it to examine a tree a voice made it clear that this was forbidden.

We also attended a performance by a visiting Russian puppet company given in Hanoi's opera house. Surprisingly some ladies wearing fur coats appeared. The puppetry was brilliant, persuading you that these were real people deserving of your attention and sympathy.

The world in the future: Berlin 1986

The Stifterverband für die Deutsche Wissenschaft in cooperation with the Deutsche Foschungsgemeinschaft – OK, you've got it, the German scientific establishment – had set up a series of conferences which brought together international scientists. The one held in 1986 was on Resources and World Development: Water and Land. These took place in a suburb of Berlin called Dahlem and therefore were known, not surprisingly, as the Dahlem Konferenzen. This was at a time when Berlin was isolated in the middle of Communist-controlled East Germany, and the city itself divided in two by the Berlin Wall. We were taken to see the Wall, on our side covered with graffiti; and I got to a concert in the superb Philharmonic Symphony Hall, including Paganini's concerto for viola – yes, he was equally a virtuoso on that.

I was Rapporteur for the Group Report on Assessment of Land Resources, our group containing many good friends including four who were to invite and support me in the future: Rudy Dudal (Belgium), formerly Head of Soils at FAO; Dennis Greenland, at that time Research Director at the International Rice Research Institute in the Philippines; Christian Pieri (France), who was to become the only soil scientist in the World Bank; and David Pimentel of Cornell University, which I was later to visit.

I had been commissioned to write a paper on computer modelling of soil changes. I began the presentation with, "In ancient Greece, one of the labours of Hercules was to cleanse the Augean stables – every day he cleaned them, and every night the horses made them dirty again. Had he been living today he might have been given the task of writing a paper on computer modelling of soil changes. No sooner did I finish any aspect when a computer search revealed a host of further papers."

The output from the meeting appeared as Dahlem Workshop Report No. 6, 52 papers, 940 pages, 1.6 kg – useful to hold down things that you want to stick together.

An exchange during the closing session may be recorded. We were discussing world population in relation to resources:

> *Speaker* It has been said that the ideal world population is three billion.
> *Dennis Greenland (from the floor)* Including us?

Breakfast, ah my fixation on breakfast! In the Swiss Cottage Hotel the breakfast buffet stretched the whole of one side of a large hall. First came the traditional English breakfast, bacon and eggs and so on; then cold meats and cheese for the Dutch, and sticky buns and syrup for Americans to mix sweet with savoury; after that, dosas and the like for the Indians, then finally noodles for the Chinese. Magnificent!

The rest of 1985 and 1986: fifteen more trips!

The network planning safari to four southern African countries has been mentioned above. There were two more trips to Malawi. What the first was I cannot now recall, but the second was to participate in a training course in conservation agriculture. This was run by Francis Shaxson, whose wedding to Annabel Hoyle, daughter of my Director of Research, we had attended there 25 years earlier. The course was held in a small wooden building in the Zomba botanical garden, where we had spent our first night in Nyasaland/Malawi in December 1958. Whilst in Nyasaland Francis had developed the methods of conservation agriculture, which you could define as soil conservation with the farmer on your side, and together with Malcolm Douglas he was to become a leader in this field. (Religious friends again: I don't know about Francis, but Annabel was a deeply committed Christian, and Malcolm and his Malawian wife Hanifa were Quakers.)

There was another training course, this time in agroforestry, run by a short-lived consultative branch which ICRAF had, made up of two foresters, Peter Wood (British) and Michel Baumer (French), who asked me to join them on the soils side. It was held in Mogadishu, Somalia, which at the time of writing is one of the most dangerous countries for foreigners.

Then there were the conferences, ten of them in two years! What was happening? Perhaps on the one hand the world at large had learnt of the existence of agroforestry and wanted to find out more; and on the other, ICRAF said, "Well, a lot of our staff are doing useful research, send along Young, he can be relied upon to present a paper on almost anything". Four of them were in Rome, one on land evaluation for forestry, one on land use planning, another called in my diary "CG" (CGIAR?[1]), whilst for the last I have neither note nor recollection. There was a forestry meeting in Bangkok, and two in India: a meeting on trees organized by the Common-wealth in Lucknow (where the Indian Mutiny took place), and a conserva-tion workshop in Hyderabad.

Now we begin to enter the world of Ripley's "Believe it or not". The IAEA (oh, surely you know, the International Atomic Energy Authority) were anxious to show that they didn't just make bombs and nuclear power stations but could assist biological research through isotope labelling (beep-beep showed where parts of a plant had got to), so they invited plant people including (What do they call it?) an agroforester. A bonus was that their headquarters were in Vienna, so Doreen came along and got some opera tickets.

As if that wasn't enough, there was the conference that (for me) never was, in Buffalo, New York State. The story starts when I became Dean at UEA.

---

[1]   Consultative Group on International Agricultural Research.

They gave Deans a Research Assistant, so that when tied up with administration they did not completely lose touch with research. I put Ian Saunders onto sorting out and coordinating an ongoing collection which I had made of card index cards and notes on research about rates of slope-forming processes, and we put this together as a joint article. The Americans set up a meeting on rates of geomorphological processes, invited Ian and me, and we re-hashed our paper. I had got from Nairobi to Rome and was about to take the transatlantic flight when a hurricane hit the west coast of the USA, closing all airports. We were put into a hotel that was so bad it had room for a complete jumbo jetful of passengers. The next morning it became clear there would be some further delay, such that by the time I arrived the conference would have finished. Ian had the bonus of presenting our paper, which was positively my last publication on slopes.

Rwanda 1987

At this point ICRAF must have got wind of my travels, for in 1987 there was only one trip, to visit our research station in Rwanda, which had somehow kept going through the genocide that had afflicted the country. Meanwhile on July 11th a very important event took place on the home front in England.

Zimbabwe 1988

Back to a travel year! Direct from Christmas leave I went to Colombo for a week and on to Bangkok for two; but neither from my diary, CV nor recollection have I any idea what this was for, so we shall be spared the details.

In Harare in June there was a TSBF conference, the Tropical Soil Biology and Fertility Programme. This had been founded by Mike Swift, based in Nairobi, with the object of improving the fertility of tropical soils through biological means.[1] This was mostly by maintaining and improving the bugs (soil fauna), of which there are a million or more in every handful of soil – hence when passing through immigration with a few bags of the stuff, I was not entirely honest in declaring, "No living matter" (the New Zealand

---

[1]   TSBF was a component of the IUBS programme, part of the MAB programme of UNESCO. Did you really want to know what these are? Read the preface to their book.

immigration officials make arrivals scrape the mud off their hiking boots). I was on the founding committee of TSBF, which in terms of scientific results produced per unit of expenditure was one of the most successful research networks ever. They did it by having the research done by top university scientists (US, South American, European, Indian), no doubt taking on locals for field observations and training.

The Harare meeting was to present the results of the first five years' work, nine papers of substance, in a book *The biological management of soil fertility* (1994). My contribution was really to criticise the former ICRAF way of doing things, which had been based on the following syllogism:

> *True statement* The objective of agroforestry research should be to design practical systems that can be used by farmers.
> *False consequence* Therefore research should consist of trials of practical systems that can be used by farmers.

This was how the donors reasoned. It led to us doing numerous statistically-controlled trials, in the hope of finding one that would work. It usually did – but worked in that specific climate and soils, and with the rainfall pattern of the years of the experiment. The correct reasoning was:

> *True consequence* Therefore ICRAF should undertake fundamental research into relationships between trees, crops, water and soils, the results from which will enable them to design practical systems that can be used by farmers.

Yes, one needs the system trials but they come next, best conducted by national research stations, and when you have a pretty good idea of what is going to work best.

Philippines, Solomon Islands, Australia 1988

This was all one trip, accompanied by Doreen. It arose because good old Jim Cheatle had been asked to organize a meeting to design a Pacific research network for IBSRAM; and who better to invite than his friend... no, I'm sorry, the leading expert on network design. That meeting was in the Solomon Islands, but I persuaded ICRAF to tack on visits before and after.

The week in The Philippines does not leave much impression on my mind. They had started agroforestry research before the existence of ICRAF. A religious NGO devised the system of hedgerow intercropping, low hedges of *Leucaena* planted along the contour as an means of erosion control. This was subsequently widely taken up by researchers – but not, unfortunately, by farmers.

So on to the Solomon Islands. The Cheatles had lived there before – Marion was a former Lady Captain of the Golf Club. (Oh, yeah, Jim was working there too, setting up a soil analysis lab.) As already mentioned, IBSRAM were not good at network research, so I hope we helped them with design. In any event, a web search shows that a certain amount of agroforestry is nowadays being practised there.

The conference took place in the capital, Honiara, but a highlight for us was a post-conference outing organized by Jim. He took us to Kennedy Island, a small island where in WWII president-to-be John F. Kennedy brought his injured crew ashore.[1] Scuba diving was on the agenda for the day, but Doreen and I were apprehensive. However, Jim's young son Callum shamed us into having a try, experience which was to prove useful years later on the Great Barrier Reef.

On the day of our departure there was a problem. Pacific islands are either volcanic or based on coral reefs. If volcanic, construction of an airport presents considerable problems. Jim therefore found a small motor boat and took Doreen, me, a Belgian professor, Charles Sys, and his wife (Charles had his own system of land evaluation), and one other delegate onto a coral atoll where there was an airstrip. "Sorry, I've got to go back to look after the others" he said, "We've arranged for an Seventh Day Adventist plane to call for you at 7.30"; and off he went, leaving the five of us on a small, uninhabited Pacific atoll.

Nothing happened at 7.30, nor some half an hour later. "This cannot happen" said Sys, "I have to get back to examine my students". "Sorry Charles" replied Doreen, "They'll have to wait". But soon after eight o'clock a speck appeared in the sky, approached and landed, and a handsome young man with a moustache got out and introduced himself. He then weighed all of us plus our luggage, even down to D's handbag. The plane was a four-

---

[1] Today it is correctly Kasolo Island.

seater so I sat in the co-pilot's seat. He was required to go through the formality of describing the emergency exit, viz. the only door where we got in, and other aspects of safety procedures, ending with, "And now before we take off, let us say a prayer: Almighty God, grant that we may be safely carried…". We gave a heartfelt Amen. The low-altitude flight across coral reefs was of great beauty.

From an island touchdown we flew to Canberra, where I was visiting the CSIRO Australia Division of Land Research and Regional Survey. They were the organization which had invented the method of land systems survey, very widely used in soil surveys at reconnaissance scale, including by me in Malawi. The Australians had used it in the 1950s and 60s to survey the vast northern part of their country. There was a political undertone to this: these areas were fairly empty of people (except aborigines), and the government were worried that if more were not done with them, it might be difficult to stop an influx of Chinese. Later they extended the surveys to their largest colony (maybe independent by then) Papua New Guinea. My objective was limited by the fact that, that having successfully finished these surveys (some 30+ of them) the personnel had been swallowed up in the Hydrology Division. However I was able to meet some surviving staff, but not the Soils Division, which was up in Brisbane.[1]

Doreen meanwhile found that Canberra had a circular bus, hop on, hop off, around Canberra's sights. I don't think these latter were full of interest, but her social skills turned the trip to good effect. She found herself sitting next to a lady who turned out to be a geography teacher. On learning we were going on to Sydney, and hoped to visit its renowned Opera House, she proved also to be a Friend of Sydney Opera, giving Doreen a phone number to ring, mention her name, and we would get tickets.

Thus it was that reaching Sydney we got to see Wagner's *Lohengrin* and, in something of a lighter mode, Britten's *Albert Herring*. Somehow we also got to see, at another theatre, *Les Miserables,* at a time when in London tickets were unobtainable. It was the 200th anniversary of the setting up of a British Crown Colony. Sydney was very full so we had to stay in an apartment in

---

[1]   This could have been my career. After the PhD I was offered three posts, with Texas Instruments, CSIRO Land Resources Division, and Nyasaland, which won out. A colleague at Sheffield, Bob Wright, took the Australia post.

the King's Cross area, which proved to be where the ladies of the street operated. One might be accosted on the way to buy bread for breakfast, an unexpected conclusion to ICRAF's best safari.

The IBSRAM-ICRAF Conference 1989

In November the world came to ICRAF, in the form of a joint conference with the International Board for Soils Research and Management, IBSRAM. This was the only time in my life that I have organized a conference, with much help from my valuable secretary, Jane Waweru.[1] It was three days of papers and discussions, published as a short set of Proceedings which gave abstracts only. The outcome was supposed to be a strengthened collaboration between the two research centres. This never came off, which in view of IBSRAM's forthcoming demise was just as well.

Conference welcoming social
"You prune them to about this high"

An excursion is always the most popular part of a conference, not just to provide a break from papers and to see something of the country you are in, but also to provide to provide opportunity for free discussion with those you want to meet. Naturally we took them to our Machakos Field Station.

---

[1] Having joined ICRAF at the lowest secretarial grade, by her own effort and efficiency Jane worked her way up to become the Director General's secretary.

During the afternoon I was afflicted by a severe stomach upset and left early by Landrover, leaving my research associate Paul Kiepe in charge of this bunch of eminent international soil scientists. November is the start of one of the two rainy seasons, the more intense one. There were two muddy dips on the track, in one of which the coach became stuck. Paul handled the situation and got them back in time for dinner, one of those occasions in life when you give thanks for avoidance of an embarrassing situation.

1990: Madagascar, Uganda, Japan, Rome and the Netherlands

At this time there begins to appear in my diary Forward Planning-Strategy-Management-Budgeting meetings, time-consuming, ominous of what was to come, but not quite yet eliminating research and travel.

In January to **Madagascar,** not so much an African country but a semi-Asian continent. From north to south it stretches 2800 km (1750 miles), three times the distance from Land's End to John o' Groats, so on a short visit you are not going to see much. The people who settled it came from Indonesia, an official language is Malagasy, although the French took it over for 60 years so there is an alternative. Malay peoples like to grow rice, but the small area that I saw lacks the broad flat plains desirable for this, so the crop snakes along valley floors. I was there at the invitation of IBSRAM, so for the moment I should withdraw my deprecatory remarks about them.

They have a major problem of forest clearance. Through continental drift Madagascar became separated from Africa a long geological time ago, and then evolved its own unique plants and animals. In particular the ecological slot 'live in trees' which elsewhere is occupied by monkeys is here taken by lemurs. The conservation community is therefore massively interested in preserving them, which means keeping the rainforest. But as elsewhere in humid regions, forest clearance and incursion by farmers is widespread. Now there is a known agroforestry-based method, tried out in Kenya, which is supposed to check this. Get the farmers in zones adjacent to remaining forest to plant their own trees on their farms; and, of course, improve their crop yields as well. I doubt if, in the absence of a good agricultural extension service and many forest rangers, this is a realistic objective, but it might be worth trying.

My main recollection is not of the conference but of going to a restaurant with a colleague one evening. Seeing on the (French language) menu 'steak tartare' we ordered this. When it came to the table and we saw it was raw minced steak, bearing in mind the likely local hygiene we had second thoughts and went for fish and chips.

In May **Uganda**, where ICRAF had set up its research station in the hilly country to the west of Lake Victoria. I knew it because we had passed through on our way home in 1962, taking photos of their long-horned cattle. They had a soil erosion problem, somewhat checked by terracing, and we were planting our nitrogen-fixing hedges on these.

Trips to **Rome** and **The Netherlands** in 1990 can be skipped ("Been there, done that"), but the visit to **Japan** was of more interest. On the way back from it I stopped over in New Delhi, intending to visit India's agroforestry research station but this was aborted when, on the railway station, money and tickets were extracted from my bag.

Japan, International Congress of Soil Science 1990

In August came the World Congress of Soil Science, held every four years. It was one of three such meetings I have clocked up, the others being Montreal, 1978, and my last international meeting, in Philadelphia, 2006. The 14th Congress, 12th-18th August 1990, was held in Kyoto, Japan's one-time capital. (Kyoto = Capital City, Tokyo = East Capital.) There was a first class Conference Centre, and as one would expect, very efficient organization. This makes it the more surprising that I can remember almost nothing about the papers! Diary entries on successive days of TARC 1, TARC 2 (AY Chairman) and TARC 3 (AY paper) fail to find their way through into my memory.

More memorable was the field trip – world congresses put on a range of these, before and after the conference, and I went on one to Osaka, 7-11 August. You drive past sometimes spectacular scenery but then stop and get into soil pits, in which there is much jockeying for position followed by turgid discussion on the placing of this soil in the local, US, French and International classification systems. There might even be mention of its agricultural value and problems, though this doesn't happen so often. However, on this occasion such discussions were shorter than usual owing to the ferocious heat, which led to mass desertion back to the air-conditioned buses.

A curiosity was passing through a landscape of undulating country entirely covered in short grass, but with neither hedges, fences nor any sign of livestock. This proved to be for the supply of turf to golf courses; we were told that some would re-lay the fairways every year. What soil characteristics favoured the location of this activity here rather than anywhere else? Very deep soils, since you were slicing off a layer annually. Andosols, formed from deep volcanic ash, have this property.

We were taken to Nagasaki, the site of the second atomic bomb, where there is a museum devoted to this. One building only remained erect in the central area, and this they have preserved untouched (as done for the former Coventry Cathedral, and a church in Berlin). After the initial deaths from blast and heat came the the subsequent radiation sickness, about which there is a heart-rending story. A young girl was among the first to be affected, and taken to hospital. The Japanese are fond of origami, paper folding, and she was told that if she made 1000 paper birds she would get better; she made 2000, but died.

Back in Kyoto, our hotel gave the story of how they were saved from being a target for the first two atomic bombs. A Target Committee had been set up in 1945, meeting first in Los Alamos and then, with President Harry S. Truman, in Washington DC. The Committee nominated five sites, including Hiroshima, Nagasaki and Kyoto. The Committee Chairman, Groves, favoured Kyoto, as a major city for military-related industry, and also surrounded by hills which would concentrate the blast. This was opposed by Henry L. Stimson, Secretary for War and the Committee's secretary. Stimpson was initially overruled, but went personally to Truman and persuaded him to remove Kyoto from the target list, despite opposition from Groves.

Why this powerful pleading to save it? Many years earlier Stimson had been US Ambassador to The Philippines. He married, and came to Kyoto on his honeymoon; his name is in the hotel register. Being such an important city in its time, Kyoto had 19 temples, many of which he visited. He wrote to his mother, "I have made obeisance to the God of tourism". Preservation of these was doubtless the basis of his argument to save the city from destruction.

There are people today who believe that the two atomic bombs, which destroyed Hiroshima and Nagasaki, should not have been dropped. They are wrong. Anyone who holds that view does not appreciate the full horror of the Far Eastern war. Fighting was continuing from island to island, troops – American, British, Commonwealth and Japanese – were losing their lives, and an invasion of the Japanese mainland would have massively increased these losses. To my mind the most powerful argument in favour of the atomic attack lay in the large number of prisoners of war in Japanese hands; a third had already lost their lives through starvation, disease and brutality, and chances of survival for the remainder were falling. I had worked with one of them, Bill Verboom, a Dutchman, who in August 1945 was in a camp on the Japanese mainland, by then on his deathbed. I asked him if they knew what had happened. He replied that they didn't know what it was, but clearly something had happened because the camp guards suddenly became very polite. It was a bold and ultimately, in terms of human suffering, beneficent decision of Truman's to drop the first atom bomb and ram home the message with the second.

Rome, Belgium and Haiti 1991

By now, planning and budgeting was increasingly dominating work at ICRAF – rightly so for its gains in the future, but at the time dominating actual research. Three overseas visits remained. One being to FAO, Rome in the week following Easter, and we tacked on a few days local leave for a visit with Doreen to Venice beforehand. The last was to a conference in Leuven, Belgium, in November.

Of more interest, the American foreign aid organization (USAID)[1] invited me to visit their work in Haiti, were they were attempting to use contour hedgerows as a means to check erosion. Haiti is the most severely eroded country in the world. The greater part of its hilly landscape was once forested but this has been almost entirely cleared and the soil reduced to a thin remainder. It was hard to find a forest remnant to show what condi-

---

[1]   In the light of subsequent events, a doubly unfortunate acronym.

tions had once been like.[1] Eager young aid workers took me to a site where, probably for the only time and place in the world, an entire valley had been filled with contour hedgerows of *Leucaena* – a German aid organization had paid farmers to do it. One could see that this form of conservation was not going to last: when runoff on the intervening cultivated strips caused breaks in the hedgerows these were not being repaired. It was as well that political conditions in the country had entered a lull at the time of this visit, for Haiti ranks high on the list of danger spots where I have worked.

The journey out was not without incident. My ever-helpful diary says, "2nd April, leave Nairobi for Haiti…24th June arrive Nairobi from Haiti", with a total blank between. The outward journey was via Heathrow, from which I took an American flight to Miami, scheduled to take nine hours. ICRAF paid business class for longer flights, but on checking in I was asked if I would mind transfer to first class. It was well that this was so. In mid-Atlantic the pilot came over the intercom, "Ladies and gentlemen, we began this flight with 371 passengers on the manifest. It may be that we shall finish with 372, as a lady has started to give birth to a baby". We therefore touched down at the nearest possible airport to Europe at Gander, Newfoundland. In an earlier age this was where transatlantic flights would leave, staggering into Shannon Airport, Ireland on the last drop of fuel. Today its large area of runways are largely deserted. A catering van was brought up and took our passenger away to have an unexpected Canadian citizen.

We were not allowed to disembark, and after an hour of more, took off again heading for Miami. Quite soon it was the pilot again. "Ladies and gentlemen, I'm very sorry but the International Air Transport Association has pointed out that our crew has been on duty for longer than the permitted time. We shall therefore have to find an airport where we can change personnel." It may have been Ottawa this time, where at four o'clock in the morning they were kind enough to let us off the plane for

---

[1] This may have happened in pre-classical Greece. Plato, in Critias, wrote to the effect, "Do not imagine that the barren hills which we see [in the Mediterranean] were always like that. Attica was once the most fertile land in the world, and streams flowed from the rich forests. But in the course of ages much of the soil washed away into the sea".

some ham sandwiches. A pilot and crew were, somewhat remarkably, found, and off we went again.

Landing at Miami 21 hours after leaving Heathrow there was another obstacle to be overcome. It seemed that Miami did not have a transit facility: you had to enter the United States. This meant going through US Customs and Immigration, not the most rapid of procedures. Checkin for the next plane, a shuttle to Haiti, was a formidable sight. The wives of Haitian politicians and businessmen who had got hold of dollars had come on shopping trips to the US. They were returning each with several vast suitcases, about the size of refrigerators (which some quite likely contained). Checkin was therefore a matter of negotiating a bribe large enough to reduce excess baggage charges.

That night in my small hotel after dinner I got talking to an Indian who was sitting on the veranda. His story was no less eventful. He had bought a ship, docked here, for which he needed a captain and crew. This was soon after the breakup of the Soviet Union, so there had been no difficulty in securing a complete set of mariners from Russia. Having secured papers for them to enter Haiti he bought a set of air tickets. Unfortunately he too did not realise that they could not change planes in Miami via a transit process, and they had no right to enter the US. The Americans sent the lot back to Russia.

15

LIFE IN KENYA

Nine years in Kenya, where to start? The first six months were somewhat fragmentary, with Doreen and the children in England during the school Spring and Summer terms, joining me in the Easter holidays. I spent a few days in the Panafric Hotel, a month in a flat near the cathedral, and then moved to a house in Lavington, a western suburb. So normal life begins in 1984 when Doreen arrives after her last term at Norwich High School, and the children come for the summer holidays, Darryl from Norwich School, Chrysogon from Leicester University.

The house in Mugumo Road, Lavington, was convenient for access to the City centre where ICRAF had their office at that time, but characterless. The stimulus for moving was when the African owner went bankrupt. He offered to sell us the house, but to have funds tied up in Kenya Shillings was not on.

By good fortune, and doubtless personal contacts, we found a place to rent in Karen, named after Karen Blixen (*Out of Africa*) where she had her house and coffee estate. The house was on Windy Ridge, and had belonged to a former Director of Forestry, Gardner. His widow still lived in the guest house, a excellent Kenya institution where you build a separate cottage in your garden so that visitors need not be on top of you all the time. It was a wonderful place to live, and the small group of shops at Karen were close by. Best of all, Karen Country Club was a short drive away.

Then Granny Gardner died. Darryl was alone in the house when this happened, and the servants called him across, his first sight of a dead person. The executors of the estate needed to sell it, so we looked around for a move. This turned up at Langata, a group of houses – one cannot call it a village, the houses had been built on six and twelve-acre plots. It was owned by old Kenya settlers, Bill and Jackie Evans, who lived in their own guest house and rented out the main residence. We had the pleasure of the company of their three dogs, without having to look after them; one of them, Webster, was so much of a crossbreed that one of his front paws faced backwards.

Our plot in Langata
Keep your eye on the ball

Super houses, but with one drawback. Soon after we moved to Karen, ICRAF left their rented offices on the 5th floor of Bruce House, in the city centre, and moved to newly built premises adjacent to the UNEP Headquarters on the northern outskirts of the city. This meant that getting to work from Karen involved a 10-mile drive twice a day on crowded and potholed roads. Had we known they were going there we should have sought a house in Muthaiga, the diplomatic area, and joined Muthaiga Club, but our lives were too firmly tied up with Karen Club to consider this.

Kenya had been independent for 20 years when we arrived, Jomo Kenyatta had been replaced by President Moi, and of course government was totally African-controlled. The expatriate community, however, was larger than at time of independence, Colonial officers having been replaced by business personnel and staff of aid organizations, like us. It was an international community, although the British were disproportionately represented. Many of the settlers remained, some still farming, others retired.

Doreen did not resume teaching in Kenya, which would have required official permission for an expatriate to undertake paid employment. Instead she took a voluntary part-time position as Museum Guide. Training began by attending the substantial series of introductory lectures on Kenya, followed by learning her way around the museum. Visiting Americans on coach tours would come, and she found an essential first step was to take them to a map of Africa and show them where Kenya was. The outstanding feature of the museum was the display of early hominid remains, collected by the leading anthropologists Louis Leakey and his wife Mary. A bonus for Doreen was getting to know their son Richard Leakey, Director of the Museum.

Club life

To write about social life one has be begin with the clubs. The leading ones were Nairobi Club, near the city centre; Muthaiga Club, best known to outsiders from literature and film, to the north; and Karen Country Club, out in our neck of the woods. There were other smaller ones, and the large Indian community had their own in Parklands, where many years ago they were required to live. The former residential zones had long since been abolished, but now served us a purpose: Darryl wrote his undergraduate Geography Project on them. Club membership was of course open to all, and one made sure that influential Africans were well represented on committees.

We had first joined Nairobi Club, which had a swimming pool, tennis, dining facilities, but not golf. After moving to Karen we maintained our membership there as it had reciprocity of up-country Kenya clubs, such as Mombasa, and also a international network. This included the Royal Overseas League in St James', which was to become our London homing spot during retirement.

Karen Country Club was centred on their fine 18-hole golf course, laid out on what had once been Karen Blixen's coffee estate. A member once remarked to me that if you took into account the high quality of the course, modest membership cost, and availability of tee times it could be considered the finest golf club in the world. There were tennis and squash courts, a swimming pool, dining facilities and a spacious bar, evening bridge, and sundry social events such as dances. Once the British army band played for us, a few military brass band pieces to start with, then dance music for the rest of the evening.

Tennis was not popular with the Africans – you got hot and sweaty – but golf certainly was, including some of our best players. Two of them played with the left hand below the right (you have to bend the left elbow on the backswing), handicaps 10 and 3. From time to time the Golf Committee would issue injunctions asking members to avoid slow play, but of course could not say by whom. There were two reasons African fourballs were apt to be slow: first, they might put money on every hole; and secondly, what a wonderful place to talk politics, away from any chance of being overheard.

Our main focus was tennis, including a mix-in every Saturday. Some recollections. Once, Doreen and I were beaten by a substantially older couple, John and Barbara Dods. By way of congratulations I said to Barbara, "How many grandchildren have you got?" "Nine direct, or sixteen if you count steps." Then there was a Danish couple who were good friends, and with whom we had exchanged dinner invitations. At a critical point in a deciding set there was a line dispute, he saying his shot was in when it was out. Our view prevailed – but they never spoke to us again. A Frenchman had a Maurice Chevalier accent, possibly put on to amuse the English. Playing him singles, at one point he executed, and remarked, "Ze drerp shot". I have always been fast on court, rushed up to reach and return it, whereupon it came back over my head with the comment, "Ze lerb".

Gradually golf took over. I often say that I took up golf at the age of 56, in 1984, which isn't strictly true, as I had played as a boy with my father, although never as a club member nor with a handicap. Thanks to a few lessons from Gary, the Club professional, I got down to handicap 18, staying in the range 17-19 whilst out there. There was a competition every Saturday, most sponsored by an airline or business, and if you wanted to play golf on that day you entered it. I may have won it once or twice.

Besides Karen there were at least four more golf courses in Nairobi, depending on where you take the boundary. In the whole of Kenya at the time there were 28 courses, of which Doreen and I played 18. The the most prestigious (but a less good course than Karen) was Muthaiga, where the Kenya Open was held. At the opposite extreme was Magadi, run by a soda-lake mining company, where there was no grass at all. As tees would not penetrate the hard soil you carried a 'nudger', an inch of hosepipe on which to put your ball on both tee and fairway. The most memorable hole was at Molo, where you stood on a hilltop 100 feet or more above the green.

An institution at Karen, as at many British clubs, was Quiz Night. This was quite riotous, as with tables of eight the difficulty of persuading your table captain that you really did know the answer was considerable. Once one of our team brought along her nine-year old daughter as a spectator. At the end of this evening she remarked, "Mummy, that was amazing – a lot of grown-ups behaving like little children". At the first to which we went, soon after joining the Club, the interval task was to write a limerick based on a given opening couplet. I produced:

> At Karen we play many sports
> Some play in long trousers, some shorts
> Some wear plastic bits
> To keep up their ... morale
> But it's topless that's best on the courts

I thought this was pretty good, but was surprised at the enthusiastic reaction, "That's marvellous, Tony". What I was not aware of was that the best tennis player in the club was Dick TOPLIS.

Part of the fun at quizzes is to dispute the given answer. One night the answers were being read out by an attractive blonde. A question was, "What is the English for the French langouste?" to which the (somewhat inaccurate) answer as given as 'prawn'. Voice from a table: "Giant prawn". Lady quizmaster: "The size is immaterial". Voice from another table: "That's not what you said to me last night, Mary."

The Nairobi Choir was another bonus. Rehearsals in the Cathedral meant a trip nearly to the City centre, but compared with most British choirs there was no attendance requirement. The choir was quite large, maybe 24 sopranos and basses, fewer in the other voices; not from my natural voice but because of the shortage I sang tenor. There were a few Africans, not many. One day I found myself sitting next to one and asked what he did. The reply came in a southern American drawl, "Ah'm a Seventh Day Adventist dentist".

We were wonderfully conducted by Barry Jobling, a small man who looked as if he had some wasting disease, but with a powerful voice. He had started at music college studying piano but then turned to singing which he found much more interesting – from subsequent experience I fully agree, the ratio between the interesting aspect of expression and the boring one of learning notes is so much higher. We lost Barry when he married a young American to get her British citizenship.[1] We performed Bach's B Minor Mass on the tercentenary of his birth in 1985, with German soloists flown out courtesy of Lufthansa.[2] The most exciting was the first performance in Africa of David Fanshawe's *African Sanctus*, in which recordings of drumming and music made from different parts of the continent are played, sometimes as interludes but often at the same time as the choral parts. The Crucifixus is sung to a thunderstorm together with viciously twanging guitar sounds. In contrast, 'Our Father' is set as a simple, very beautiful, popular-style song. Hear this work when you can.

Barry's wedding reminds me of a another marriage of convenience. In the Club, one of the better bridge players was a very overweight lady, Francis (her advice: "One peep is worth two finesses"). She had been left a sum of money by an Aunt on condition she married. So she married an Italian acrobat who happened to be in the country, got the inheritance, then was able to carry on with her chosen mode of life.

The local repertory company began in an old theatre which was in bad shape, and was bought by an African for redevelopment. They found a smaller auditorium, capacity only some 250, and renamed themselves the Phoenix Players, since they had arisen from the ashes of the former theatre. At first there were about six players, all European, putting on new productions every one or two weeks, so at any one time they would be holding at least three parts in their heads. Then they took on Africans, who are good actors. I recall a production of *Romeo and Juliet* where we happened to be in the front row, so close that we got spattered with tomato sauce during the duel scene. Once a year an all-African group took over the theatre with a Gilbert and Sullivan, the music jazzed up and some lyrics adapted to add

---

[1] In 2014 he was giving an annual course of talks on operas in the Friends Meeting House, Ealing.

[2] Airlines were the best sponsors for many things, from golf prizes to bringing out haggises for Burns Night.

local colour; one of the characters for whom the punishment was to fit the crime was the secretary who always answered the phone with, "He's at a meeting".

Another occasion was a production of *Antigone*. In this, two brothers are killed. The ruler, Creon, believes one of them to be a traitor and will not give him a proper burial. He exposes the body and issues an edict that anyone who covers it up will be put to death. His niece, Antigone, disobeys and covers her brother's body with earth. Creon, although he loves her, is obliged to put her to death, because otherwise it will be seen that his rule is weak, he cannot obey his own law. Tension was added to the classical situation by the fact that in this production Creon looked remarkably like President Moi, also an autocratic ruler. We saw the first night, which was very moving. The following day there were disturbances in the city, nothing to do with the play, but it meant that all further performances had to be cancelled.

Local travel

We were popular with visitors. Besides Darryl, Chrysogon and Howard we enjoyed the company of Pat and Michael, Jeannette and Jonathan, Peter and Doreen Simpson, and some of the children's friends. Weekends and local leaves offered chances to travel. The coast at Mombasa was 300 miles away, an eight-hour drive on the potholed road. An early visit was to a tented camp, decidedly uncomfortable for Doreen as her leg was in plaster from a broken Achilles tendon. A fisherman came daily to sell his catch, "Fraish!" More comfortable were the hotels, importantly with security guards patrolling the beach.

At a conference in Rome I had been urged by an older British delegate to try wind surfing, so we bought a rather old-fashioned surf board, strapped to the roof of the car. Conditions were not the easiest for learning, as facing the Indian Ocean the water was choppy, but I learnt to stay up most of the time. Accurate navigation was more difficult and, blown by the south-east trade winds, I was apt to proceed in a zigzag direction northwards towards Somalia. One day this took me quite some distance so I beached the board and started to walk back. Two ladies were lying on the beach sunbathing so I enquired in a friendly fashion if I was getting near the hotel. Necessarily I had taken out my contact lenses, so did not fully appreciate that these were Germans lying starkers. Darryl quickly became more skilled at windsurfing, would go a long way out, to distances which frightened Doreen. One day the wind freshened and it was quite difficult to get him ashore, paddling the last part of the way.

The other main destination was the game reserves, more properly called national parks. One is on the outskirts of Nairobi itself, fenced on the city side but opening onto Masai tribal grazing land. Then Tsavo West, by far the biggest; Amboseli, the most popular with tourists; and Masai Mara, Aberdare, Mount Kenya, Lake Nakuru, Mount Elgon; and the furthest north and best, Samburu.

Amboseli National Park
Darryl's 21st birthday

Some high spots. Pat and Michael came to Masai Mara, the Kenya end of the great migration of about one and a half million wildebeest (gnu) following the rains north from Tanzania, thousands of which are all over the park. On arrival at the park gate, Michael asked, "Where can we see the wildebeest?" A neck fight between two giraffes, to decide superiority for mating. Once, a leopard chasing and killing a Thompson's gazelle. The vast flocks of flamingos on Lake Nakuru, so large and dense that the pink areas can be seen from when flying into the country, an unusual case of birds being visible from 33000 feet. When we had the IBSRAM conference, Doreen was in charge of the wives programme, so took them there, unfortunately on a day when their leaders had said, "OK, fellas, it's Lake Bogoria today", and they had nearly all gone. Early on, when Chrysogon had come out before Doreen, I took her to Lake Naivasha where you can get a rowing boat which leaves you on the island in the lake. Chrys was enchanted at us being the only people on the silent island, able to approach the antelopes until we came within their flight distance.

At Mount Elgon our host was a farmer, Tony Mills, one of very few still remaining in an area which had once all been settler farms. "In those days you could look out over the land with not a wathu (African) in sight." He took us up the mountain in his jeep, showing us the nest of Kenya's finest bird, the fish eagle. On the way back down the track was blocked by a stationary elephant, obviously dying (which is when their teeth wear out) but too ill to move. The land on either side was too steep to divert. It took repeated revving and pseudo-charges before it moved a few steps and we could get by.

Not all weekend trips were to national parks. I mentioned the golf course at Magadi, site of the soda-mining company down in the rift valley. One weekend they held a sports festival, in which you could choose to compete in a range of events. The programme included a relay race in the swimming pool, the only time I have done competitive swimming. I have to do a sort of sidestroke, as when I try crawl, the leg kick produces absolutely no forward impulsion whatever.

Another time we were camping, had gone off for the day, and on return saw a large snake approaching the tent. It put its head under the canvas and went a short way in. We peeped in cautiously thorough the entrance. It looked up, peered round, presumably was disappointed at the absence of edible prey, so turned round and exited near the point it had come in, thus presenting from outside the spectacle of a snake both entering and leaving the tent.[1] Reaching that camping spot had involved crossing a stream by the usual African bridge, larger tree trunks between banks covered by thinner ones across. On returning we found that this bridge had been removed, a nearby informant telling us this was because we had not paid the owner of the land to camp there. Standing around were a few small boys, whom Doreen approached and asked the oldest whether there was any other way of reaching the road. They were taken into the car and navigated us through

---

[1]   There's a place in the Canadian Rockies where you can see a train doing this, into and out of a tunnel in order to gain height on the side of a mountain.

bush (short-tree savanna) until we reached the track which counted as a local road, crossing the stream by no more than a shallow drift. We rewarded them suitably – and told them not to depend on casual income but to work hard at school.

On Mount Kenya

Once there was a trip with ICRAF colleagues to Mount Longonot, an extinct volcano with a caldera. We walked around the rim of this. A Swiss meteorologist called Till Darnhofer had with him his Alsatian dog; three-quarters of the way round the dog seemed to be limping, and we found that the volcanic ash had ripped open his paws. Till lifted up the dog, put him round his neck and carried him, looking like a shepherd in the bible. There were spectacular visits to Mount Kenya, one with the Smith family. Darryl reached a higher altitude than I was able to.

Then there was the Geology Club, in fact largely a Dutch Camping Club, who would go off for weekend trips. We joined them once, to walk to the top of a mountain which had holy significance for the local tribe. When we got there it turned out that permission had been withdrawn, probably because the financial compensation we had offered for encroaching on its holiness was not sufficient. We were fortunate to be there in the final years when it was possible to go off into the bush and camp. By the time we left or soon after, the state of security put paid to stopping in anything other than a protected site.

My Kenyan cousins

It is a matter of regret that only the last two years of our time there did we learn of the existence of my Kenyan cousins. We had known all along from my father that they ought to be there, but it was only when we mentioned this to Tony Mills that he, knowing all the remaining settler farmers, told us where to find Timothy Llewelyn. After a bit of family history hunting, it turned out that Tim was my second cousin.

Our grandmothers were sisters, Hilda and Gertrude, both daughters of Captain James Buchanan. Gertrude married Charles Bailey, who ran C. H. Bailey and Co., ship repairers and chandlers in Wales. Clearly he made good because in the 1901 census he had six servants. When Charles died, about 1914, his widow went out to Kenya to avoid a large tax bill (again according to my father). Gertrude had six children one of whom, Elizabeth, ran away to Gretna Green to marry Leonard George Edward Llewelyn (George), son of Sir Leonard Llewelyn, who was born a miner, decided he would work his way up to own the mine he worked in, did so, and was knighted for saving the lives of his men in a colliery accident. He had a daughter Elizabeth (Beth), born the same year as my father, 1900. She divorced George and took her children out to Mombasa in 1934. Gertrude, my father's first cousin, followed her daughter out in 1935, ran a horse-breeding business, and was still living in Nakuru in 1990, though we never got to visit her.

One of the children, Tim, became a farmer in Kenya, growing wheat on the high-altitude land at Nanyuki, below Mount Kenya. He married Gillian Gascoyne. So these were my second cousins to whom we wrote, were invited to stay, and went to their farm. Ringing the bell brought a servant who let us in, and after a time a head came round the door, "Oh...sorry... just a moment" and disappeared again. When she came back we learnt that the timing of our visit was spectacularly unfortunate, as the previous night their barn had burnt to the ground. This could reasonably explain Gill's odd manner, but talking to mutual acquaintances afterwards we were told that it was normal whatever the circumstances.

We were shown into their guest house (what a fine institution this is) and later met by Tim, who in contrast was charm itself . He showed us round the farm, including the foundations of Gertrude's former house, and a portrait of her. The house was built to an unusual design, in which all the rooms could only be entered by separate doors from the outside. Not long afterwards Tim was killed when his private plane crashed.

Tim had told us where to find Biddy Davis, née Bailey, also a second cousin, and living in what you might call the outskirts of Nairobi. Havn't we come across a Bailey before? Correct. Brother and sister Bailey married sister and brother Llewelyn, a situation which can cause genealogical computer programs to give up in despair. Robin Davis was an artist, making his living from engravings (e.g. of animals) on black slate – nothing very unusual about that. Biddy was a different matter: she must have weighed some 18 stone. Her profession was breeding dogs, mostly labradors. In England you would expect to find this carried on in kennels. Here, whilst there was a wire enclosure for the latest puppies, most of the dogs were in her garden or house, many occupying every sofa and arm chair in the drawing room. Biddy also judged cattle at agricultural shows. They were extremely welcoming, and we enjoyed their hospitality on two visits, one when on a return visit to Kenya after leaving ICRAF.

Biddy told a story about when two burglars had come into the house. In these circumstances most Europeans would retreat and let them get on with it. Biddy seized a long pole, possibly a bamboo, and started to set about them, whereupon in surprise they made off. This incident had been witnessed by two giant tortoises who lived in the garden. For a week after-wards they wouldn't leave her, following her about wherever she went.

Subsequently we have had long Christmas letters from her. Robin died and Biddy in due course had to go into a wheelchair. This didn't stop her continuing an active life, including going off with friends camping.[1]

---

[1]   There is an archive of these letters on file.

White Mischief: our connection

The 'Happy Valley' set was a group of British semi-aristocrats who led a hedonistic life in Kenya, giving a bad name to the settler community as a whole. We have tenuous connections. George Llewelyn married four times, probably in the order Beth, Molly, Diana, and Sybil. It is Sybil who was said to be part of, or linked with, the Happy Valley group. Although still living in 1993, we did not manage to meet Sybil (after all, I had a job to do).

We did, however, have some connection with the story subsequently told as *White Mischief*. In 1941 Sir Henry Delves Broughton was married to the much younger Lady Diana (with this lot, if you refer to a marriage you need to give the date). He learnt that Josslyn Hay, Earl of Errol, was flirting with Diana. After dinner and boozy evening at the Muthaiga Club, Errol took Diana to her home in Karen. Broughton followed, and hid in the back of Errol's large Buick with a gun, until Errol left to drive back to Muthaiga. The road from Karen begins with a straight stretch, and Errol was accustomed to drive at 70 miles an hour. Now when you are in a car travelling at that speed you do not shoot the driver, so Broughton waited until he slowed down on reaching a junction. There he shot Errol, and the car overturned into a ditch, where Errol's body was found the next day. Although not very fit, Broughton sprinted back to his house to establish an alibi.

At his trial for murder, quite an event, he was acquitted. It was said after the verdict he whispered to a friend, "I am a very good actor". Later he confessed privately more than once, the first time to a 15-year old girl, Juanita Carberry. Back in England, in December 1942 he killed himself with an overdose of morphine.

Our connection? First, most times that we drove out of Karen, including to work every day, we passed the road junction, with the ditch still there. Secondly, while we were there a film of *White Mischief* was being made, shot locally, with a stunning cast: Greta Scacchi, Joss Acland, Charles Dance and John Hurt. Muthaiga Club refused to let them film there, so they built a replica on a dairy farm. They appealed for extras for the race course scene, and Doreen and I volunteered. The day began with 'casting' (what we should each look like), 1940s haircuts and styles, costumes and makeup. I was chosen (for the second time in my life) as a policeman, with clothing which included shorts which, in the words of a beer advertisement of the time, allowed the air to reach places which other shorts did not. The Director warned us all that a key requirement for extras was the ability to wait about for long periods.

Filming *White Mischief*

Also in the cast were some Maasai warriors in full regalia, who were required to arrive in the back of a Rolls Royce driven by John Hurt. At lunchtime they were seated in the grandstand. Waiters from the Nairobi Hilton, in evening dress, brought round sandwich boxes for us and for them, a spectacular contrast in fancy dress.

After lunch, assembled at the far end of the racecourse were most of the race horses that Nairobi could summon up. At the critical moment these came thundering down the straight and we, the crowd, left off chatting and ran down to the rails, shouting and throwing out hats in the air. As this looked daft the Director called for a retake, in which only those with birth-days in January and February were to participate in hat-throwing. After 12 hours we all went home, for a fee of £16 each.

SOME KENYA STORIES

Two of these are based on hearsay and may not be accurate – and they are certainly politically incorrect. The middle one was well authenticated during the succeeding Presidency of Mwai Kibaki.

The Body in the Lake

This counts among the biggest blunders on record. The President wanted to get rid of a Minister who was being too uppish, so arranged to have him shot. This left a dead Minister with a bullet wound through the head, so those responsible felt they should dispose of the body. They poured petrol on it and set it alight. This left the charred body of a dead Minister with a bullet wound through the head, so they decided it could be safely lost in Lake Victoria. Now you need to know that this has an area of 68 800 square kilometres – to use the standard measure of comparison, three times the size of Wales. So they took the body up in a plane and dropped it over the lake…**and they missed**. The body was found by a boy in the reeds.

The Goldenberg Affair

During his time in office President Moi introduced a scheme to encourage exports to hard currency countries. Anyone doing so would received 20% of the value of any such exports as a subsidy in Kenya Shillings. A certain Kamlish Pattni negotiated that for exports of gold and diamonds his company, Goldenberg International (really!) would instead get 35%. To augment Kenya's very small production he smuggled in gold from the Congo, getting the Commissioner for Mines and Geology to certify that this came from Kenya – which it didn't. He then got the Commissioner for Customs and Excise to certify that boxes full of gold and diamonds had left the country – which, in the numbers stated, they hadn't. Finally he bribed the Head of the Central Bank of Kenya (and some 10 of its staff) to say it had received huge sums in Swiss Francs – which it hadn't. This made him able to claim the 35% export compensation, which amounted to a fifth of Kenya's national product, and pay off more than 20 people he had bribed, including two of the President's sons.

Habeas Corpus

This story was told to me by an Australian, and gains flavour if read with an appropriate accent. The Luo come from the west of Kenya, by Lake Victoria, and they have strict burial customs. A Luo woman was told that her husband had died in police custody. She wanted him to receive appropriate tribal rights so she went to court, saying, "Isn't there something called habeas corpus, that means I can have his body back doesn't it?" and the judge ordered the Police to give it to her. So the Police dug up all the people they had shot recently and when they found what they thought was the right one, gave it to her. But someone, maybe the tribal pathologist, found a bullet hole in his head, which had entered via the back of the neck and exited through the forehead. When confronted with this evidence, the police replied, "Well you see he was bending over, of course, shot trying to escape".

Wedding bells 1987

The summer of 1987 saw a very different and delightful holiday for us. Chrysogon had graduated from Leicester in Engineering after specialising in electronics and computer engineering in her third year. Her first job was with Philips in Cambridge where her immediate team leader was Howard Smith. He was not a permanent Philips employee but had been seconded from his post with Logica (now CGI). Hence once again the glorious play of chance that shapes our lives.

Doreen flew home 17th June to make arrangements, I followed 30th June, and the wedding was on Saturday 11th July – auspiciously a full moon.[1] The reception was in the restaurant of the Sainsbury Centre for Visual Arts at the University of East Anglia. Welcoming the guests, I noted that Howard was a computer expert, which some people think, wrongly, has a lot to do with mathematics. It does, however, have much to do with logic. "So I turn to the words of a great nineteenth century logician: "Contrariwise," said Tweedledee, "If it was, it would be; and if it were, it might be; but as it isn't, it ain't".

The gardens hold Henry Moore bronzes. It was a brilliant sunny day, and to add to the joy of the occasion, when we were on the lawn with drinks,

---

[1] And the day when world population reached 5 billion.

Concorde flew across right overhead. Chrys kept their honeymoon destination secret, "Somewhere you've not been" – in fact I had done a mid-ocean unplanned stopover in the Seychelles, but it was on a different island.

The extension of our family to the next generation would begin with the birth of Madeleine on 28th March 1991. By a happy chance we had planned to take leave and flew to Venice that day. After our short Easter holiday there Doreen flew to England to see the new baby. I went on to a prearranged consultancy at FAO Rome.

Three years later Oliver was born, on 15th February 1994. We had left Kenya by then, and the story of his arrival is told below. As I write Madeleine has graduated with a Masters in Maths from Oxford and now works in the research and software development branch of IBM. Oliver read Philosophy and English at Warwick, followed by a Master's degree at UCL. Howard's middle name being Neil they have both added this to their surnames.

Leaving Kenya

Why did we leave? I should make it clear that this was my decision, Doreen would have liked to stay longer. The reason was a mixture of push and pull factors.

ICRAF was going through a planning stage, with seemingly endless meetings for programming and budgeting. They had also recently introduced a ten-year rule: international staff, who up to then had held more or less ongoing posts, would henceforth be replaced after 10 years unless a special case for them could be made – 'Ten years, not tenure' you might say. At the same time they were wanting more heavy science, more technical experimental work, which was going to make my 'synthesis and writing' skills less in demand. (Something similar had happened before after 15 years at UEA.) I could have applied for Director of Research but this would have meant I couldn't do any research myself; and secondly, 1 don't think I would have got it.

At the same time I wanted more of what UK and Europe could offer. It was becoming more and more doubtful how long our unoccupied house in Norwich would last without major burglary. Financially our position by then was sound, and there would be opportunity for further consultancies. So whilst remaining on ICRAF's payroll into early 1992, based on leave not taken, we in fact left Kenya on 18th December 1991.

So for the second time, following the School of Environmental Sciences at UEA, I had joined an institution soon after its inception, and left when it had become large and successful.

ICRAF farewell presentation
"The vultures are hovering"
Left ICRAF's second Director General, soil scientist Pedro Sanchez

INTERLUDE: OCCASIONS

REACHING BACK

This is basically how far back can one reach with people whom I have met or have had some connection, or in a few cases events: name-dropping if you like. Most of the items are found earlier in the text.

1933 Queen Mary, on coming out of Harrod's (where she used to shop but not pay), saw me in my pram with a uniformed nanny and remarked, "What a pretty baby".

1945 heard the first radio broadcast of Britten's *Peter Grimes*.

1947 at St Christopher School heard a lecture by Maria Montessori, founder from 1909 of the educational system for young children which bears her name.

1948 I had gone to Lord's with John Manson to watch MCC v. Australians, hoping to see Don Bradman get a century; he was out for 98.

1951 my first tutor at St John's College was Sir James Wordie, a member of Shackleton's Antarctic expedition 1913.

1951-52 Jonathan Miller was loping about St John's College, reading medicine while appearing in *Beyond the Fringe*, which I saw on the London stage. In 1965 met him at a drinks party in Sussex. He was to go on to be a leading director of opera.

1952 shared a bathroom, in St John's College (there were only three) with Manmohan Singh, to become Prime Minister of India 2004-14, the first Sikh to hold his office. I never encountered him because he did not wish to be seen without his turban so would cross the court to bathe at 5.00 a.m.

1952 in Cambridge, heard US evangelist Billy Graham call upon people to be saved. I wasn't.

1953 went to a public lecture in Cambridge by Fred Hoyle, St John's College, who was responsible for continuous creation theory, an alternative to the 'big bang', a name which he created, initially as a term of disparagement, in a broadcast in 1949.

On February 28th 1953 I would have been in Cambridge on the day Francis Crick and James Watson walked into The Eagle pub and announced, "We have found the secret of life", the double helix structure of DNA. I was, however, totally unaware of this.

1958 spent 30 days on the *Braemar Castle*, London-Beira, with Dr Brydon, who said he was a doctor to Queen Victoria, and had heard Gladstone speak in the house. For the validity of these claims, see Chapter 9.

1959 Roy Welensky, second Prime Minister of the doomed Federation of Rhodesia and Nyasaland, spoke to a meeting in Zomba, then the capital of Nyasaland.

1965 supervised a dissertation on African Music by Virginia Wade, subsequently to become Wimbledon singles champion 1977.

1967 met Leonard Woolf, husband of Virginia but also a socialist and writer of note, at a drinks party at his home, Monk's House, Rodmell, Sussex (now National Trust). The party was in honour of the High Commissioner of Sri Lanka, Malalasekera, and Sussex University, on being approached to nominate a guest, searched in vain until the Geography Department told them Doreen and I had recently returned from a spending a week there. Also present was Malcolm Muggeridge, then editor of the *New Statesman*.

1970 well before the world attention to climatic change, a conference on the terrestrial element in the global carbon cycle was held at was held at the Wood's Hole Oceanographic Institution (WHOI !), Massachusetts. Among those present was Dave Keeling, who in 1958 started measurements of atmospheric carbon dioxide on Mauna Loa, a high volcano in Hawaii, after difficulty in securing a grant.

1980 in St John's College Senior Common Room met Sir Harold Jeffries (d.1989), mathematician and doyen of geophysicists, author of *The Earth (1st edition 1924);* he would not accept the existence of continental drift because, at that time, there was no plausible mechanism for it.

2010 in St John's College Senior Common Room, met Maurice Wilkes, credited with invention of the world's first stored-progam computer to offer a service to users (Cambridge researchers), EDSAC, 1948.

And going further back:

My father spoke of seeing the bass, Chaliapin, as Boris Godunov, "This huge man, staggering about the stage shouting more than singing, Dushka! Dushka!"

My mother spoke of seeing Rachmaninov, "No histrionics, he just gave a perfunctory nod to the audience, sat down at the piano, and played".

MUSICAL OCCASIONS

Over the years Doreen and I have been to some outstanding musical performances:

February 1962 Joan Sutherland in Bellini's *La Somnambula* (includes the Mad Scene): La Scala, Milan.

November/December 1962 Margot Fonteyn and Rudolph Nureyev, pas de deux from *Le Corsair*. Royal Opera House, (Tickets from my father and Peggy).

21st December 1974 Rostropovich, first performance of Britten's Cello Suite No.3, Snape Maltings. Ben Britten, ill with a heart problem, was in his box, adapted from an oven.

1990 With the Nairobi Choir, sung in the first performance in Africa of David Fanshawe's *African Sanctus*.

1997 in Norwich, Wagner's *Ring* cycle, at the Theatre Royal, Norwegian State Opera (visit said to have been negotiated by John Major); interval picnics in the car park.

2011 in Norwich, heard the Beethoven sonatas complete, over 10 recitals, Francois-Frédéric Guy.

2013 on the 100th anniversary year of Mahler's death, 2013, heard Symphonies 1, 2, 5, 6, 7, 8, 9, 10 (incomplete) and *Das Lied von der Erde*, mainly London Philharmonic at the Royal Festival Hall.

MEMORABLE MOMENTS

Most exciting

Without doubt the most exciting moment of my life was seeing Mo Farah win the 5000 metres at the 2012 Olympics. I had been to the same event at Wembley in the 1948 Olympics and moved mountains to get tickets for the same event, which was on the last Saturday of the athletics (four family members applied, including a 'Michael Young'). Chrys, Darryl and I were three rows back opposite the finishing line. When Mo came through on the last lap and held his lead, the roar in the stadium was unbelievable.

London Olympics 2012, not Usain Bolt

Later that afternoon Usain Bolt took the last leg to win the 4 x 100m relay for Jamaica. In 100m and 200m events he slows down (relatively speaking!) over the last ten metres. For this relay, he was visibly giving it everything he could right up to the line.

Most moving

The most moving occasion was on TV. We were on leave from Kenya when on 9th November 1989 the Berlin Wall was breached. It had been built in

1961 to separate communist East Germany from the West. After an evening when confusing instructions reached the guards, at midnight they opened a barrier. It was highly moving to see Germans from the East, many of them young who had grown up entirely under communism, pour through and greet their countrymen in the West.

On New Year's Eve 1940 (1941?) the BBC broadcast Harry Lauder singing *Keep right on to the end of the road*, and I was able to understand the added meaning in the context of the War.

In 1965 I was reading Charlotte Bronte's *Jane Eyre* in the Malayan jungle. She is at this dreadful school and her best friend is ill – it doesn't say with what, but we know that it's tuberculosis from cold rooms and sparse food. Jane gets into her friend's bed, puts her arms round her and they go to sleep. In the morning there is a tremendous fuss – because, of course, the girl has died. I just went around in a daze for a time.

Every time I try to recite John Betjeman's *In a Bath teashop* my voice breaks before the end.

Many moving moments have come when listing to music:

> Dido's lament, *"When I am gone"* from Purcell's *Dido and Aeneas*; including at a schools performance with Madeleine and Oliver in the cast.
>
> Mahler's *Adagietto* from his 5th symphony
>
> The trio from the last act of Strauss's *Rosenkavalier*
>
> At an amateur show in Nairobi Club, Noël Coward's *Mad about the boy* was sung so movingly that for the first time I can recall, tears ran down my cheeks.[1]

Funniest

The greatest laugh, both for Doreen and me, was not at a comedian, but seeing Natalie Dessay in Donizetti's *La fille du regiment*.

---

[1] Don't let anyone tell you this is a homosexual lyric. It is from the 1932 show *Words and Music*, where it is sung by women in a cinema queue waiting to see the romantic star Rudolph Valentino.

Jokes without words are good. Three clowning events, two seen, the other read about, are in the text. Otherwise, how about:

> *Peter Cook (senior RAF officer):* I want you to lay down your life, Perkins. We need a futile gesture at this stage. It will raise the whole tone of the war. Get up in a crate, Perkins, pop over to Bremen, take a shufti … don't come back. Goodbye, Perkins. God, I wish I was going too.
> *Jonathan Miller (pilot):* Goodbye, sir — or is it — au revoir?
> *Cook:* No, Perkins, it is not.

Jokes are not good in print, they have to be spoken, usually fast, so you won't get 'best joke' which is the one about the three-legged chicken. There is also the problem that my sense of humour is not everyone's, and can sometimes give offence. Let's be content with this, from Norman Wisdom:

> I was walking along the street when I saw this feller lying flat on his face looking down a manhole I said can I have a look he said go ahead I said I can't see a thing he said I know it's been like that all day.

Aren't you glad I stopped there?

16

ALLIANCE FRANÇAISE 1992-2000

The post-Kenya period covers more than 20 years, all of which might be described as 'living in Norwich, with travels'. So what did we do, or rather try to do, first? Learn French.

This had been my worst school subject. Later I tried a little more success-fully to learn German because in the inter-war period ability to read German had been considered desirable for a PhD, and I didn't appreciate that those days were over. Subsequent attempts to learn Chinyanja (Malawi), Malay and Swahili had not been much more successful. So we both decided to go for it, with the added joy of living and travelling in France. In 1992 there was a further incentive, to stay out of England long enough not to terminate the resident-abroad status for tax purposes that our spell in Kenya had established.

So from January to April we lived in Amboise, in the Loire valley, studying with a Eurocentre language school. This was both the best and the worst of the eleven courses we were to take: the best because everything was fresh, and the area delightful; the worst because we were in a class of 16, which to put it mildly doesn't allow for enough conversational interaction. The other students were from many countries and a lot younger than us. This intro-duced us to the immersion system, where students are forbidden to say a word in their own language (at some institutions there can be a fine). Morn-ings were classes, afternoons private study with video's available. One morning we were exhausted by the mental effort and glad to get away to a crêpe; only to learn subsequently that there was another class before lunch.

It was cold, and in the gîte which they had arranged for us, when you turned up the heating it threw the switch fuse. One day we returned and the landlady greeted us with, "J'ai une petite surprise pour vous". She had laid a wood fire. We lit it – and the room filled with smoke. One day her husband was cultivating some vegetables in the garden and I sought to exchange some conversation. "Le problème" he replied, "C'est les moines". Puzzled at why monks should be damaging his crop, dictionary research showed that these were les moineaux, sparrows. We struggled, for the most part unsuccessfully, to follow French TV on which they speak too fast – the quiz programme "Questions pour un champion" was a favourite. There was a small but select cinema, in which once we formed half the audience. We embarked on some wine connoisseurship, including an excellent Loire red, St Nicholas de Bourgeuil.

During a really cold spell Pat and Michael came out to visit us. After shivering on the Chateau of Amboise we went to Tours, to find ourselves in narrow streets with high buildings on either side, which the sun had not penetrated all winter, it was like being in a refrigerator.

But for all the problems, linguistic and climatic, it was for me one of the happiest periods of my life. Doreen expresses surprise at this. It was the combination of doing something entirely new and intellectual, and following the life of visitors to France, shopping, restaurant meals, and the like.

The rest of 1992 was something of a helter-skelter year, taking in Menton, Florence, Crete, a week's skiing in Risoul, Montpellier, two months in Nairobi 'house-warming' for residents on leave (John and Barbara Dods), and two FAO consultancies, in Jamaica and Bangkok, plus some short periods in Norwich. Some of these we'll pick up later, but a word on others. Menton was a stopover on the way to Italy. We chose the Hotel Prince de Galles where we had spent part of our honeymoon 35 years earlier, and to prove it there were our names in the Visitors' Book. Montpellier was meant for practice in French, but was also chosen as I had contacts with their Institute for Mediterranean Agriculture. One night we got tickets to their old opera house – just two toilets in the whole building, I don't mean assemblages, just room for two occupants. Getting there in good time we went off to a bar, returning half and hour before the performance. All was very quiet, and some usherettes directed us to our box, making "Sh" signs, for strangely the performance was already under way. We had come the night after the clocks went forward for summer time. After that we enjoyed

Il ritorno d'Ulisse in patria (Monteverdi). Earlier, in Tours, we had seen *Les tentations de Saint Antoine* (Soler), the temptations of St Antony out in the desert, an enterprising production in that the desert was represented by a circus ring, with sand for the horses and an equilibrist on a swing in the background.

And why Crete? Not a holiday. I had been invited to lecture on agroforestry at the only centre for Mediterranean agriculture which operated in English. The air fare plus a small emolument paid for our 2600-mile return car journey, plus ships Ancona-Piraeus and Patras-Crete.

Could this be called our "Grand Tour," as made by 18th-century aristocrats? Well, it was the nearest we are likely to get to this, remaining in Europe from 24th January to 6th April, 2½ months.

Back to the French. Over the next twelve years we took ten more courses. Two were one-offs, at Avignon, where the Rhone flooded (we were staying the other side of it in a poky little room at Villeneuve-les-Avignon), and at Rennes. We found out why are there so many courses with a single teacher: the government required anyone who wished to work as a au pair to sign up for a language course.

The remainder were at centres to which we returned several times, and were much more rewarding. At Artemare, in the Jura, was one called Accents, run by Pam Bourgeois, English but married to a Frenchman. They offered 'French with…' courses, language in the mornings and another activity in the afternoons. The first was French with Hill Walking, still exercising the language by chatting with the guide. I remember a dog rushing out barking furiously at me at this invasion of his territory. Surprised that I did not jump away but admonished him, I enquired the French for to bluff which is easy. So I continued, "Il bluffe. Quelquefois il y a une problème, si le chien pense que c'est moi qui bluff". From there we went straight on to a subsidiary centre based on a traditional house in Forcalquier, north of Aix en Provence, for French with Golf.

We had both done a little downhill (Alpine) skiing but felt that the muscles were no longer up to this. Then Hubert Lamb (founder of the Climatic Change Research Unit at UEA) suggested we try cross-country (Nordic skiing, ski-de-fond) which he and his wife were still doing when older than us. Opportunity arose when the Artemare centre offered French with ski-de-fond. They had the good fortune that one of their language teachers was a Nordic ski expert – he had once coached a local girl from beginner until she reached the French Olympic team. We followed their course twice, in February 1994 and 1995, managing the strenuous physical effort and making some progress. A bonus was that their teaching area was adjacent to the local gym which had a sauna. After the 1995 course we had hired a flat in Cannes. However, Doreen contracted severe flu and totally lost her voice. We drove there in total silence, except for whispered remarks – this wasn't necessary for me but when the other person is whispering it is hard not to do so.

That ended skiing for us, and also turned out to be the end of Artemare courses. They had hired a marketing manager, the salary for whom put them in financial straits. He proposed that past students bought a bond, to be set against future courses. Wishing to support them we did so, and soon afterwards they went bust.

We learnt of another centre further south at a small village called Fondeveille, not far from Lyon. This was run by two ladies, one of them in a wheelchair. It was excellent from a language point of view, and also a very amiable atmosphere. The teacher had married a man from Birmingham, who did the cooking and housework. We followed courses there in 1997, 1998 and 2000. Later they moved south to Nyons, in the Drôme valley (which had an appelation controlée for its olives), where we did our final French course.

Did we accomplish our objectives? To become fluent in French, no; to be able to have a simple conversation, yes. Our abilities rose, then reached a plateau, which would only be surpassed had we lived in the country for a prolonged period. Doreen was clearly better than me, not so much in vocabulary and grammar but because she was better at talking, and at picking up what other people meant.

There was an adjunct to the French courses, buying wine. Consulting our copy of the *Guide Hachette* we would tour around the small villages of Beaujolais and Burgundy, tasting and buying a dozen or so. The boot of our car would take 144 bottles, so all our luggage was on the back seat. This was the start of our wine connoisseurship at a very elementary level. We focus on the ten Beaujolais cru, with Fleurie, Julienas and Chiroubles as favourites; together with Burgundy, Loire, and for whites, Alsace and South Africa.

Once we hit one of those remarkable coincidences which occasionally crop up. We were in a small winery and exchanged a few words with the one French pair who were there. He asked, "What is the English for fruité?" After replying that it was simply 'fruity' I remarked that his English was such that he must have lived there for a time. "Yes, for a year." "Where was that?" "At Oxford." "Oh, a few weeks ago I was invited to lunch at a college there." "Which one?" "St Anthony's." "My college." "Well, my name is Anthony and I was lunching at St Anthony's College with Anthony Kirk-Greene." "My supervisor!"

17

SETTING THE WORLD TO RIGHTS?
CONSULTANCIES 1992-2001

So there I was, unemployed again. But as I had gambled when leaving ICRAF, a flow of consultancies continued for the next ten years. Most were for FAO, six in Rome, two around the world, and two as authorship contracts. Besides serving to bring in some income, these expanded the range of my knowledge of land resources, bringing in more on land degradation together with work on land use planning and national soils policy. Others were for the World Bank, UNEP (that's good old Jim Cheatle again, via his wife Marion who worked there), and a commercial company in the USA, Winrock International, who were looking at the global carbon cycle.

In 1997 I reached 65, the FAO retirement age, and they had a rule that for such individuals the maximum fee was $100 a day, on grounds that many consultants were their own retired staff to whom they were paying a pension. European law on age discrimination cut no ice with them, so that became the rate I received. However, for authorship jobs, Freddie Nachtergaele colluded in letting me claim that these took longer than they really did. It would be boring to run through all these consultancies so this is a selection only.

A national soils policy for Jamaica 1992

National Soils Policies were a new project for FAO, only two previous countries being covered.[1] After briefing in Rome it was off to Kingston, Jamaica, where matters were largely in my own hands. The idea was to liaise with the

---

[1]   One of these was Syria. At the time of writing the country is in a state of civil war, making National Soils Policy an extremely low priority.

national Soil Survey, find out what they thought should be done, and write it up. I was assisted by a Jamaican lawyer called Winston Churchill, who covered the legal aspects: what were the laws relevant to land use, and were they enforced (to which the answer was no). This was a fascinating task, involving an instant appraisal of the geography of Jamaica. Soil mapping of the whole of the country had been done in colonial times, but it was reassuring to learn that the local survey had done extensive land evaluation exercises. At the end of a period of discussions and a field visit, a conference was arranged to present and discuss the policy. It was intimated to me that all government meetings began with a prayer, it being an honour to some junior employee to be asked to say it.

I stayed in the Liguania Club. Early morning tea in bed is an essential, so my usual practice when staying in hotels is to take a kettle, powdered milk and tea bags. In Jamaica this ran into difficulty: they have the US standard of 110 volts. So that was four weeks of tepid tea. Fitted in one round of golf, on a course which is one respect is like St Andrews: nine holes out in more or less a line, then nine back. However, the first nine head towards the central mountain range, so you are going continually upwards, exhausting in the heat. On 6th September the BBC Antiques Road Show came to Jamaica, nothing very spectacular turning up. As the paper put it the next day a lady said, "Me show 'im me old Grannie's teapot, him say it not wort' nuttin."

UN agencies like to hold conferences, one of which was hosted by the Club. I have a photo of the display poster, showing showing that lack of a focus need be no obstacle. It showed, "UN CONFERENCE ON CONFERENCES".

To the best of my knowledge the Jamaican government subsequently 'adopted' the Soils Policy, which didn't actually require them to do anything but may have provided guidelines on matters concerning land use.

Land degradation in South Asia: Bangkok and travels, 1992-93

This was a major consultancy, sponsored by FAO, UNDP and UNEP, to report on the state of land degradation – soil erosion and fertility decline – and importantly, "its effects upon the people", in eight countries: India, Pakistan, Sri Lanka, Bangladesh, Nepal, Bhutan, Afghanistan and Iran. Based on Bangkok, it had been set up at the instigation of Frank Dent,

Regional Soil Management Officer, RAPA. I had to go to the Internet to find what this was, working through the Reidvale Adventure Play Association and a dozen other meanings which achieved higher rankings on google searches before finding it to be FAO's Regional Office for Asia and the Pacific (ought to be ROAP but there's no knowing with acronyms). In principle a joint consultant was an elderly Indian called J. S. P. Yadev, though in practice I wrote the lot, acknowledging that he had "contributed detailed material".

I quickly bagged the most attractive countries, Sri Lanka and Nepal, for field visits. Yadev would do his own country, so I was landed with Pakistan as well. Afghanistan and Iran were ruled out on political and military grounds, whilst Bhutan I would have loved to see but arranging to go there is difficult. There was no point in anyone going to Bangladesh since FAO's most dedicated consultant, Hugh Brammer, had spent half his working career there.[1]

How on earth could one person tackle such a huge area? Well, there had been a major international survey, GLASOD, the Global Assessment of Soil Degradation, followed up by a more detailed regional assessment for Asia, ASSOD. Hence FAO knew (for the first time) the severity of degradation; what they were interested in was, "…its causes, and effects upon the people" – in other words, should and could anything be done about it.

The work was done in two tranches, both based on Bangkok, on one of which Doreen came and joined me. Bangkok was an unattractive city, desperately overcrowded. Hotel air conditioning only partly protected us from the air pollution. One got about, or tried to, by tuk-tuks, small three-wheeler taxis although even these, when told where you wanted to get to, would sometimes indicate that this just wasn't possible. One couple, I was told, were invited out to dinner, but the delay was so great that at midnight they spotted an hotel and checked in for the night. A popular way to get about was by river ferry, across or along the broad Mekong, full of boats but not to the extent of a log jam, and very cheap.

Doreen came with me on the field trips for this project. The first was to Sri Lanka, mostly up into the Kandy hill country. Then came Pakistan, to the capital, Islamabad, obviously a holy place in the Moslem religion, with the

---

[1]   As I write he is 90 but still producing copious reports.

added complication that the visit took place during the month of Ramadan. During daylight hours food could not be served in public, although the hotel would bring meals to our room. As soon as dusk came, stalls sprang up serving sweetmeats and the like. Whilst I had talks with government and agricultural officials, Doreen found a handy place to spend the day in the library of the British Council; when she had sat down, the rest of the table could not be occupied by men. Once in the hotel she was going down in the lift when it stopped at the second floor; a man saw her, bowed, but of course could not do such a shocking thing as going down in the lift with her. She was not required to cover her head in the street, although out of politeness put on a Queen-style coloured headscarf. They arranged a field trip up into the foothills of the Himalayas, desperately overgrazed. Arriving at a village were were in some consternation when a boy appeared with a rifle. This, however, was for visitors like us, for a few pennies, to fire darts into balloons.

In retrospect, such was the enormity of the task I am pleasantly surprised I completed it. I based my analysis on a 'causal nexus' between land, population, poverty and degradation. This would fit very well into Chrysogon's Southbeach Notation[1], with six red boxes:

Increase in rural population + Limited remaining land —> Land shortage

leading to the vicious circle:

Land shortage —> Poverty —> Non-sustainable land management practices —>
Land degradation —> Making land shortage worse

Somehow or other I cobbled together a 100-page account, published somewhat obscurely as *World Soil Resources Report* 78. As so often in the consultancy world, once the consultant has completed his allotted task he doesn't know what, if anything, this led to. Personally, however, I used this 'causal nexus' in the future, right up to my last substantive publication, on population, in *Geographical Journal* of 2005.

---

[1] www.southbeachinc.com

That one went down well!

Shorter jobs, 1993-94 – and another express journey home

Four shorter consultancies followed, two at FAO, Rome, one in The Netherlands and another in the USA, involving the carbon cycle which was later to become so prominent in the climate change debate. The last of the four was in Rome, again with Doreen, where there was an 'expert consultation' on land use and land cover classification, and the tame hack was asked to write the report. Land cover is what it says it is: forest, crops, settlements, etc., easy to map from satellite imagery. Land use is more subtle, for example a catchment with a land cover of forest might have uses of forestry, water catchment, conservation of plant and animal resources, or collection of minor forest products.

At the end of this work – well, I hope it was the end – a phone call reached us that Oliver has been born. We sped off in the VW and in three days, 19-21 February, made it from Rome to Coulsdon. Overnight stops were in Frejus, on the French Mediterranean coast, and Laon on northern France, which gives successive days' drives of 480 and 580 miles – great to see you, Oliver!

The World Bank, Washington DC, 1986, 1992 and 1995

The World Bank has always been extremely weak when it comes to natural resources. There is a Forestry Division, but apart from that they stagger along with just one staff member who knows anything about soils. Called Senior Agro-Ecologist (there wasn't a junior one) this was held successively by two British, John Coulter and Ian Douglas. The economists who make up most of their staff sometimes deign to employ consultants from other disciplines, to supply them with data which they then convert into economic terms, turning them into the cost:benefit ratios to form the basis for investment decisions.

I made three visits to Washington DC, the first while still at ICRAF and accompanied by Doreen. In Washington I was put into an apartment hotel (DoubleTree?), effectively a serviced apartment, in walking distance from the Bank building. The nearest supermarket to buy food was in the Watergate Building, site of the burglary which led to the impeachment of President Nixon. At weekends you could walk across the Potomac to the old sector, Georgetown. This included the Bioscope, a cinema showing early films, and it was there that I saw the best film ever, Jean Renoir's *The River*.

The first visit, in 1986, was for a training course in Land and Water Resources Management. "Well, fellas, someone's said that 'sustainability', which has become all the range, isn't just about economics, it's supposed to include looking after the soil (erosion, maybe) and water, so to please them we ought to brush up on these." As to whether my contribution was about soils or, more likely, telling them what agroforestry was, memory is hazy. The second, in 1992, was a short seminar on Managing the Fertility of African Soils.

FAO earlier had decided to try and determine land quality indicators, objective measurements (like soil organic matter) which might tell people how 'healthy' the land was. They held a meeting on this is 1993 – in August, not the best time for working in Rome, the regular staff took their annual holiday then, and remaining staff tended to crowd into the few rooms which, because of instruments or the like, were air conditioned.

Then the World Bank decided to have a go at it. By this time the Senior Agro-Ecologist was a Frenchman, Christian Pieri, distinguished in the area of tropical soils through work in the fearsome dry lands of French West Africa. A charming, intelligent and hard-working man, he came from Corsica (as did Napoleon). As the Bank didn't initially know much about it they got together a small group to cudgel away at land quality indicators. Presumably someone in FAO advised Christian that I was good for both pre-meeting preparation of papers and writing a report afterwards. There were some esoteric discussions on exactly what land quality indicators were, one senior American repeatedly saying, "Well, it's the quality of the land, isn't it?", which didn't do much to advance our objective of measuring this.

But don't let's worry about the professional side as I don't think the project got very far. During these sessions, Doreen was able to visit the excellent museums to be found in Washington, and learnt how to negotiate the metro. One day in the street an older couple stopped and asked her if she knew the way to Foggy Bottom. As this was a main tube – sorry, metro – junction, she was able to tell them. "Oh, do go on talking" said the lady, "I just love your accent".

The system for pricing food in the World Bank canteen is of interest. As in a normal buffet you take a tray and put the items selected on it. When you reach the till, quality is of no object; you place your tray on scales, and are charged by what it weighs.

Once more to Rome: it's LADA 2000-01

What do you do with a LADA? You climate.

No, not the notorious Russian Lada car, nor Latent Autoimmune Diabetes of Adulthood. This has to be the Land Degradation in Drylands project. The acronym doesn't work properly, but neither do later attempts to improve on it such as Land Degradation Assessment for Dryland Areas. Initially it wasn't meant to be confined to drylands but to be global in scope, but the funding came from some dryland-focused source. We got round this by defining drylands as almost anything bar steamingly humid rain forests.

FAO divided responsibility for planning it between the Soils Service and the Remote Sensing Unit. Unfortunately they chose the head of Remote Sensing, a Frenchman, to be Director – life for me, as lead consultant, would have been easier if Freddy Nachtergaele from Soils had been chosen.

There were two problems. One is that remote sensing experts tend to have only a limited knowledge of the real world. The other was that this was one of those individuals who are constantly changing their mind on what they want, usually when you have completed papers for an interim review meeting due to take place in a day or two's time.

There had been some FAO authorship contracts in 1999 and 2000, one co-authoring and editing *Land Resource Potential and Constraints*, which led to the establishment of FAO's TERRASTAT database (statistics on land use etc.). The LADA project became my last, and I think longest, FAO consultancy, preparing papers for the planning meeting, attending this, and afterwards assisting with report-writing. The period in Rome ran from November to December 2012, the nicest time to be in the city. After Christmas there was some editing from home ('editing' often means correcting foreign English).

A distinctive thing about LADA was that it was implemented, initially with about six countries (including China) saying they would take part. It appears to be still in operation (though people don't always delete obsolete web sites). It seems to have expanded and become GLADA where the G stands for Global. The fact that something actually got done makes a pleasing end to something like 25 FAO consultancies and meetings, since in I went there in 1973 at my own initiative to find out what the Soils Service did.

And for the honour only

After LADA my professional work was nearly all writing. Two lecture invitations came along. Rothamsted Research, England's national agricultural research station, invited me to deliver the 2010 Russell Lecture. This was quite an honour, which made up for the fact that there was no fee. I chose as the title, "The study of soils in the field: what is its role today?" The reception could be described as 'polite'. I could see a glazed look coming over the eyes of the audience, most of whom worked in laboratories and had not been down a soil pit since their undergraduate days. They didn't suggest I should prepare the lecture for publication.

In the same year I was asked to give the talk at the annual meeting of the Nyika-Vwaza Society, a non-profit organization which helps conservation in those two national parks in Malawi. It was held in the auditorium of the Royal Geographical Society, where I had spoken before. My title was, "Thin on the ground: land resource survey in Malawi and the Commonwealth". The reception could not have been more different from that at Rothamsted. I invited along every ex-Colonial soil surveyor I thought might be still alive, including one of my former students, Peter Goldsmith, who had made a career in soil survey. Two of the guests were notable. There was Hugh Brammer who, after a lifetime in soils survey and land evaluation in Ghana, Zambia and Bangladesh, at 80, was still living the only life he knew, work. Then I was overjoyed to meet the only woman soil surveyor in the Colonial Service, Helen Brash.[1] She had been recruited to Ghana by C. F. Charter, not the most likely person to favour a woman, who to her horror promised her parents she would be give a desk job and not allowed to go into the field. She persuaded him otherwise, and there is a regional survey in her name. After the first tour she married. This was too much for Charter – he preferred bachelors, on grounds that, "A married soil surveyor is half a surveyor". Helen became a geography teacher, first in Ghana and then in England. Chrysogon, Howard and Darryl were there, and in a blind-bid auction Chrys secured a painting of the Nyika that had been donated to the Society. They even published the talk.

It was a wonderful occasion, and a fitting end to a professional career that had begun in Malawi 52 years earlier.

Talking about the golden age of soil survey
With Maurice Purnell, Helen Brash, Hugh Brammer

---

[1]   Married name Helen Sandison.

18

SCRIBBLE, SCRIBBLE, SCRIBBLE

"Always scribble, scribble, scribble! Eh! Mr Gibbon?"
Boswell, referring to Decline and Fall of the Roman Empire

From beginning to end of my career I have been writing. My Publications List fails to record that this began with an article, *What man? No hat upon your head?* which appeared in the St Christopher School magazine for 1949 under the authorship of "M". The quotation is from Shakespeare, the (no doubt ludicrously funny) text refers to a school rule that those attending classes held out of doors in summer should wear a hat, and "M" refers to my non-existent middle name. To my surprise the *Old Scholars Notes* in 2012 reprinted this as being of interest, and in the subsequent issue I confessed to being the author.

An interval of about ten years ensued before the next publication, this time geographical: *Waiting for the rains* appeared in the the magazine of the Shef-field University Geographical Society. Written after my first year in Nyasa-land, it described how the temperature rises, the vegetation dies, and tempers become frayed in the build-up to the start of the rainy season.

From then on I have been writing throughout my life. In the earlier part this was based on my own research, surveys and consultancies. Later on, I guess it got around that I could write, and I was increasingly asked to take on work that was basically, "Read up what is known about such-and-such, and write a summary of it". In retirement this became largely of my own voli-tion, although a few professional requests trickled in up until 2014. But having got into the habit I couldn't stop writing – hence this book!

What good has this done anyone? Leonard Woolf is mainly known as the husband of Virginia Woolf, but he became a literary critic and devoted much time to the Fabian Society (early socialism) as their man on foreign affairs. In the last of his five volumes of autobiography he wrote, "Looking back at the age of eighty-eight over the fifty-seven years of my political work in England, knowing what I aimed at and the results, I see clearly that I achieved practically nothing…I must have in a long life ground through between 150,000 and 200,000 hours of perfectly useless work".

I cannot do it in hours. Say 7 books, 11 monographs, 3 books for schools and 130 papers, that works out at some 5000 pages or 250 000 words. But how long did it take to write a page? That varies enormously between, at one end of the scale, gathering together all that is known on a topic and synthesizing it, and at the other end reworking a previous paper – if you've written, say, "Agroforestry for soil conservation" it doesn't take much extra time to write, "AF for SC on vertisols" or "…in Zambia". So I can't do an estimate of hours spent writing. Suffice to say that much of my working life has been directed at publications, either as an account of the results of fieldwork or, in some cases, with the writing of summaries of knowledge as the primary objective.

How was it done? Nowadays everyone keeps references on a computerised database, and writes in a word processing package. Neither of these were available when I started.

For most of my career a my references went onto card index cards, with reduced abstracts written on them, subjects added, and a subject index made on larger cards. As computerised methods advanced I realised that this would be far more efficient, but to change over would have meant too much work. Also, keeping to index cards reduces the amount of screen-staring, so I stayed with them. When the time came for a clearout, by measuring the thickness I reckoned to throw out over 10 000 cards.

As word processing had not been thought of, I invented my own system. This was to write on one side of the paper, on alternate lines, and start each paragraph on a new sheet. In that way minor changes could be inserted on the blank lines, major insertions by a number leading to matter on the back, and the paragraphs could be shuffled. Some people take sabbaticals to write their books but I never had one. I am no good at working late into the night, unless it is a purely routine task (like the hand calculations for my PhD). Being an early bird I used to get up around 5.30-6.00, get the

Englishman's essential, a cup of tea, and fit in a writing session at my best time, before breakfast. Later of course I changed to word processing, with the invaluable fact that I had learnt touch typing as a boy. Even today, ask me where the letters are and I can't tell you – only my fingers know. Early on I read that you should decide who your intended readership are, and write what they need. Reviewers seems to appreciate the result of doing this.

Publications

Out of just over 150 publications, 25 were about the geomorphology of slopes, about 70 in the broad area of tropical soils and land resources, 55 on agroforestry (that's where there were some pot-boilers), and two, after retirement, on population. Let's look at them briefly, beginning with the seven 'heavies', the academic books[1].

Books

Slopes (1972). An outcome of the background reading for my PhD. This was in the days when you could hope to read everything that had been published on a subject – and often really read it, not just the abstracts. It is systematically arranged and clearly written, but being directed at an intended readership of geomorphology students, is hardly exciting. There are no jokes. Circulation 6000.

Tropical Soils and Soil Survey (1976) I think through the agency of my supervisor, Benny Farmer, Cambridge University Press asked for a book on tropical soils. Being a soil surveyor, not a laboratory boffin, I extended the title and focused on what people would find in the field. This is not a light-hearted text, but beneath each chapter heading was a quotation, supposed to show my erudition and sense of humour. Examples:

> Chapter 13 Soil Classification: "Scientists who are otherwise reasonable and unemotional are liable to behave quite differently when discussing this topic." (Mulcahy and Humphries, 1967)

> Chapter 19 Methods of Soil Survey: "And Moses sent them to spy out the land of Canaan, and go up into the mountain; and see the land what it is…whether it be good or bad…fat or lean". (Numbers xiii 17-20)

---

[1] Further information about my publications can be found at my website www.land-resources.com

Chapter 14 Problems of soil evolution: "Quand on ne disputait pas, l'ennui était excessif" (Unless you argue, life gets boring.) Voltaire, Candide.

Circulation 3500, of which 2000 in hardback.

Soil Survey and Land Evaluation (1981) This was written jointly with my UEA colleague David Dent, who was more familiar with temperate soils (he particularly studied soils of mangrove swamps having the natural advantage, when the tide came in, of being six foot seven inches tall). There is more original material here, as I had made improvements in methods of soil survey, and was one of the pioneers of land evaluation. Circulation 4200.

Agroforestry for Soil Conservation (1989). This was written as part of my work at ICRAF. When asking for it they were thinking that soil conservation meant erosion control, but I extended this to the equally or more important aspect of preservation of soil fertility. There were no royalties but sales were 2300, and in addition it was translated into French and Chinese.

Agroforestry for Soil Management (1997). After leaving ICRAF they asked me to write a revised edition of the preceding, but in fact much of it was rewritten so I changed the title. Not being on their payroll they said I could keep the royalties. For the first time in my books, this was largely based on abstracts. Circulation 2600.

Land Resources: Now and for the Future (1998). This was my major objective in retirement, to set out all I had learnt about soil survey, land evaluation, land use planning and policy. It's written readably, with some (relatively) light-hearted material. Circulation 4200, some of it in paperback and latterly ebook.

Doreen, who read everything through, censored the jokes, so you must go to the endnotes to find many of them. But this extract got into the text.

The economic value of soils can be illustrated by the following hypothetical conversation between a land sales agent and a purchaser:

"Here, Sir, is the piece of agricultural land you have bought for $5000, exactly one hectare."
"I see. Excellent climate, gently sloping, close to markets. But something looks wrong – there isn't any soil."

"I regret, Sir, that the previous owner took the soil with him. Very concerned about natural resources is Mr Coke."

"So to carry on my intended farming activities, I shall need to buy my own soil?"

"Anticipating your need, Sir, I have obtained quotations from suppliers. The market rate is about $10 per cubic metre."

"So to cover one hectare to a depth of one metre I shall need to pay, let me see... another $100 000?"

"Regrettably so, yes, Sir."

Thin on the Ground: Land Resource Survey in British Overseas Territories (2007). This was my own idea. There had been a golden age of soil survey in British colonies, in which I had taken a small part in Malawi. I wanted to put this on record, as an achievement of the Colonial service. Many of those who had taken part were still alive and I wrote to about 100 of them, asking for CVs, achievements and recollections, the last to include weird and wonderful happenings. It's my best book, objective achieved, and the most readable (the less serious recollections are grouped at the end of each chapter). But oh dear, the circulation! On the advice of an eminent soil scientist I chose as publishers The Memoir Club, and they produced an excellent book, well printed and illustrated. What I had not realised was that that publisher's name would lead people to think that this was recollections of an old Colonial, a genre which formed most of their output. After sales had reached 450 the publishers ran into financial problems, and I cannot currently get any information from them. But there you are: no-one can write it again, many of the respondents have passed away, so it stands as a record for the future.

The title *Thin on the Ground* owes its origin to a UEA student essay, which suggested an original way to improve soil fertility: "In the tropics, soil surveyors are often spread thinly over the ground".

Except for the last mentioned, the circulation figures are respectable for academic books. They pale into insignificance, however, before those of three books written for schools. When we had returned from Malawi a publisher approached us to write something for schools there. Doreen and I jointly wrote a very conventional textbook, *A Geography of Malawi*, which went through two revised editions, selling in all 93 000 copies. Then after a Geographical Society talk in Sheffield a local schoolmaster, Dennis Riley, approached and asked if I could supply photographs of tropical vegetation for a book he was writing. We combined and jointly wrote *World Vegetation* (1966), which ran to 83 000 sales. Finally, Doreen and I contributed to series of short school textbooks with *Slope Development*, two editions of which sold a more modest 20 000 copies.

Building on the success of *World Vegetation* a long-standing friend at the University of Swansea, Mike Bridges, produced *World Soils*, which I suspect well exceeded my sales figures. Later on a publisher asked a Norwich schoolmaster, David Wright, to organize an atlas for British primary schools; I don't know the sales figures but they would have been at least an order of magnitude higher than mine. The Ian Fleming of academic text-books is D. G. Mackean's *Introduction to Biology* (1964), continually updated for 50 years, and with sales that must run into millions.

Monographs

Grouped under this heading are a range of publications shorter than books but longer than journal articles. They comprise:

- Nine reports of soil surveys. These begin with the two maps and supporting monographs on the surveys of Northern and Central Malawi, and later include the Jengka Triangle project survey for a consultant company, Hunting Technical Services. Only nine survey reports, when I call myself a soil surveyor? But only totally dedic-ated souls spend their whole working lives getting into soil pits. Most try to get out of these (literally and metaphorically) and move into something else – in my case land evaluation, land use planning, and land resources policy.

- Fourteen reports for FAO, some arising out of conferences, others commissioned by them in authorship contracts. ("UNEP wants this damned report, who can we get to write it?" "Ask Young, he churns out anything".) Some appear as jointly authored, that is to say FAO printed them as their output, acknowledging in introduction that I had written most of it. The one I am most proud of, *A Framework for Land Evaluation* (1976) is an honourable exception to this, written jointly with Robert Brinkman.

- Four reports for other organizations, including the World Bank.

Journal articles

Getting papers published by refereed international journals are the very stuff of academia, the means of career advancement. Lip service is paid to your contributions to teaching, but everyone knows it's the publications list that counts with appointment committees. I had 130 of these; the mind boggles when one thinks of the effort involved in just one. The topics moved with time from the geomorphology of slopes, through soil survey and land evaluation, into the post-1983 ones on agroforestry.

The first was *Scree profiles in West Norway* (1956), only short but which did make a substantive contribution to knowledge (abstract in Chapter 7). The last (to date), *Land resource survey in Malawi and the Commonwealth* (2010), the outcome of a talk given to a charitable organization, the Nyika-Vwaza Trust.

The article which, like Martin Luther, I would like to nail to the doors of FAO, the World Bank, and aid organizations, is *Poverty, hunger and population policy* (*Geographical Journal* 2005). It took the best part of a year, off and on, to write; but clearly, from subsequent attitudes to population growth, its impact has been minimal. If the United Nations population body, UNFPA, the British organization Population Matters, and people as respected as David Attenborough cannot influence population policy, what hope have I got? Politicians simply will not touch it.

Number of publications is a very poor measure of contribution to knowledge. Granting this, it is possible that in simple numbers of publications I was the most prolific author on three appointments: Sussex Geography Department, East Anglia Environmental Sciences, and certainly at ICRAF.

And what about climatic change, doesn't everyone write about it? "But Young" you say, "You're not a climatologist, and you've never published anything on it". True, but in the first place, climatic change concerns the whole of the physical environment and its interactions with humanity, and hence lies at the core of geography and environmental science. Secondly, I have the capacity (not always seen among those who write about this subject) of looking at evidence and arriving at conclusions impartially. I attended two of the earliest conferences on the global carbon cycle.

So here, very briefly, is my previously unpublished article on the subject.

A mantra for climatic change

'Global warming', a rise in mean global temperatures, took place from 1910 to 1940, then again from 1975 to 1998. From then until 2015 there has been no significant trend, upward or downward, in global temperatures. Look for yourself at the data.[1]

Measurements of atmospheric carbon dioxide were only made from 1958, when Dave Keeling set up a measurement site on a high volcano in Hawaii (after some difficulty in securing funding).[2] It is highly likely, however, that the atmospheric concentration has been rising since the industrial revolution.

So it was observed that from 1975 to 1998 the atmospheric concentration of also carbon dioxide steadily rose, and so did mean global temperatures. Scientists know that a correlation between two sets of data does not necessarily mean cause and effect. However, once the correlation *for this period* was pointed out, the Intergovernmental Panel on Climate Change was set up, and we had much talk of global warming. The media and politicians jumped on the bandwagon, and to this day political correctness requires that one should accept it. People who question it may be blackballed.

Problem: the concentration of carbon dioxide, and other greenhouse gases, has continued to rise at an unchanged rate to this day, but global temperatures have shown no further significant rise. Once this slowly came to be realised, activists had to switch from 'global warming' to 'climatic change'.

Climate is not constant. It changes, not only over geological time but over the historic period. Think of the medieval warm period, with vineyards at monasteries, or the very cold winters when the Thames froze over which so impressed Charles Dickens. You can read about these changes in the book by Hubert Lamb, founder of UEA's Climatic Research Unit, *Climate, History and the Modern World* (1982).

---

[1] www.cru.uea.ac.uk

[2] Keeling's say-so when I met him at a conference on the global carbon cycle at Wood's Hole, Massachusetts in 1970.

There are many causes of climate change. Human activity, through coal-fired power stations and other industry (and keeping cows) is just one. Even if the obvious measure of reducing carbon dioxide emissions were to succeed (which is unlikely), that would not remove the other causes.

Most accounts refer only to the possible negative effects of climatic change. There are also positive effects: higher atmospheric carbon dioxide stimulates plant growth, and thus crop yields and forest growth, higher temperatures reduce heating costs.

So here is a mantra for climatic change, to be recited by all concerned with this vitally important subject:

- **The climate has always changed.**

- **It will go on changing.**

- **And nothing that politicians can do will stop it.**

It follows that investment funds are best directed not at trying to stop climatic change, but at mitigating its negative effects and taking advantage of its positive effects.

Writing Land Resources I: Cornell, Guelph and San Francisco 1995-96

The Leverhulme Emeritus Fellowship is intended for academics when they retire to gather together their accumulated wisdom. I applied for this and got it, very likely with the help of Dennis Greenland FRS, a good friend who has long supported my work. This was for travel and expenses to write the land resources book.

I intended to spend six weeks at Cornell University, Ithaca, New York, which has Departments of Natural Resources and related fields, although as usual I actually chose it through a personal contact with a friend met at FAO. So in April 1995 Doreen and I rented an apartment and I started making staff contacts, discovered that to get food in America, say a lunch sandwich, you have to answer a string of questions (white or brown, butter or mayo...), and found that the town centre was almost dead, killed by supermarkets. Discovered that Cornell, like other Ivy League universities, had a large intake of Chinese students. Gave a lecture on agroforestry (there was a fee for this, and it had taken a massive effort at the American Embassy in London to obtain a visa for paid employment). We saw a production of *She stoops to conquer,* their attempts at English accents being so excruciating that we left at the interval. At the weekend we drove into the Finger Lakes region of upstate New York, found a small museum which had photographs pre-dating the invention of photography, and took lunch at a diner which illustrated the mathematical concept of infinity: no matter how much food you removed from your plate, the size of the remainder was unchanged.

Then after a week there was a phone call from Chrysogon: my father had died. He had for long suffered from high blood pressure, so it was no surprise that at the age of 94 years and 11 months he had an aortic aneurysm (a burst in the big artery which takes blood from the heart). He was at the Abbeyfield home in Richmond where he had been living for many years, felt bad, was taken to hospital, and died the same night. Chrysogon, bless her, sat by him all the time. She was able to explain that we were in America, and he said that we were not to return.

But of course we did. There was the death certificate to obtain, and then his room to clear up, not a big task as he had already got rid of so much. Being a tax lawyer, Dad had taken steps to provide for his own care during his life-time and then avoid paying any inheritance tax on his death. So that was, sadly and regrettably, the end of our time at Cornell.

That left the rest of the Leverhulme Fellowship, and the following year we set off on a two-stop American visit. The first was two weeks in Guelph, Ontario, which for many years had had a Department of Natural Resources, one of the earliest universities to do so. Arriving in mid-February it was of course, like much of America in winter, covered in snow. We lodged in a private house, which offered Canadian breakfast, which I recall as something like savoury pancakes with sausage, maple syrup and jam. Given snow boots it was an easy walk to the university, passing the junction of Norwich Road with Norfolk Avenue and the Wymondham shopping centre – East Anglians must have settled there at an early date. For leisure it offered a cinema that was also a bookshop and café. At the weekend we drove to Niagara Falls, a spectacular site as it was all frozen, huge stalagmites of ice had built up. A restaurant lunch in Niagara turned out to be basically potato chips (British meaning) on thick bread, hardly a balanced meal.

The final part of this whistle-stop tour was at the Stanford University, California. The objective was to meet Paul Ehrlich, who had written *The Population Bomb* and *The Population Explosion*, a fellow spirit in his view that world problems of hunger, poverty and environment couldn't be solved without checking population increase. Stanford is a top university, on a level with the American Ivy League, but that is not its only distinction. If Stanford students and alumni had competed as a nation in the 1992 Olympic Games they would have come ninth in the world; having Carl Lewis was a good start. They have a high grade shopping centre on campus too.

I went straight to Paul Ehrlich's secretary who said yes, he was very environmentally conscious, he lived nearby and came to work by bicycle. So could I arrange to see him? Not at the moment. Professor Ehrlich was currently guiding a world tour of alumni, using up rather more in aeroengine fuel than the consumption of his bicycle. Doubtless at the end he would be collecting their tax-deductible cheques.

It was a useful time for meeting and talking to a range of their staff, though only Ehrlich on the last day. We used the bus to travel about, though found that by and large buses were only used by those of a lower station to us, Mexicans and poor whites. One woman got on dragging a large trolley load, which she announced was all the possessions from her house: if she left them behind they would go. I liked the display in buses of icons with red lines through them, indicating that there was to be no smoking, no spitting, and no shooting people.

A bonus came when we went to San Francisco, by rail with double-decker carriages. One was advised not to walk from the railway station to the city centre as the streets between were not safe. On the spur of the moment we got tickets hard to get in London, for *Phantom of the Opera*.

Writing Land Resources II: Bellagio 1995

I had assembled material for the Land Resources book without yet writing anything. Opportunity to do this came from getting a Rockefeller Fellowship, so I became a Rockefeller Feller. These were to give four weeks time, uninterrupted by teaching or administration, to academics who had a book or paper to write. You stayed in a villa at Bellagio on the shores of Lake Como, the villa itself on a hilltop surrounded by a terraced garden. Spouses were included. The standard of accommodation was higher than any hotel in which we have been. Doreen was particularly taken by the provision of about six towels each, changed daily. Lunch was a simple pasta, so as not to interrupt your writing, but dinner a full Italian meal with best wines. One did *not* go off to Venice or elsewhere at weekends, though we did manage a boat across the lake. In the evenings my efforts at piano sight-reading were popular in singalongs, through availability of a pile of music by Irving Berlin, Jerome Kern and the like. There were also international games of scrabble, including American spellings.

There were other Fellows of interest. They liked to have the arts represented and we had a composer and an artist. The composer was Canadian, Linda Bouchard, who by now has a substantial string of compositions to her credit. I remember her remarking, "When I started to get into music I went to the works of the great composers, and discovered they were mostly male, white, and dead". At her presentation she played recordings of her works adding, "Now you'll know how to recognize my stuff, it goes da-da-da-da da-da-da-da." Which is true: the Internet comments, "Her music is characterized by timbral explorations and percussive explosions" – meaning it goes da-da-da-da… BANG!). You can listen to her stuff on YouTube.

The artist was an elderly Hungarian, Josef Brezney. Aged 79 at that time, he was to die in 2012. His project seemed to be to take some early religious picture and disaggregate it into tiny squares, the same number in each colour as the original but reassembled in a square at the top. I am not clear what this showed. He held a sale of his works and we bought two, one a watercolour of Lake Como painted during his time with us.

The rest were academics, most of them American. One was researching on managerial adaptability. What this meant was that American companies had found that some of their executives who did a good job at home found difficulty adapting to conditions in foreign companies – they would fly in their own loaves of bread, or something like that. They wanted to know if they could separate the good from the bad adapters before posting them overseas, so as not to send the latter. The funding must surely have come from the companies – his research grant was 1½ million dollars.

Most notable was Dan Schorr, journalist and broadcaster. He was to die in 2010 and his *Times* obituary begins, "Daniel Schorr was the bane of American presidents, the FBI, the CIA, the Kremlin and, at times, his own bosses". During the Watergate scandal, when handed a copy of Nixon's notorious 'enemies list' he began reading aloud the top 20, only to discover his own name at number 17. "I broke into a big sweat," he later wrote, "This was the most electrifying moment of my career…a greater tribute than the Emmy list" (he had received three Emmy awards for his coverage of Watergate for CBS News). In 1975 he revealed to CBS that the CIA had attempted to assassinate Fidel Castro, Patrice Lumumba (the Congo Prime Minister) and other Third World leaders, but failed, "Albeit not for want of trying". Knowing his family had come from Russia, I asked about his name. His parents were Russian-Jewish emigres, coming to New York some time before 1916. His father arrived at the immigration desk and was asked his name. "Gedaliah Tschornemoretz". "Spell that." "S-C-H-O-R-…" "OK, OK bud, Schorr, you're in."

Dan was Moscow correspondent for a time, during which he became a personal friend of President Kruschev. He told us the following story. Once he said to the President, "Mr Kruschev, I understand you may summon a meeting of the Central Committee of the Communist Party. I was about to take a holiday by the Black Sea, should I postpone it?" Kruschev thought for a moment before replying, "Mr Schorr, you take your holiday; and if *absolutely necessary* I will postpone the meeting of the Party". Dan was a great guy. I once remarked to him, how difficult it must be to compress summaries of a news topic into the five minutes of a radio slot. "Five minutes?" he replied, "I was given two." It was during his fellowship that he started on his book, *Staying Tuned: a Life in Journalism.* Possibly he is the most eminent person whom we can say we got to know.

Clearly I couldn't write a book in three weeks. What I was able to do was to decide what would be the 15 or so chapters, and write summaries of what each would contain. This gave a flying start to long hours spent in the study, followed later by proof-reading and the boring but important task of indexing.

Wives (partners, spouses) were encouraged to have their own projects, and Doreen's was to sort, date and list all the letters we had written to our parents from abroad. The biggest packs were from Nyasaland, nearly all on aerograms, which without telephone connection was the only means of communication. On our foresighted requests, both our mothers kept all of these.

All things considered, the spell in Bellagio was the most enjoyable time of any during retirement.

Did all this do anyone any good?

So after all this writing, have I finished up as cynical as Leonard Woolf? To look at the positives:

- The books all met with favourable reviews, often highly so. It has to be said, however, that most of these were written by colleagues, friends and in some cases former students. Except for *Thin on the Ground* the sales were acceptable for academic works.

- For the monographs, having co-authored *A Framework for Land Evaluation*, FAO kept coming back and asking for more. At a nominal $100 a day, what had they to lose?

- With one single exception, and ill-advised submission right at the start, every single paper that I submitted was accepted for publication. How common is this?

A negative side is that although good at writing, I am not good at persuading people to do what I want them to. Some senior academics go on lecture tours, getting institutions like the Royal Society to let them hold forth. I lack this authority and persuasiveness, so have to operate not by the verbal sword but by the pen. We've already looked at the knotty question of whether anyone makes use of soil surveys. Did my attempts to improve methods of soil survey, looking at crop yields or other measures of performance at the same time as mapping soils, persuade institutions and surveyors to change their ways? You'll have to ask them.

One apparent success was the campaign to cast doubt on the amount of 'spare land' which FAO said was available for agriculture (Chapter 12). In their major overview *World Agriculture 2010* they still quote their own data but concede that, "Doubts have been cast on these in some quarters". I am honoured to be considered a quarter.

The big non-success was trying to get institutions and governments to appreciate the massive negative influence of population increase, but then the same fate has befallen the efforts of even major institutions. If people who have the ear of the media like David Attenborough cannot bring about a change in attitudes, it is no wonder that I can't.

19

GEOGRAPHERS SEEING THE WORLD
1997-2007

Two jobs, the Colonial Service and ICRAF, together with many consultancies, had taken me to a good many countries, to some of which Doreen had come too. This was the best sort of travel, having a built-in contact with the local people, both government officials and farmers. It makes conventional tourism dull by comparison. I had even managed to fit in a round-the-world trip from Nairobi when attending the World Soils Congress in Japan. There were also three returns to Nairobi, house-warming (looking after houses for the Dods and the Pickerings whilst they were on leave) and playing golf. I don't know my country count by then but it must have been over 70. By now, leisure travel has taken it to 81.

Why did we want to travel any more? Basically because we were geographers, and didn't think much of sun, sea and sand. So we took our first long-haul holiday, much enjoyed it, and embarked upon seven more.

Round-the-world I: Australia, New Zealand, Tahiti, California 1998

An ambitious trip to start with, eight weeks and four countries. The main objective in Australia was the Great Barrier Reef, being advised to avoid Cairns so driving up to Port Douglas. Seeking to get rid of jet lag by sunshine we went straight onto a lounger around the hotel pool. "I see you're from Norwich" came a voice. We were carrying our oddments in a John Lewis bag.

Going on a small tourist boat out onto the reef, we were grateful for Callum Cheatle's tuition in scuba diving. There was a safety instruction. From the boat they call out on a loudspeaker from time to time, "Are you alright?" The reply is, if you are OK, hold one arm up in the air; if you are not, wave both. Everyone who has done it, and many more who have seen it on television, knows how magnificent are the colours of the fish on a coral reef. I was far from happy on seeing below me a giant clam, supposing that if I touched it it would slam shut – could this happen, I don't know? The lady in charge told us that Gordon Brown, Labour Party number two (later to become Prime Minister) had come with his friends and hired the entire boat.

Down to Melbourne, stayed with Doreen's college friend Norma Pigott whose husband Colin had, not professionally but as a hobby, become the leading authority on migration of Australian sea birds – they fly to Siberia to breed.[1] On to New Zealand, North Island magnificent: volcanoes, hot springs, and the town of Napier, flattened by an earthquake in 1931 and rebuilt in Art Deco style. South Island had one idyllic spot, Wanaka, where we could have stayed much longer in the wooden guest house huts. The mountainous west coast was disappointing, most of the potential scenic views hidden by tall forest. New Zealand was delightfully old-fashioned, and with long distances between settlements. I can see why, if you grow up there and are ambitious, you become a leading rugby player, soprano or detective story writer: anything to get out.

Next stop Tahiti, too hot and humid, with no air conditioning in our hotel. Doreen liked it but for me the only place to be was in the ocean.

Over to California, to meet my school friend John Manson and his partner in Santa Barbara. We flew from Los Angeles via Phoenix to Flagstaff, the take-off point for the Grand Canyon. After a night in a less than top class hotel, the first morning there was brilliant sunshine, giving us the true glory of this magnificent natural spectacle. Photographs and film cannot match the sheer scale of the views. The next morning we woke up to a blanket of snow. It was misty too so the views weren't great, and we went to an Imax film of canoeing down the gorge.

The following day we had to fly back to LA. First leg, Flagstaff to Phoenix, was on a small plane. It was snowing. The snow piled up on the wings,

---

[1]   Recent tracking by radio collars has shown that some birds remain on the wing, over ocean, for up to 7 days.

which prevented takeoff. A man with a hosepipe was attempting, in a desultory manner, to remove this snow; but as soon as he cleared it from one wing, another layer had accumulated on the other. We watched with some anxiety as failure to take this short flight would mean we would miss our prepaid connection from LA to UK. Eventually the rate of snowfall eased off enough to satisfy safety regulations and we were off, reaching home as planned. A great trip which left us keen to try more.

John Manson

Like my other best friend at school, Leon Fish, John Manson also had something of a tough time in life. His father died when he was nine. His mother, Simone, Belgian, taught French at St Christopher, and John had the longest time as a pupil at the school, from Montessouri at 2½ to sixth form at 17. Like Leon and me, he was mad keen on sport.

When he was 17 his mother took it into her head to go out to California to follow Krishnamurti, a way-out thinker, theosophist possibly (one found that sort of thing in Letchworth). She took her children with her. Then one day she went for a walk in the Sierra Nevada and disappeared, just never returned, nor was a body found. So there were John and his brother and sister, still at school, in a strange country with no parents.

I think John got a job as washer up in a restaurant. By good fortune this was owned by a husband and wife of great goodwill, who more or less adopted him (we met them when he took us to dinner there on our visit). He got to the University of California where, besides academic success, he was the leading goal-scorer in their football (soccer) team. He worked his way through college by acting as a golf caddy: no trolleys, one caddy for two players, two heavy bags, "It was hard work". On graduation he got a job with the General Telephone Company, remaining there for his working life. He negotiated compensation with landowners who would be affected by telephone works, a surprising job for a non-American.

John never lost the keen interest in sport which we began when at school. He went to ten of the twelve athletics days at the 1948 London Olympics, one of them with me. Although long since an American citizen he avidly supports British sportsmen – athletics, tennis, golf – and we exchange emails. He refereed high school soccer games, common in California, until the age of 80 at least.

Malawi 40 years on 1999

My first tour in the Colonial Service, as Soil Surveyor, Nyasaland (soon to become Malawi) began in December 1958 and ended somewhat over three years later in February 1962. Mostly through ICRAF I had made seven further visits up to 1989. It seemed interesting to return and do a 40-years-on tour of the country in January-February 1999.

There was a professional objective. I was by then deeply involved with the 'spare land' controversy, refuting the received view that one way to solve food shortages was to take previously uncultivated land into agriculture. Malawi was a prime example of a country that was supposed to have such unused land. When we arrived in 1958 the population was three million. By 1999 it was close to ten million and farms were desperately small, 48% of them less than half a hectare. Driving along roads familiar from my soil survey work in all three Provinces, Northern, Central and Southern, the effects of this were striking. Previously one would pass through empty bush for long stretches between settlements. Now it was rare to be in a spot where there were not fields, huts, or people on the road. I worked this up into an article, basically arguing that the only long-term solution to Malawi's problems was to check population increase.[1]

There was a second, more personal, aim, to take photos (colour slides) from the same viewpoints as those we had taken before, to see how the vegetation, agriculture and people had changed. This didn't come off very well; the rainy season was late so skies were often cloudy.

As a holiday trip it was fine. Starting from Zomba where we had lived before, we stayed in the hotel on Zomba Mountain. But when you said you were going for a walk on the plateau you were required to take a security guard; Africans walking up to collect firewood (illegally) could not be trusted. In Zomba itself as soon as they found that I was Young of 'Young and Brown' (the soil survey) we were welcomed with open arms. Doreen, who had formerly worked in the Education Department, was shown around

---

[1]   Malawi 1959-1999 – a 40-year perspective. *Newsletter of the Tropical Agriculture Association*, September 1999, 20-22.

it. Our former house had become the Statistics Department. We drove north as far as a small hotel on the Lake Shore near Nkhata Bay (it had acquired an 'h').

That was Malawi at the beginning of 1999. This was referred to as the last year of the millennium. Certain pedants pointed out that as there was no year Zero, this should have been 2000, but no-one listened. My school friend Philip Drazin (Maths Prof at Bristol) booked himself onto a small island east of New Zealand so that he could be the first to see in the new millennium.[1] Computers were supposed to crash, because up to then they had recorded dates as two year digits only, e.g. 20/07/99. This potential disaster passed without serious effects.

The list, "Where did we go on holiday?" then says March, New York (opera and a musical); July, Yzeures-sur-Creuse; October, Wexford opera festival. Yzeures-sur-Creuse was the birthplace of the coloratura soprano Mado Robin, and there was a small museum to her there. Quite a year for us.

In September I broke a femur, clearing out gutters on a lean-to ladder which slipped on the patio during rain, taking my feet with it. Doreen was out, I couldn't move, but summoned up my best singing voice to cry, "Help!" Before passers-by came to my aid Doreen came home and rang for an ambulance. A young man on a bicycle arrived, giving the impression that the NHS had gone over to Viet Nam's version of an ambulance, a stretcher slung between two bicycles. However he proved to be the advance guard, phoning the ambulance service to report how near to death's door the patient was.

Another US trip planned for September had to be cancelled, so no long-haul trips that year. Oh, we did go to Cornwall (the holiday list says, "post-AY prostate op."), our last French course at Fondevielle, and Doreen joined me in Rome for an FAO consultancy, spread over November-December so she became an expert on the antiquities, churches and art.

---

[1]   Philip liked to be present for astronomical events. Some time ago he had booked himself into a Cornish hotel years in advance in order to view a total eclipse of the sun.

Utah and western national parks 2001

We hit on the national parks of Utah as the next objective. Flying to Denver, Colorado, there was opportunity to meet my cousin Richard who is a year older than me. I don't know what training he had to get into the safety line, but he got a job as Safety Officer with a bauxite mining company in Jamaica, work which must have been of considerable responsibility. There he met and married Phillippa, a Jamaican from several generations of mixed parentage. Phillippa is an artist in silks, designing wonderful scarves and the like.

When politics rendered Jamaica a chancy place to be, I think Richard's next job was in oil shale mining in western USA. From there he moved to become Safety Officer for San Francisco Airport, responsible for safety on the ground, not in the air. On retirement they found that San Francisco was an expensive place to live and moved to Cheyenne, Wyoming, from where they drove down to meet us in Denver.

When hiring a car in a strange country the first stages are manic: how to get out of the airport and find your way to the road you want, not knowing the signage system, the US practice of overtaking on the inside, and getting used to left-hand drive – Doreen was for ever screaming that I was in the middle of the road. Also there were no hotels on the highway, so we had to dive off on spec to find an hotel for the night.

Utah has at least four national parks, all with superb scenery and good opportunities for walking. The first and finest was Arches, where you find natural stone arches. There was one place where you could walk up a moderately strenuous path to see the best of these. On reaching to top Doreen noticed that nearly everyone else was considerably younger than us. At one point there was some kind of stone ledge, and a young couple politely put out a hand to help us across. The following exchange ensued. "May I enquire how old you are?" I gave my usual reply, "Well, I'm pushing 70, but (wink) my wife is younger". "Gee – may I take your photograph?" So Doreen and I are now a US National Monument.

On to Colorado and Nevada, seeing for real the pediment landscapes that had constituted an important part of our geographical (geomorphological) education. Cheapest hotel room? Las Vegas, something like $35 – they expect you to play their machines. Finally the Grand Canyon again, this time from the north side. We managed to descend on a path about 1500 feet before the prospect of the steep return climb made it wiser to turn back.

Anything else that year? Well, there was Corsica, Helsinki, and Copenhagen in December, the last two for opera. At the latter it was Rossini's *Il viaggio a Reims:* no plot to speak of (some travellers on the way to Reims stop and sing to each other) but reams (sorry!) of magnificent arias, most leading to an extended Rossini crescendo – it's not often performed because it calls for nine top-class soloists.

Round-the-world II: across Australia, Tasmania, Fiji 2002

I can see how some people like Australia, open spaces, plenty of sunshine. Two of our friends have settled there, my cousin Valentine in Sydney, and Doreen's college friend Pat Minton in Melbourne. A drawback is the large distances between somewhere and anywhere else. Nowhere is this more so than when the somewhere is Perth. The train to Sydney, the Indian-Pacific, takes three days. The distance is over 2000 miles, which would get you from London not only to Moscow but half way to the Ural Mountains as well.

First stage Western Australia – or rather, Perth and its immediate environs, since Western Australia is ten times the area of UK. Perth is a lovely city, easy to get around, and we came across a brilliant street pianist who could play anything you asked; I tried a Billy Mayerl which he rattled off, after-wards agreeing it was difficult (it's full of consecutive fourths). Went to see a colleague from the golden age of soil survey, Cliff Ollier, Bristol Geography degree, who then masterminded the first national soil survey in Africa, that of Uganda (1959-62). Cliff left soils for his first love, geomorphology, with excursions into anthropology. After I had got the low-down on the Uganda survey for my book, Doreen asked him, "Cliff, what do you do when you are not working, what are your hobbies?" "Well, you could say they are my work. I'm just so fortunate that people pay me to do what I enjoy doing."[1]

Spent a week driving around the south-west corner of Western Australia, scenery beautiful but nothing spectacular; some dolphins put on a display for us swimming along the beach and back. I like the restaurant practice that you order and pay at the counter first. I think it was there that we were in a

---

[1] I later got the same reply from the doyen of soil survey, Hugh Brammer.

restaurant and asked the waiter what were traditional Australian dishes. He was delighted at this interest by two pommies, and got the chef to serve us (off the menu) kangaroo and crocodile.

Next onto the Indian-Pacific railway (it connects the two oceans). A cabin with bunk beds, then you walk along the corridor to a lounge and dining area. At meals we met a retired soldier and his wife. A surprise was that this shortish, softly spoken, and most charming person proved to be a regimental sergeant major. The train rumbled along, jogging you to sleep at night, with daytime stops where you could roam about (not forgetting the departure time). One was at an abandoned mining camp in bleak semi-desert, where a notice remained announcing a nine-hole golf course.

Sydney: failure to adapt to the local environment

The centre of Sydney is a wonderful area, spread around the vast harbour. Captain Cook remarked that it would accommodate all the world's navies, and for the millennium year something like that was there, headed by the aircraft carrier Ark Royal. We were guests of my cousin Valentine and his Australian wife Helen. The youngest of Uncle Edward's three boys, Valentine, made a career and a life in Sydney, and through his daughter Joanna is now populating Australia with, at the time of writing, four Young descendants, by marriage called O'Brien.

Tasmania next stop, staying in heritage guest houses. It is unusual in still having mixed agriculture, crops and livestock on the same farm. Harrowing tales of the early treatment of transported convicts. The Tasmanian Aboriginals were made extinct by some combination of European diseases, war and something like genocide, possibly also it was said by the those remaining, on being confined to a camp, just choosing not to have children (seems unlikely).

Home via Fiji, Doreen loves hot tropical islands. I have an abiding memory of the hotel breakfast, one of those huge buffet help-yourself systems which I love, guests drifting around, sudden sallies at the toaster to seize what they might or might not have put in. The Australians had a glazed look in their eyes, vainly searching for vegemite, their version of marmite. Its absence being reported, the Royal Australian Air Force saved the situation by flying in emergency supplies.

And so eastwards across the Pacific to complete our second round-the-world trip.

ICRAF's 25th anniversary, Nairobi, and on to the Garden Route in South Africa 2003

The International Council for Research in Agroforestry (ICRAF) had been founded in 1978 on the instigation of a Canadian who invented the term. The founding staff, all 12 of us, were invited but without financial support. Disappointingly (but not surprisingly), apart from my Director-General Bjorn Lundgren (and I expect they paid for him) I was the only one to attend. It was good to see our little band, starting on the fifth floor of a city-centre building, had expanded to a fully-fledged member of the international agricultural research community. I made a short speech, saying that four things I had urged upon them had been accomplished: the change of 'Council' to 'Centre'; changing the old logo which looked like an arrow falling into a fir tree into something which could be Acacia trees in a farmer's field; abandoning the former over-emphasis on alley cropping; and importantly, bringing in more foresters and more hard experimental science – a change of emphasis assisted by my departure.

Having got across the equator we went on to South Africa, from Capetown along the Garden Route, getting some golf in on the way (with caddies again!). Motoring on the main coastal road was somewhat different from at home: if a car comes up behind you pull over onto the reservation.

New England 2004

The New England trip had been planned for 2003, but on the train to London I got an attack of atrial fibrillation. After an emergency debate on the platform we boarded the same train back to Norwich. The rearranged trip had to be a year later as tourism in New England is based on 'leaf peeping', viewing the spectacular autumn colours – though our Virginia creeper in the garden is just as fine. In Boston the main street we walked along had an odd arrangement of shops being sunk below pavement, sorry sidewalk, level, most of them nail parlours and restaurants.

On to a circular tour clockwise around four of the six states of New England. West across Massachusetts to see the Clark Art Gallery in Lincoln, north through Vermont to Burlington, on the eastern shore of one of the 'finger lakes' of New York (they are glaciated valleys), east across New Hampshire, then just the south-west corner of Maine. Memory doesn't bring up much apart from the trees, my diary is as usual when abroad completely blank, so you'll have to go to Doreen's journal for anything more.

North Island New Zealand with Hong Kong 2005

This trip started with a surprise. Needing to change planes, we gave ourselves a day in Hong Kong. By an amazing piece of serendipity this turned out to be Chinese New Year, experience from Singapore having shown that this was more or less the only day when they don't work. The main activity in the morning was for small groups of young girls to gather and sit around on the pavement talking, one of them having brought noodles and the like in those stacked tins the Chinese use to carry food. In the afternoon we were promised a procession, so cameras at the ready. Well, yes, there was, lanterns and dragons and the like, although all very organized, with police hovering about, not at all like Notting Hill or Rio.

Tongariro National Park

On the previous visit to New Zealand we had guessed wrongly, allotting one week to North Island and two to the less interesting South Island, so this time we stuck to the former. Auckland came as a surprise, streets full of Chinese. Met two of my school friends from St Christopher, Oliver Barton and his sister. Oliver had made a career there as a motor engineer, largely with a local bus company.

The motels are cheap, friendly and frequent. It's a long way from one place to another in New Zealand, and there was a problem driving. Large areas had what geomorphologists call feral relief (meaning wild), steep valleys running one into the other. Roads across these areas were necessarily a continuous succession of bends, so much so that I became dizzy and sick, and had to rest before going on.

First highlight was the central hot springs area, Rotorua. There was a spa area with a range of pools of different temperatures, you could move between them at will. After a long walk in Tongariro National Park we reached a volcano, finding there was a chairlift to take you up the lower slopes. It was late afternoon by the time we took this, and walking upwards regrettably had to turn back before reaching the rim of the smoking caldera. Also fitted in Mount Egmont in the south-east, and Ninety-Mile Beach in the northern peninsula. Then there was a small forested national park with a map showing walks of a modest two or three kilometres. What it didn't show was that most of these paths were some thirty degrees steep. This time we didn't attempt a westward Pacific route for the return.

World Congress of Soil Science, Philadelphia 2006

Our holiday together in 2006 was a modest week's trip to Brittany, crossing from Portsmouth. Viewed the 'calvary', stone carvings of the crucifixion, a form of Breton art found on many of the churches. The Monts d'Arrée were hard to detect, so we just enjoyed the village atmosphere, language and meals.

In July I had been asked to be chairman for a session devoted to soil survey in the History of Soil Science section at the World Congress of Soil Science held in Philadelphia. By now lacking any institutional connection there was no chance of financial support, but I went along out of obligation and hoping to pick up material for my book on soil survey in the tropics. The conference hall was a cavernous place, converted from the abandoned rail terminus. Concurrently it was also hosting the conference of American chefs, well-built individuals in full white cooks' uniforms including tall hats. No big deal, but I did learn of an early study by the US Soil Bureau (as it was then), a 16-km wide north-south transect of Puerto Rico in 1902 – one year later than the earliest tropical soil survey, by the Dutch in the East Indies. Owing to a stomach bug I had to drop out of their mid-conference field trip, but was told by former UEA colleague David Dent that it was no great shakes. So thus ended, I can confidently say, my international conferences.

Australia: Northern Territory, The Ghan, Adelaide and Kangaroo Island 2007

Having crossed Australia from west to east by the Indian-Pacific it seemed worth while to do it from north to south from Darwin to Adelaide. This was by means of another early railway, the Ghan.

There was an aspect of this region of great interest in the history of soil survey. It arose out of the use of air photographs for reconnaissance during the war. Three organizations independently realised that these supplied a way of surveying which was far more efficient than conventional ground-based studies. At the time the Australian government was worried about the lack of use of their 'empty' lands in the North and Centre, and embarked upon a series of surveys to discover their potential, carried out by CSIRO Australia.[1] They started by mapping what could be seen from the air, mainly landforms. Having drawn boundaries in this way, then sallied off in landrovers to find out what these enclosed – soils, vegetation, and what land use there was. This became known as the land systems approach. The first of the Australian studies was Survey of the Katherine-Darwin region 1946 (not published until 1953). It was to be followed by a series of surveys, covering vast areas of northern Australia and also extended to Papua New Guinea. In the ensuing years it was widely adopted for surveys at reconnaissance scales.

These included my survey of Malawi which, to use a measure widely adopted for comparative purposes, covered an area more than five times the size of Wales, which could not possibly have been achieved without the land systems approach. It was therefore of much interest to see what the country around Darwin and Katherine was like. It has be be said that this was not very inspiring, but then for ancient geological and geomorphological reasons much of Australia is about as mountainous as Norfolk.

We started by hiring a car to see something of the national parks, brightly coloured cliffs and sites of aboriginal rock paintings. This was October and it was blazing hot. Driving in Northern Territory had the benefit of very low traffic densities – that's and over-statement, away from the few towns you hardly see a car. What you did encounter was road trains, lorries pulling three or four long trailers weighing up to 200 tons, the longest legal vehicles

---

[1]   Commonwealth Scientific and Industrial Research Organization.

in the world. To overtake one of these you needed to be able to see nothing was coming on a straight section of about three kilometres.

The national parks here were notable for us for a different reason. Visiting a very scenic river, my heart started beating irregularly. This was atrial fibrillation, which had started years back as a consequence of the trauma of breaking my femur. It makes you feel very poorly. There was a river lookout, only 100 feet up a steep path, which I had to take short stretches at a time.

The first discernible settlement beyond Darwin is Katherine, 300 km south. Although appearing on atlas maps, Katherine has a population of about ten thousand. It has been repeatedly subject to flooding, to an extent that it was debated whether to abandon the site and build it somewhere else. This was where we boarded the Ghan. To Adelaide was a shorter trip, only 3000 km compared with 4000 km from Perth to Sydney. As before we had a bunk bed cabin, but with a problem. The margin of the upper bunk was a strip no more than six inches high, and with my known capacity for disaster I could not risk falling out. I therefore bedded down on what there was of the floor, which was not very much. We didn't meet a regimental sergeant major this time.

Close to the half-way point the Ghan reaches Alice Springs. You can leave it there and take a coach to see what was once Ayers Rock, now renamed Uluru. This mass of rounded rock is of some geomorphological interest, as a lone remnant of an erosion surface higher than the one which constitutes most of interior Australia. I don't suppose the Aborigines realise this, but they do recognise it as a holy place. You can stay in Alice Springs long enough to make this trip, hoping that the next train will arrive and not leave you 1500 km from anywhere. We opted not to take this stopover, and instead took a walk through Alice Springs to the museum, with its display of early aboriginal art (which fetches astronomical prices on the antiques market).

So to Adelaide and some pretty farming country around. Last stop was Kangaroo Island, Australia's second largest island after Tasmania. No big deal, but the warden in charge of a tourist feature at the far end was so pleased at anyone coming to see him that we had a personal account of the island's history. Its bees are very special. They are Italian Ligurian bees, colonies of which were imported in 1884. The original Ligurian bees in

Europe are no more, having cross bred, so the ones isolated on Kangaroo Island are unique. Selling honey is the main tourist attraction.

That was long-haul trip number eight, and for a combination of reasons, mainly health, the last to date. After that our travel was more limited: Tenerife (with Darryl and family), Seville, Cornwall (twice with Pat and Michael), Jersey, the Dorset coast, Vaucluse (with the Smith family), and the Loire valley (with Chrysogon and Howard). Also, with the main objective operas, Amsterdam, Barcelona, Brussels, Lille, Paris – and Valencia, where besides the opera, a show by performing dolphins brought our world travels to an end.

20

BACK HOME: NORWICH

When my father died (in 1994 at the age of 94 years and 11 months) I found he had left an account of what he called, "The more interesting years of my life". On reading this I discovered that these ended in 1928, four years before I was born. I am tempted to say that, apart from following the lives of our family, my 'interesting years' ended on retirement from full-time work in 1992.

Which should mean that this account should now stop.

What we did to keep ourselves occupied is not very gripping for readers. I've written about the French language episode and the long-haul holidays so that leaves what we did, and in some cases are still doing, in Norwich. Let's start with the two least successful.

Ballroom dancing We went to extra-mural classes for a term but it didn't work out for three reasons: the teaching was not good (too many extra steps, no coaching on style); the fact that there was no ballroom dance hall in Norwich where we could go to practise; and, it has to be said, a degree of incompatibility on the dance floor between Doreen and me.

Tap dancing I've always loved watching this, and seized the chance to try it out at classes. Fun for a while, but it didn't last more than about a year. Again the teacher was not very good (didn't prepare structured classes), she twice bungled entry for the bronze level, and then breaking my femur put an end to this one.

Music theory I gave thought to working towards a degree in music, going to see the head of music in Bath Spa University (not the more eminent University of Bath); but that would have meant not only moving house but giving up all other activities. Norwich City College offered tuition for Music A-levels, but all their classes were on days when I had regular golf. I tried private coaching with the retired music teacher of Norwich High School, Pat Clouting, and got as far as a scraped pass in Associated Board Grade 8. But I had a basic problem: whilst I could sight-read on the piano, and to some some degree sight-sing, I had never learnt to look at a music score and hear it in my head, so that option was not viable. My compositions were limited to two songs, settings of poems by Philip Larkin and John Betjeman.

Singing Doreen and I have sung in choirs all our lives. In my case this started during my PhD with the Sheffield Bach Choir. The best time for us both was the Nairobi Choir, which met in the Cathedral. Highlights were Bach's *St Matthew Passion*, with German soloists courtesy of Lufthansa; and the first performance in Africa of David Fanshawe's *African Sanctus*. The choir was mainly expats, with not many Africans, mostly in the ladies' voices.

In Norwich I sung once with the University Choir in Walton's Belshazzar's Feast, but could never meet the rehearsal turnout requirement of the Norwich Philharmonic. I always sang tenor in choirs, largely because they were so short of them. In retirement, however, there was no question that I had to sing bass.

Doreen and I went to two opera workshops in Cambridge, ambitious efforts in which shortened versions were performed after rehearsals from Friday evening to Sunday morning. The first was *Eugene Onegin*, with soloists from the Royal Opera; I sung Prince Gremin's aria and was in the chorus which, as well as singing, did the dance for the ballroom scene ("Here in the country…"). The second was Peter Grimes, including the tricky chorus in 7/4 time, "Old Joe has gone fishing"; I grabbed the part of Ned Keene, the Apothecary. Both were a great experiences.

I also went to several weekend workshops in which everyone sung chosen songs which then received comments from teacher and audience. At one I sung the 'death of Boris' aria from *Boris Godunov*, at the end of which he falls to the ground dead. I did this so realistically that I broke my collar bone – but carried on; it made my performance at the last session, again as Prince Gremin, particularly realistic as he is a retired military man and my arm was in a sling. Once I went to workshops twice in the same venue, at the first of which I sang Pimen's aria from *Boris Godunov*. In this the aged monk Pimen tells of meeting an old shepherd who relates that he was once blind, but visited the grave of a child, one of the princes whom Boris has murdered to get the throne (Pimen's objective: to scare Boris). Two years later someone who was taking a different course came up and said, "Wasn't it you who sang that song about the little child"? Touching.

I passed the Grade 8 singing exam with merit, but later gave up because my teacher left Norwich, and I didn't much like her successor. It was great while it lasted.

Which brings us to activities current in 2015

Art classes I took these up as a replacement for singing. Basically there was a class called "Painting Day", five hours, in which you could do what you wanted, with advice from the tutor. Most amateurs start with watercolour, but beginning so late in life I went straight for oils. It cannot be said that any spectacular hidden talent emerged but a number of viewable paintings appeared, mostly landscapes and portraits, some abstracts.

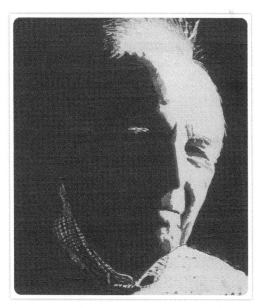

Self-portrait

Golf As I write this takes up more time for both of us that any other hobby, and is likely to remain so as long as fitness is retained. We are neither of us ace players, but golf is the only sport in which the handicapping system really works, as a result of which we have won a number of competitions at Eaton Golf Club. Doreen is particularly deadly in team events, ladies and mixed, and I come in when there are competitions which make allowance for age. In 2013 I won the 70 and over class in the Eaton Seniors Open. The St Johns' College golfing society meets once a year and there are two prizes. The main one is for best stableford score, which I won on the first year of entry. There is also a cup for 'age plus stableford points' which in 2013 I won by a margin of ten strokes. In 2000 Darryl challenged me to a game, his idea being to keep the old boy fit. So we instituted the Semper Juvenis Cup, so named because it will always be won by a Young, and we have played for this annually to date; in the first year I gave Darryl four strokes, but by 2014 this position had been reversed.

Receiving prize for best score, age plus stableford points
St John's College Golfing Society

Bridge I had played at Hammersmith Bridge Club when in the army in 1951; my partner John Manson travelled by train from Letchworth, returning about midnight. Doreen and I played once a week, sometimes more, in Kenya. In the early years at Norwich the demands of our respective professions for evening work left little spare time, but after retirement we joined a local club. To begin with it was an evening activity but then clubs with after-noon sessions started up, when one felt fresher. There are two systems of rating one's ability, master points and national grading. Master points are gained if you come in the top six in any session, and they accumulate. We have moved from Club Master to County Master and now to simply Master level. National grades are percentage figures based on the most recent sessions. Our grade is close to 50%, meaning that of the 45 000 or so members of clubs affiliated to the English Bridge Union we are about average. This is pleasing considering that most people play far more than us.

Learning My professional life has all been learning new things (geography, soil science, land evaluation, agroforestry), and the bug of learning has also been a leisure activity. As a boy I got hold of Pelican books, the non-fiction section of Penguins. What they were about didn't matter too much, their editor was good at selecting authors so most were interesting and, to my slant of mind, enjoyable.

So in retirement I struggle to widen my knowledge by learning, often things that for reasons of weak maths and science are beyond my full competence. Two fascinating areas are the worlds of the large and the small: cosmology and nuclear physics. On the first of these, I doubt if one person in a hundred among the general public (and *a fortiori* among priests) appreciates the sheer size of the universe. It's not enough just to quote billions of stars in billions of galaxies, you have to build up to it starting with the eight minutes it takes the Sun's light to reach Earth. Even a light year is a gob-stopping concept. The current consensus is for the origin of the universe in the big bang but there are a few dissenting[1] astrophysicists, and I'll join them. Grounds for scepticism? Well, there's the 'singularity', meaning "Sorry, our equations don't work at that time" (Hooray! That must be God??). Then there's dark matter: it's basically crazy to invent a material supposed to constitute 90% of the universe but which no-one has ever detected, just because, oh dear, the equations don't work for the rotation of galaxies either. Having been in the same college as Fred Hoyle and heard him give a talk, I'm happier with his idea of continuous creation.

At the other end of the dimension scale there's the very small, the nuclear and sub-nuclear world. Again, to appreciate the size of this, the scaling

---

[1]   Dissenting, yes, that's the word for me!

down, is a problem. Let's start with Planck's Constant, $6.626 \times 10^{-34} \ m^2 \ kg/s$; and then having got something surely small enough, they go and halve it in their equations. For someone without the maths, to gain some notion of quantum theory is a real struggle. And boo to the Schrodinger equation, hooray for the Dirac version; that's partisan, since Dirac's room at St John's College was on the same staircase as that on which I had my tutorials. The best guy for explaining this, Jim Al-Khalili, is of the highest ability and has spent a lifetime in nuclear physics; yet he ended a TV programme by saying, "I believe there is something fundamental that we do not know".

Recently I asked for a birthday present a book that would stretch my under-standing. Taking me at my word, what I got was Professor Sir Roger Penrose, *The road to reality: a complete guide to the laws of the universe*. Having spent most of my undergraduate lunchtimes playing table tennis with him I had a fellow feeling; but without advanced maths, you just have to feel your way through to his conclusions. As my religion is science, possibly this is my bible.

I realise I've been name-dropping: Dirac, Hoyle, Penrose! What a pity I wasn't a frequenter of The Eagle, the Cambridge pub where, during my time there, it is said that Francis Crick walked in and announced, "We have found the secret of life", the discovery of the double helix structure of DNA. Trying to understand the developments in this science since then has been a third focus of interest. I can grasp its basic method of division, recombination and thus reproduction of life, but just how analysis of a genome is done, and still less genetic engineering, is beyond the conception of a layman.

Of all the developments in knowledge that I would find most exciting it would be to find life elsewhere than on earth. It is very unlikely to resemble the life forms found in science fiction, more probably it would be like bacteria or other single-celled organisms, which was all there was for three-quarters of the period of life on earth. What would be of massive scientific interest would be to learn whether extra-terrestrial life is based on some-thing other than DNA.

It's not only science that I try to learn about. A limited amount of history, mostly 20th century, especially the Second World War, to find out what was happening when I viewed it from sources at the time: radio news (very formal then), newspapers (advances by our troops – and the Russians – shown as thick arrows on cartographer-drawn maps), and excitingly, the newsreels at the cinema.

What's the objective of all this learning? None! I don't expect to be writing about it, nor using it professionally. I've spend my whole life learning one thing after another, and can't get out of the habit. It's just for my own enjoyment.

Chrysogon, Leicester, BSc Engineering, 1984

Family

But none of the above, travel and leisure, rivalled our main interest: family. During times at work, you could say it was matched by our careers; but after retirement, following the lives of the family came increasingly to the fore. Having grandchildren whose ages span 13 years has given us plenty of interest in following their lives. As our age advances, I suppose we are moving from a position of doing what little we can to help the family to one of trying not to be too much of a burden on them.

Darryl, Sidney Sussex College, Cambridge, BA Geography, 1989

A number of our friends fill their Christmas letters with accounts of the doings of their families, most of whom we do not know. So it would be possible here to write admiring accounts of the growing up, education and careers of our children and grandchildren, a kind of family CVs. But as the readership of this account is not intended to stretch beyond the family, and they all follow each others' doings as well as we do, that is unnecessary. Let us settle for the graduations of our two children.

Wedding bells again 2000

Darryl is four years younger than Chrysogon but took longer to make up his mind about which girl to marry. His wedding was therefore eleven years after hers, in the auspicious first year of the new millennium. Like Doreen and me, Catherine Cox was a fellow geographer from another university (Southampton), and like Chrysogon a former Girls Day School Trust pupil (Sutton High). Darryl and Catherine met as fellow employees in their first job, at the BBC. Catherine has two sisters one, Melanie, living in 'mile high' Denver, Colorado (we never thought of Nairobi that way), the other, Helen, who at the time of writing is playing first violin with the BBC Symphony Orchestra.

The age spread has resulted in Darryl's children, Jamie and Lauren, being respectively ten years younger than Chrysogon's, Madeleine and Oliver. This has given Doreen and me the joy of following the growing up, education and in due course careers of two pairs of grandchildren separated by half a generation.

Anniversaries

Our silver wedding anniversary came just after that short-lived spell with the World Bank in northern Nigeria, and on the actual day, August 3rd 1982, we flew off for a family holiday in Crete.

The 40th wedding anniversary in 1997 was the first of several great family occasions. We rented a seven-bed gîte at the village of Goudelin in Brittany, having previously reconnoitred the area, booked a restaurant lunch, and found a B and B as overflow accommodation. There were 12 of us: Chrysogon, Howard, Madeleine and Oliver (CHOM), Darryl, Pat and Michael, Jeannette, Jonathan and Debbie.

2002 brought Tony's 70th birthday, a small family gathering at Dormy House Hotel, Ferndown. I played my last ever game of squash, against Chrysogon. (The hotel burnt down two years later!)

For the golden wedding anniversary in August 2007 we booked a celebration at Cannizaro House, a hotel near Wimbledon. Let's put on record the guests:

> Tony and Doreen
> Chrysogon and Howard Smith, Madeleine and Oliver Neil Smith
> Darryl, Catherine, Jamie and Lauren Young
>
> *Pat's family:*
> Patricia and Michael Fair
> Jeannette and Neil Fuller, Olivia and Monty
> Jonathan and Deborah Fair, Georgia and Benjamin
>
> *Doreen's cousins:*
> Mary Cotterell
> Delia and Howard Williams
> Diane Gibb

Tony's cousins:
Elizabeth Young
Valentine Young (over from Australia)

Cousins' children:
Jane and Anthony Fletcher
Thomas and Janet Young

Parents in-law:
Arthur and Beryl Smith
Peter and Maureen Cox
Maureen's mother, Kathleen Tyrrell (aged 91)

Invited but not able to come:
Tony's Cousins Andrew and Carole Young, Helen Young (in Australia), Pamela Lack, and Richard and Phillippa Lack (in USA); and Doreen's cousins Nancy Lee and Carl Pohly (in USA).

It was, and has remained, our fullest family reunion, a great occasion!

Golden wedding, with Darryl and Chrysogon

The Smith/Neil Smith family

The Young family

Subsequent anniversaries were more modest. Tony's 80ᵗʰ birthday was a lunch at the Royal Horticultural Society's garden at Wisley for the children and grandchildren, Doreen's a garden party at Chrysogon's house in Purley for a somewhat larger group. There was another big family gathering at Jeannette's house in Kingston upon Thames in August 2013 for Pat's 70ᵗʰ birthday.

If you hadn't been what you were, what would you like to have been?

Walter Mitty fantasized about being a sailing ship's captain, a Mississippi gambler ("Ah hev four aces." "Well, that's mighty strange pardner, cos Ah hev five."), an emergency-room surgeon, an RAF pilot ("Just a scratch – set the bone myself."), and a fashion designer ("Just between ourselves, entre nous, I – hate – women"). Most of these would not suit me, although as an undergraduate I did give consideration to switching into training for medicine, but realised that my scientific basis was nothing like strong enough.

A wider choice is offered by Flanders and Swann's song, *The sloth*:

> I could climb the very highest Himalayas
> Be among the greatest ever tennis players
> Always win at chess or marry a princess or
> Study hard and be an eminent professor.
> I could be a millionaire, play the clarinet,
> Travel everywhere,
> Learn to cook, catch a crook,
> Win a war, then write a book about it
>
> I could paint a Mona Lisa
> I could be another Caesar,
> Compose an oratorio that was sublime
> The door's not shut
> On my genius but
> I just don't have the time!

Some of these I have tried as hobbies: hill walking (but not serious climbing), play the clarinet (and piano, classical and trad jazz), tennis, painting, a very small amount of musical composition. Considered as a profession, the most pleasant life as a professional sportsman would be that of golfer, but the strain of having to produce one's physical best most be tremendous.

Win at chess I early realised that if you're going to become good at chess you have to be brilliant when young and then dedicate your life to it, to the exclusion of all else. So we keep to bridge which can be played pleasurably at a middling level.

Be a millionaire If your want to make a lot of money, then that must be the sole objective. As the impresario Lew Grade once said, "At an early age I made up my mind to earn enough to lead the life I had decided I would become accustomed to". Years of dedicated work over long periods, at times 18 hours a day, are needed. Observation of the lives of those who have achieved financial success suggests that a having a deprived childhood is an advantage. Personally I have never been what could be described as rich, but on the other hand, have never not done anything I would like to have done on account of lack of money.

Win a war/be another Caesar To be a soldier rightly demands that you obey orders unthinkingly, very far from my mindset.

Learn to cook To be a chef requires combination of skill with enormous energy.

Catch a crook I have a great admiration for the police, but to be a policeman you need to be the sort of person who, on addressing a lad with, "Now then, now then, what's all this?" doesn't get the reply, "Garn, f--- off". It helps to be heavily built, wear a uniform with phones attached, and carry a gun, but it's natural authority that counts.

Marry a princess (or something similar in the aristocracy). For example, I might have been the Duke of Devonshire, except that:

- My father was not the Duke of Devonshire.

- I did not go to Eton, nor to Balliol.

- In the army, I did not serve in the Guards, nor win the Military Cross.

- Through absence of opportunity, I did not marry one of the Mitford sisters.

- I do not normally wear high-quality Norfolk tweed suits.

- My father, at the age of 53, did not choose to saw up fallen trees, and die of a heart attack.

So I am not the Duke of Devonshire.

Some jobs are very hard to get. Organist at Notre Dame, Paris is one. When the post falls vacant they appoint some brilliant young man who, since he is at the top of his profession, doing what he enjoys, and doubtless also gets a good screw, has no wish nor need to move on. Louis Vierne, who was blind, was appointed in 1900 and died whilst playing 37 years later. Down the road at the Eglise de la Sainte Trinité the composer Olivier Messiaen became organist in 1931 and held the post until he died 61 years later.

I believe also that it is pie in the sky to think of becoming a *Times* crossword puzzle setter. Besides the necessary ability, the turnover rate is extremely slow.

Nothing to do with the sea, thank you. Nor airports, all hassle, hassle. Nor the diplomatic corps. Nor carpet laying.

Coming nearer to reasonable alternative careers, in my third year at college Dad introduced me to the head of a firm of chartered accountants, a profession which I could have entered. It has the advantage that everybody wants an accountant, so you could get into management of, say, sport, music, education. But not being attracted I left this to another Geography graduate, Darryl, who later reported that he had to learn more in the one year of being articled than in the three years of his degree. In any event, not having the flair for buying low and selling high I would have been useless in business or commerce. I'm not bad at investment, though.

A career in music would have been great from the point of view of what I enjoy, but at what level? I played the piano, but solo pianists need phenom-enal natural ability combined with vast application. I would like to have learnt the violin as a boy, from the aspect of being welcome in amateur orchestras. With better training in music theory, including the ability to 'read' a score (hear it when seeing it) I might have gone into something in the music line. For a pleasant but undemanding job, I can think of nothing better than a presenter on Radio 3 – what could be more relaxing than Essential Classics at 9.00 a.m.?

If asked, "If you were not yourself, who would you like to have been?", my answer is not a top sportsman nor, "Eef I were a reech man" but Antonio Pappano, conductor, Music Director of the Royal Opera House, and to all appearances a thoroughly amiable guy. Mind you, learning every single note of, say, Wagner's *Ring* must be an enormous strain. Less ambitious might be Paul Martin, antiques expert, television presenter (Flog it), and when it comes to interacting with people, everything that I am not.

Most realistically, there I was, with some ability at manipulative arithmetic, sitting right at the start of the computing age: Fortran, card input, and doing some programming during my first job. I even had the opportunity of old-boy influence, since one of the four St John's geographers with whom I shared tutorials went into ICL. So I could have been in on the ground floor.

But no. A lecturer in my third year, Vaughan Lewis, and my tutor, Benny Farmer, awakened the geography bug, and my professor at Sheffield, David Linton, confirmed it. After a shaky start there was no stopping me, and the job in Nyasaland set me up for life. I had the idea that academics were well rewarded, which is only true if you have a college post at Oxbridge. My salary only became comfortable when it was in tax-free dollars at ICRAF.

But for interest, variety, and opportunity to see the world – see above!

FAMILY TREES

As a supplement to Chapter 4, *The Family*, this section puts on record the genealogy of the Young and Lack families.

The format shown is not as familiar as the usual 'boxes and lines' form of family trees, which would require a sheet of paper at least one metre square. The system shown compresses the information into a much smaller space.

The generations are numbered. Everyone with the same number belongs to the same generation. The symbol + shows wives or husbands. For example on the first page of John Young's descendants, all the 4s (Austin, Beatrice, Sidney Michael I, Catherine and Miriam) are brothers and sisters. The children of each of these are generation 5. They are brothers and sisters if from the same parents, as Sidney Michael II, John, Geoffrey and Edward; or cousins if from different parents, i.e. if 5s are separated by a 4, as with Denys and Yvonne Shoppee, and Harold Wagstaff.

Still confused? If so, start with yourself, and first work upwards to your parents (one number less) and grandparents (two numbers less). Then find your brothers and sisters (the same number as you), and your cousins (also the same number as you, but separated by a lower number.

You may find you have a large number of third and fourth cousins, some of whom you did not know about.

There will certainly be errors, omissions and additions to these trees. Please send me any that you find.

The Young Family

The genealogy of the Young family was traced by my Great Grandfather Sidney Young, doubtless by sitting in vicarages and perusing the originals of parish records. I have added the later generations.

Descendants of John Young V

The Youngs have been divided into two trees, separated by John Young V (meaning the fifth of that name). John V was the last to be wholly resident in the Isle of Wight. His son, Joseph Young, was born there but moved to the mainland and died in Chatham, Kent. All of the 157 people on this tree are descendants of John V and Miriam Goodall, and are thus related.

1 John Young, V (1753 - 1823)
+ Miriam Goodall (1748 - 1796)
   2 6 other children Young
   2 Joseph Young (1794 - 1872)
   + Catherine Pratt (1805 - 1874)
      3 John Young, VI
      3 Six other children Young
      3 Anne Young (- 1895)
      3 Sidney Young (1843 - 1914)
      + Elizabeth Maria Gooch (1842 - 1924)
         4 Austin Travers Young (1867 -)
         + Edith Louise Taylor (1872 -)
         4 Beatrice Elizabeth Young (1868 -)
         + Gerald Augustine Shoppee (1858 - 1896)
            5 (Commander) Denys Charles Gerald Shoppee (1892 -)
            + Letitia Mildmay
            5 Yvonne Emily Shoppee (1894 - 1983)
            + (Major) Thomas Henry Edward Oakes (1895 -)
               6 Ursula Yvonne Oakes
         4 Sidney Michael Young, I (1871 - 1955)
         + Hilda Hardcastle Buchanan (1877 - 1963)
            5 Sidney Michael Young, II (1900 - 1995)
            + Joan Berrett Lack (1899 - 1982)
               6 Anthony Young (1932 -)
               + Doreen M. Rolfe (1933 -)
                  7 Chrysogon Rosamond Young (1963 -)
                  + Howard Neil Smith (1957 -)
                     8 Madeleine Rose Neil Smith (1991 -)
                     8 Oliver James Neil Smith (1994 -)
                  7 Darryl Anthony Rolf Young (1967 -)
                  + Catherine Jane Cox (1968 -)
                     8 James Jackson Young (2001 -)
                     8 Lauren Josephine Young (2004 -)
            + Peggy Carlotta Francis (1913 - 1976)
            5 (Jack) John Lancelot Young (1902 - 1963)
            5 Geoffrey Ernest Young (1909 - 1994)
            + Olive Nethercott (1913 - 2000)
            5 Edward Buchanan Young (1910 - 2000)
            + Francis Sprague (1909 - 1992)
               6 Bernard Young (1938 - 1993)
               + Elizabeth Ann Leisk (1939 -)
                  7 Patrick Young / Godfrey-Young (1964 -)
                  + Angela Bromfield
                     8 Simon Oliver Young (1990 -)
                     8 Rosemary Jayne Young (1992 -)
                     + Patricia Godfrey

```
            7 Martha Young (1966 - )
            + (Bill) Julian Canham
                8 Luke Canham (1997 - )
                8 Annabel Canham (1998 - )
            7 Thomas Luke Young, III (1969 - )
            + Janet Elizabeth Astill
                8 Elizabeth Frances Young (2007 - )
        6 Andrew Young (1941 - )
        + Cecily Freeman
            7 Teresa Young
            + Nigel Bishop
            7 Nicola Young (1966 - )
            + Rodney Pring (1967 - )
                8 Eleanor Pring (1995 - )
                8 Henry Pring (1997 - )
                + Carol Herriott (1951 - )
        6 Valentine Young (1945 - )
        + Helen Andrews (1946 - )
            7 Joanna Young (1973 - )
            + Nicholas James O'Brien
                8 Olivia O'Brien (2007 - )
                8 Ruby Valentine O'Brien (2008 - )
                8 Henry James O'Brien (2012 - )
                8 Georgia Helen O'Brien (2013 - )
            7 Andrew David Young, II (1975 - )
            7 Timothy John Young (1977 - )
4 Catherine Young (1874 - 1875)
4 Miriam Goodall Young (1877 - )
+ Harold Walter Wagstaff (1872 - )
    5 Harold Maurice Wagstaff (1908 - 1979)
        6 Barbara Wagstaff
        + Holden
            7 Two Children Holden
        6 Christopher John Wagstaff (1936 - )
            7 Marianne Wagstaff
            7 Robert Wagstaff
            7 Alister Wagstaff
    5 Richard Kenneth Wagstaff (1910 - )
4 Christopher John Young (1883 - 1968)
+ Margaret Harrison (1895 - 1981)
    5 Elizabeth Margaret Young (1925 - 2007)
    + Oscar Conrad Risius (1916 - 1987)
        6 Andrew Risius (1951 - )
        + Fran Wright (1947 - )
            7 Eleanor Risius (1985 - )
            + Chris Gross (1985 - )
            7 Deborah Risius (1988 - )
        6 Ruth Risius (1952 - )
        + Tim Aldous (1948 - )
            7 Catherine Aldous (1978 - )
            + Sean Taylor (1966 - )
                8 Oliver Taylor (2009 - )
                8 Imogen Taylor (2012 - )
            7 Lizzie Aldous (1979 - )
            + Mark Wheelhouse (1980 - )
            7 Rachel Aldous (1982 - )
        6 Isabel Risius (1959 - )
```

```
    + Trevor Hyde (1946 - )
        7 Lindsay Hyde (1986 - )
        7 Nicola Hyde (1988 - )
        + Simon Dingle (1987 - )
        7 Johnathan Hyde (1992 - )
5 John Harrison Young (1928 - )
+ Jean Rosemary Getliff (1932 - )
    6 Richard Getliff Young (1958 - )
    + Jane Margaret Buckley (1956 - )
        7 Gloria Ruth Young (1992 - )
        7 Daniel Peter Rowan Young (1996 - )
    6 Hugh Christopher Young (1960 - )
    + Rachel Margaret Pearce (1961 - )
        7 Sophie Natasha Rachel Young (1997 - )
        7 Katherine Emma Young (2000 - )
    6 Peter John Charles Young (1970 - 1993)
```

The Young family in the Isle of Wight (1558-1823)

Sidney Young traced a substantial family tree living in the Isle of Wight, most of whom are only very distantly related to the present family. The second tree therefore only shows the direct ancestors of John V. All of them were born and died in the Isle of Wight, mostly in the village of Carisbrook, the later generations at Pan Mill, Whippingham (now a suburb of Newport).

Thus the Young family has been traced back to Jone Young (maiden name not known) who died in 1558. My father found some manorial records of John and Richard 'le Yonge' from the 14th century which, from the subsequent use of these names, he considered likely to be ancestors

The name has remained common in the Isle of Wight. Taking the 1881 census (before people moved about so much) as a basis, in Great Britain as a whole there were 64 000 Youngs, 0.2% of the population. The Isle of Wight had 560, 0.75% of its population and the third most common surname.

```
1 --- Young
+ Jone --- ( - 1558)
    2 Thomas Young, I ( - 1586)
    + Edith --- ( - 1595)
        3 Richard Young, II ( - 1608)
        + Elinor Payne
            4 John Young, III (1583 - 1635)
```

```
            + Sarah --- ( - 1630)
                5 James Young, I (1620 - 1672)
                + Elizabeth ---
                    6 Richard Young, III ( - 1727)
                    + Catherine --- ( - 1737)
                        7 Richard Young, IV
                        + Elizabeth Pitt
                            8 Richard Young, V (1708 - 1793)
                            + Sarah Tipps (1710 - 1799)
                                9 John Young, V (1753 - 1823)
                                + Miriam Goodall (1748 – 1796)
```

The Lack Family

I traced this tree myself, largely from printed and mimeographed records, before the advent of computerized genealogical data.

The Lack surname is much less common, just over 1000 in Great Britain in 1881. They are, however, concentrated in two counties, Northamptonshire (200) and Norfolk (147). Moreover the latter are focused on the north-west part of the county. Among them were John Lack who ran a business of saddler and harness-maker in Swaffham, taken over by his son William and grandson John Gildon. Most of their descendants come from the eight children of John Gildon (generation 4), giving rise to a family tree of 175 people. The family shows a strong focus on education, leading to notable individuals in three areas: medicine, natural history, and art.

The link between the Lack and Young families comes, of course, with the marriage between my father and mother. By coincidence they both fall into generation 5 of the Young and Lack trees, so cousins can be traced between the two families.

Descendants of John Lack (1767-1835)
of Swaffham, Norfolk

1 John Lack (1767 - 1835)
+ Ann Kidall (1778 -)
   2 William Lack, I (1795 - 1859)
  + Mary Elizabeth (Eliza) Goold (1804 - 1891)
     3 John Gildon Lack, I (1823 - 1892)
    + Suzanna Maulkinson (1830 -)
       4 Maud Lack (- 1901)
      + John Thompson (1858 -)
       4 John Gildon Lack, II (Jack) (1859 -)
      + Lizzie Cornell
         5 John Goold Lack (1888 - 1975)
        + Dorothy Freeman (- 1964)
           6 John Reginald Gildon Lack (1916 - 1992)
          + Ruby May --- (1921 - 1998)
          + Kathleen Diana Freeman (1912 - 1999)
         5 Gladys Maud Lack (1890 - 1978)
         5 Reginald Lambert Lack (1891 - 1916)
        + Elsie Radcliffe
         5 Winifred Gertrude Mary Lack (1901 - 1991)
        + Terence Conrad Newth (1904 - 1994)
           6 Timothy Conrad Newth (1936 -)
          + (nee Smythe) Brenda Bullock
             7 Timothy Newth
             7 Jane Newth
           6 Jonathan Gildon Newth (1939 -)
          + Joanna Brooks
             7 Benjamin Newth (1965 -)
            + Alison ---
               8 Daisy Newth (1998 -)
               8 Ella Newth (2000 -)
             7 Daniel Newth (1968 -)
            + Gay Wilde
             7 Rosalind Newth (1980 -)
             7 Eliza Newth (1982 -)
             7 George Newth (1985 -)
             7 Lottie Newth (1988 -)
      4 Frederick William Lack (1862 - 1918)
      + Mary Keer Berrett (1863 - 1950)
         5 Hilda Mary Lack (1891 - 1972)
         5 Victor John Frederick Lack (1893 - 1988)
        + (Babs) Beatrice Snell (1905 - 1982)
           6 Richard Lack (1931 -)
          + Philippa Goffe (1939 -)
             7 Stephen John Lack (1963 -)
            + Beth Hudspeth
             7 Rosalie Ann Lack (1965 -)
            + Gregory Roensch
           6 Jeremy Lack (1933 - 1999)
          + Pamela Leithead (1940 -)
             7 Andrew Victor Lack, II (1965 -)
            + Sally Thorpe (1962 -)
               8 Isobel Georgina Lack (1996 -)
               8 Thomas Joseph Lack (2000 -)

       7 Michael Lack (1969 -)
     5 (Gypsy Diddie) Mercie Keer Lack (1894 - 1985)
     5 Joan Berrett Lack (1899 - 1982)
     + Sidney Michael Young, II (1900 - 1995)
        6 Anthony Young (1932 -)
        + Doreen M. Rolfe (1933 -)
          7 Chrysogon Rosamond Young (1963 -)
          + Howard Neil Smith (1957 -)
            8 Madeleine Rose Neil Smith (1991 -)
            8 Oliver James Neil Smith (1994 -)
          7 Darryl Anthony Rolf Young (1967 -)
          + Catherine Jane Cox (1968 -)
            8 James Jackson Young (2001 -)
            8 Lauren Josephine Young (2004 -)
  4 Edith Lack (1863 -)
  4 Gertrude Lack (1864 -)
  + George Durrant
    5 Spence Durrant
    5 Mary Durrant
    5 Daughter Durrant
  4 Mabel Lack (1867 -)
  + Reverend Cragg
  4 (Ettie) Ethel Lack (1869 -)
3 William Lack, II (1825 - 1902)
+ Maria Louisa --- (1832 - 1902)
  4 Harry S.(?) Lack (1855 -)
  4 William Thomas Lack, III (1856 -)
  + Emily J. --- (1865 -)
    5 William G. Lack (1898 -)
  4 Mary Louisa Lack (1859 -)
  4 Edward Ernest Lack (1861 -)
  + Harriatt W Freestone (1860 -)
  4 Frederick John Lack (1867 -)
3 Mary J Lack, II (1831 - 1901)
+ Thomas Goold, II (1824 - 1901)
3 George Lack (1834 -)
3 Anna Lack (1836 - 1901)
+ George Dunger, I (1834 - 1901)
  4 George William Dunger, II (1861 -)
  + Ellen --- (1864 -)
    5 Maud Dunger (1884 -)
    5 George Dunger, III (1885 -)
    5 Alice Dunger (1886 -)
    5 (Maggie) Margaret Dunger (1887 -)
    5 Tom Dunger, II (1889 -)
  4 Anna Dunger (1864 -)
  4 (Maggie) Mary Macrave Dunger (1868 -)
  + Jack Nunn
    5 --- Nunn
  4 Tom Dunger, I (1869 -)
  + Nancy (Tots) ---
    5 Joanna Dunger
    5 Daughter Dunger
3 Emma Lack (1836 -)
3 (Harry) Henry Lack (1839 - 1897)
+ Emily Case (1840 -)
  4 (Bertie) Harry Lambert Lack (1867 - 1943)

+ Kathleen Francis Rind (1877 - 1961)
   5 David Lambert Lack (1910 - 1973)
   + Elizabeth Theodora Twemlow Silva (1916 - 2015)
      6 Peter Lack (1952 -)
      + Diana Ridgley (1954 -)
         7 Alexander Lack (1995 -)
      6 Andrew Lack, I (1953 -)
      + Sally Cooke
         7 Jennifer Lack (1987 -)
            8 Sophie Lack (2007 -)
            8 James Lack (2015 -)
         7 David Lack (1989 -)
         + Helen Moorhouse
         7 Aidan Lack (2001 -)
      6 (Martin) Paul Lack (1957 -)
      + Katharine (Katy) Taylor
         7 Christopher Lack (1989 -)
      6 Catherine Lack (1959 -)
   5 (Katreen) Kathleen Lack (1912 - 2009)
   5 Christofer Lack (1913 - 1996)
   + Hilary Wilson (- 2011)
      6 Vivien Lack (1942 -)
      + Brian Hughes
         7 Christopher Hughes (1967 -)
         7 Alexander Hughes (1969 -)
         + John Hefferman, I
         7 John Hefferman, II (1981 -)
         7 Michael Hefferman (1982 -)
      6 Julian Lack (1950 -)
      + Elizabeth Rees
         7 Amanda Lack (1970 -)
         7 Nicholas Lack (1974 -)
         + Catherine Smith
         7 Amelia Lack (1998 -)
   5 Oliver Lack (1918 - 1985)
 4 (Willie) William Lack III (1869 -)
 + Hermine ---
   5 Valerie Lack
   5 Nancy Lack
3 (Lummie) Thomas Lambert Lack (1842 - 1935)
+ (Nellie) Ellen Wright Taylor (1846 -)
3 Margaret Sherwood Lack (1845 - 1904)

SOURCES

This account is based on:

- My curriculum vitae, for dates of jobs and consultancies.

- A document, "Where did we go on holiday?", originally written for the children, then maintained.

- My diaries, from 1963 onwards. These are just engagement diaries, not the sort that politicians write when they expect to make money from memoirs when they are thrown out. They are apt to go blank when I am on travels.

- Photographs, good for jogging memory and getting incidents into the right years. 30 photograph albums and about 7000 colour slides.

- Memory. Having got places and dates from the above I relied largely on memory, on grounds that if I did not recall something then it wasn't of interest.

Two other sources contain considerably more information and better accuracy, although for reasons of time I have not used them here. Taken together they possibly amount to more words than the 100 000 in this text.

Doreen's journals

Starting in Nyasaland in 1958 Doreen often kept journals when we were overseas. There are 19 handwritten journals, some combined into one book. These give more detail and, importantly, more accuracy than my accounts.

1.   November 1958-October 1959: Voyage by ship, London-Nyasaland, and early days in Nyasaland.
2.   1959-60: Local leaves from Nyasaland: Northern Rhodesia, Southern Rhodesia, Tanganyika, Kenya.
3.   1962: Zomba-Bath by Volkswagen.
4.   1965-66: Malaya.
5.   September 1966: Malaya-England journey home: Bangkok, Calcutta, Nepal, Afghanistan.
6.   1974: Kenya, Tanganyika, Malawi.
7.   1979: Western Canada.
8.   1983-85: Kenya.
9.   1986: Malawi.
10.   1986-88: Kenya.
11.   September 1988: Philippines, Solomon Islands, Australia.
12.   1998: Round-the-world: Great Barrier Reef, New Zealand, Tahiti, Los Angeles, Grand Canyon.
13.   January-February 1999: Malawi 40 years on.
14.   May 2001: American West, Utah and other national parks.
15.   October 2002: Perth, Indian-Pacific Railway, Tasmania, Fiji.
16.   2003: Kenya, South Africa (Cape Province).
17.   2004: New England.
18.   2005: Hong Kong, New Zealand North Island.
19.   October 2007: Northern Australia, then Katherine-Adelaide by the Ghan, Kangaroo Island.

Letters home

In Nyasaland we asked our parents to keep our letters home, mostly aerogrammes. Without a telephone, these were our only means of communication. They kindly did so, then and on subsequent overseas trips. In 1995 at the Rockefeller centre in Bellagio Doreen sorted and listed these. They consist of seven box files:

Tony to Doreen 1953
Introduction and Nyasaland 1958-62
Kenya 1983-91 us to the family
Kenya 1983-91 Chrysogon and Darryl to us
1964-71 including Niger, Malaya, Singapore, Brazil
1970-82 including Sokoto 1982
1991-92 family to us; Chrysogon from Leicester University; and postcards.

Made in the USA
Columbia, SC
22 September 2018